ENCYCLOPEDIA OF AMERICAN IDEALISM

TOWARD A NOVEL METHOD AND SYSTEM OF PHILOSOPHY

*Dialectics, Epistemology, Metaphysics, Cognitive Science,
Psychoanalysis, Phenomenology, Metalinguistics,
Aesthetics, Ethics, & Politics*

G.R. TOMAINI

978-0-6452126-9-3

Encyclopedia of American Idealism:

Toward a Novel Method and System of Philosophy

G.R. Tomaini

Thema Classification: QD (Philosophy), JQDHR (Western Philosophy), QDX (Popular Philosophy).

MANTICORE PRESS
WWW.MANTICORE.PRESS

Dedicated To
My Teachers:

G.W.F. Hegel

Drucilla Cornell
Derek Parfit
Theodore Sider
Cornel West
Slavoj Žižek

CONTENTS

CHAPTER II

CHAPTER III

i. OF THE ACKNOWLEDGMENTS

WHAT triggered me? After drunkenly almost meeting my fate at the hands of a few mere stairs, I presented myself with an ultimatum: either contribute to the discipline now, or take the chance that, due to fate, I may never will. Thus, I wasted no time in weighing where to publish my philosophical system. At first, I was to submit the work to Union Theological Seminary's graduate student journal, because — I figured — they would accept anything I threw at them. Once the manuscript exceeded forty pages, it became a journal article; once the manuscript exceeded one hundred and fifty pages, it morphed into a book. Getting a book published as but a mere graduate student would be byzantine; *nevertheless, I persisted.* To start, I must acknowledge all of my dear friends who made up what we called the Asbury Circle: Royce, Beebee, Anthony, Jared, Doreen, Rick, Jack, Meg, Jean-Luc, Kelsey, and Bill Gorge. Erina Van Wetering — my Japanese grandmother through mutual adoption — was another cherished gift from the cosmos who lived in Asbury. Many a fine cherry-Chambord cocktail was enjoyed at Coach Michael's penthouse in Asbury Park, too: my dear friend from the LGBTQ book club in the city. Special thanks to Myke K. for being such a wonderful presence in my life over the past two and a half years. Of course, it goes without saying that Barbara, Richard, Matthew, and Joan need to be acknowledged, too: how could they not be? It was Richard who taught me how to play chess at three years old: my first encounter with dialectical reasoning. Barbara, on the other hand, taught me to always go for the jugular: and that's what this encyclopedia is all about. Special thanks to Danton — my Hegelian Freedom Bonsai Tree, and his brothers, Georg Hegel the Cactus, Immanuel Kant the Cactus, Mr. Jingles the Money Tree, and most of all, applause for Le Piston, a plant who needs no introduction. Once I got to Rutgers College, I collided with the world's second-best Analytic Philosophy department. Originally, I was a Finance major in the Business School, aiming to one day dip my pinky toe into the decadent pool of hedge funds; after Finance, I switched to Economics; after Economics, I switched to Philosophy and Political Economy. In my freshman year, I met the notorious Prof. William C. Dowling, who taught me Semantics, Ricoeur, and the Oxfordian tutorial method; my friends and I would sip either tea or sherry with him, depending on what best suited our needs at the time; during the night, of course, we would sup at the veritable Rutgers Club.

I also met visiting Yale professor Henry Sussman — the famous deconstructionist — who taught me the masters of suspicion: Marx, Nietzsche, and Freud. Prof. Andy Murphy taught me the great political theorists: Hobbes, Rousseau, Kant, and Mill. A lecture delivered by Oxfordian professor Jeff McMahan, that I attentively listened to, on Just War Theory, became the bedrock of this work's focus on Just Mind Theory, Just Rule Theory, Just Environment Theory, and Just Economy Theory. Prof. Doug Husak inspired me during his seminar on Moral Responsibility, to write up the theory of subliminal prioritization. Prof. Branden Fitelson taught me Logic in a truly superlative fashion. While I did have the opportunity to study under the brilliant epistemologist Ernest Sosa, and did so, I never took any seminars with Alvin Goldman, another towering epistemologist. Prof. Richard Serrano, the renaissance man, and I had many debates over Napoleon and his influence on the arts and humanities. Profs. Ted Sider and Barry Loewer taught me Metaphysics, again, in truly superlative fashions; their good friend and visiting Columbia professor David Albert, too, was a tremendous influence. Profs. Camp and Kirk-Giannini shared their enthusiasm for Austinian pragmatism across a handful of graduate seminars — an enthusiasm that was delightfully contagious. The infamous Political Theorist and True Philosopher Drucilla Cornell taught me Jacques Derrida's deconstruction and the philosophy of Georg Wilhelm Friedrich Hegel. Drucilla had many influences: an attendee of Ronald Dworkin's regular seminar on the Philosophy of Law, her daughter was also Derrida's godchild, to say the least of their friendship that started at Essex. My deep appreciation for Derrida's philosophy led me to plan an international conference entitled *Derrida, Who?* in which world-famous Columbia Professor Gayatri Chakravorty Spivak agreed to be a panelist for. Unfortunately, due to the cancellation of a Junior Princetonian, the conference had to be canceled — looking back on it, if I had been more experienced, the event could still have gone on. The Dean of Students, Mark S. Schuster, again employing the Oxford tutorial method, sat me down once a week to learn the philosophy of Michel Foucault. That same year, now my third, I encountered the infamous Derek Parfit by way of his student, and — coincidentally — the Department Chair of Philosophy, Larry Temkin, a preeminent philosopher in his own right; how I will forever hold dear the seminar I took with them so many years ago! Parfit's *On What Matters* deeply triggered me, because I knew there was something wrong with the work, but I couldn't yet articulate what precisely that was while Derek was still alive. Parfit's work inspired my own *Holistic Theory of Personal Identity*, as well as my synthesis of Benthamite Utilitarianism, Kantian Deontology, and Aristotelian Virtue Ethics: *Leibnizian Virtue Cyclological Speculative Optimalism*. Another undergraduate conference that I threw — this time with Peter Singer — interrogated animal rights and so on, and it subsequently changed my life.

Profs. Martha and Robert Bolton were some of the most intense Philosophers in the entire department, in my opinion. Martha taught Locke, Descartes, and Leibniz, although was chiefly a Lockean historian. It was through Martha I was taught Leibniz, the most cunning of all the Philosophers, whereas Hegel is the most profound of all the Philosophers. I found Robert's graduate seminars on Aristotle deeply informative: Robert is the one who taught me dialectics, in fact, during a seminar on Aristotle's *Organon*. Prof. Louis Sass taught me Husserl, Heidegger, Freud, and Lacan across two graduate seminars. His book, *Madness and Modernism*, is among the most profound I've ever read. Prof. Michael Levine taught me Nietzsche and Heidegger in a graduate seminar that I audited on the Eternal Return: those with the ears to hear may understand what knowledge exactly the course dealt with, as it were. Finally, during my tenure as President of the Rutgers College Undergraduate Philosophical Society, I invited Slavoj Žižek, Judith Butler, and Seyla Benhabib to deliver lectures, unsuccessfully, I'm afraid. Thanks be to my good friends Ryan, Claire, Emma, Facundo, Jerry, Josh, Michael, and Anthony; Jerry and I met Theological Facundo under auspicious circumstances: it was 3:00am when we waltzed into Nirvani's Kati Roll establishment; in my left hand I carried a pack of Newport cigarettes, and in my right hand I clutched Hegel's *Science of Logic*: we got along famously. Ultimately, while an undergraduate at Rutgers College, and during such time as I was a Federal McNair Fellow, I audited twenty-five graduate seminars and enrolled in six. Next, after a two-year personal sabbatical, came my enrollment at Union Theological Seminary and my collision with the following esteemed individuals: President Serene Jones; Distinguished Reinhold Niebuhr Chair — Professor Gary Dorrien; and the Distinguished Dietrich Bonhoeffer Chair — Professor Cornel West. All three molded my thought in profound ways, and encouraged me to ponder a life of greater degrees of activism and community service. All three had and continue to have immense impacts upon my academic trajectory. President Jones's enthusiasm for the theology of John Calvin inspired me to take up theological questions; Professor Dorrien, time and time again, proved his encyclopedic knowledge, and his book *In A Post-Hegelian Spirit* remains a powerful source of information. Professor Cornel West, perhaps by the *Cunning of Reason* itself, returned to Union just as I was entering my second year there; I had written to Professor West for his autograph in high school and he obliged. I attended a lecture he delivered on political philosophy at Rutgers, and his enthusiasm for non-Analytic strains of philosophical research left an indelible mark upon my trajectory; at Union, four classes with Professor West furnished me with a new vocabulary for interrogating both Philosophy and Justice-at-large. Cheers to my Birkbeck interlocutors: Jodi Dean, Étienne Balibar, Costas Douzinas, Esther Leslie, Sisonke Msimang, Achille Mbembe, Stephen Frosh, Sarah Nuttall, Jacqueline Rose, and Slavoj Žižek himself. Profound respect and admiration for the brilliant and wonderful intellectuals Jean Mathee and Laurie Rodriguez, who together taught me so much. Immense love and thanks go to both Gwendolyn Taunton and Wendy Lochner. Especial thanks to Michael and Max for reading every word of the manuscript as the project unfolded. And — lastly — what should I have done, without *House Balenciaga*?

G.R. Tomaini
London, United Kingdom

ii.   OF THE PREFATORY REMARKS

DR. CORNEL WEST

THE first use of the word "encyclopedia" in early modern European letters is found in the inimitable Francois Rabelais — the greatest comic writer of excess, disorder and surfeit in any language! As Mikhail Bakhtin and John Cowper Powys (the two towering readers of Rabelais) have taught us, the poetic and philosophic explosion unleashed by Rabelais, and augmented by the indispensable Laurence Sterne, were revolutionary acts of imagination, transgression and social reconstruction. Greg Tomaini is a highly ambitious poet-philosopher obsessed with encyclopedic scope yet mindful of how contingency and incongruity undercuts any grand system in philosophy. This manifesto is a fascinating, fun and fallible effort to imagine, transgress and reconstruct our chaotic world of discourse, politics and spirit. Because it is the work of a young thinker still couched in the language and jargon of one's teachers and mentors, this creative work may be confused as inchoate or reduced to incoherence. I am convinced that beneath the apparent surfaces of frenetic formulations lurk an emerging poetic vision and philosophic worldview that is thoroughly democratic in content and character. Despite the nearly compulsive attempt to encompass the insights of philosophic giants of the past and present, Tomaini enacts and embodies the clash of the encyclopedic and excess, order and disorder, system and surfeit. And in our moment of massive imperial decay — in the American, Russian and Chinese empires — sheer chaos and frenzy are shout through so many of our efforts to see, feel and act wisely. In my humble opinion, this tortured and tormented book is a noteworthy effort to push forward a faltering yet precious democratic project!

Cornel West

Union Theological Seminary
New York City

13

iii. OF THE INTRODUCTORY REMARKS I

Leibnizian Reconstructive Imaginary Dialectics Contra Hegelian-Heideggerian-Schmittian-Derridean Deconstructive Negative Dialectics; or, Of Analytic-Modernisms Contra Continental-Postmodernisms: Beyond So-Called Analytic and So-Called Continental Philosophical Modalities: Toward an Imaginary Dialectics Rooted in Leibnizian Harmony: Toward Reconstruction

THE *Encyclopedia of American Idealism* aims to defenestrate the influence that the Hegelian philosophical program has had over philosophy for the past two centuries. Employing the metaphilosophy of Gottfried Leibniz, Hegelianism as a system can be eviscerated, rather than ignored, as has been the tendency as of late, for the most part, outside of the Brandomian Pittsburgh School of Hegelianism. Ransacking the Hegelian philosophical system, its jewels are taken and thrown into the intellectual hopper that, too, absorbs innumerable other Western philosophers, who are indiscriminately assessed based on the merits of their philosophies, whether Pragmatic, Continental, Analytic, or Historical.

A genealogical trajectory at the end of which lies international *harmony*, the *Encyclopedia of American Idealism* advances the literature in the following domains: Dialectics, Epistemology, Cognitive Science, Psychoanalysis, Phenomenology, Metalinguistics, Aesthetics, Ethics, and Politics. This begins with a Leibnizian Reconstruction of the Ancient Greek question interrogated by Isaiah Berlin and Ronald Dworkin: the question of the fox versus the hedgehog; whether it is better to be like the fox, who knows many things, or the hedgehog, who knows one big thing. Here, neither option is selected: instead, the Wittgensteinian *Duckrabbit* emerges as the winner of the race: philosophy from the point of view of the *Duckrabbit* is inherently versatile: it both knows one thing and many things, for it is a *nuanced systemizer*. In *Anthropoepistemology*, Metaphysics and a so-called First Philosophy trace the lines of thought employed by Descartes, Saint Anselm, Lewis, Goldman, Sosa, Plantinga, and many more toward the formulation of a Whiteheadian-Derridean *Process Epistemology*, and the realization of the *Pragmatic-Cognitivist Consciousness*, contrasted with its antithesis, the *conspiratorial consciousness*. In the *Anthropocognitivity* division of this work, the domains of Cognitive Science and Metalinguistics are interrogated: Marx, Austin, Lacan, Althusser, and Fodor loom over the dialectic, toward the identification of the *Hegelian-Lacanian*

Linguistic Superstructure, grounded upon the Lacanian symbolic register. Then, in the *Metapolitics*, which has three divisions — *Aesthetics*, *Ethics*, and *Politics* — philosophers are taken to trial for their philosophies: these being, notably, Kant, Hegel, Rand, Habermas, Nietzsche, Rousseau, Foucault, and Nussbaum. In the *Aesthetics*, there is a general discussion of Aesthetic Phenomenology and the Work of Art, as well as an improvement upon Chalmers's *Extended Consciousness* thesis. Also, in the Aesthetics, the phenomenologies of John Keats and the Marquis de Sade find their synthesis in the phenomenology of none other than George Gordon, Lord Byron, who embodies the *fashionable consciousness*.

Die Unterfrau, functions as a foil to Nietzsche's *Ubermensch*, and embodies the *revolutionary consciousness* itself. In the *Ethics*, following the reasoning of Parfit — Benthamite *Utilitarianism*, Kantian *Deontology*, and Aristotelian *Virtue Ethics* are syncretized into a new *General Theory of Ethics*: *Virtue Cyclological Speculative Optimalism*, grounded in the *Theory of Justice as Leibnizian Harmony*, a *harmony* of the identified eighteen ideal principles of morality, which, in the *Politics*, develop from mere ideals into concrete rights; these eighteen ideal principles of morality are none other than: *perfection, gravitas, hope, autonomy, dignity, grace, utility, civility, peace, trust, hospitality, decoloniality, beauty, defocality, dehierarchality, experimentality, improvement,* and *harmony*. *Process Epistemology* develops into *Process Ethics*. At the tail end of the *Ethics*, the concept of the *Boltzmann god* is introduced, which has great implications for the rest of the work, and inaugurates the *Birth of God Theology* research program, contrasted with *Death of God Theology*. Ultimately, in the *Politics* division of this work, *Just World Theory*, which is comprised of four components, these being, *Just Mind Theory, Just Rule Theory, Just Environment Theory,* and *Just Economy Theory* is presented.

Before *Just World Theory* is interrogated, the *Holistic Theory of Personal Identity* is represented as a counter to Siderian *temporal parts theory* and Parfitian *personality nihilism*; the theory argues that there are seven chief components of personal identity. The four theories inherent to *Just World Theory* are grounded in an *Aristotelian Metaphysical Theory of the Individual and of the Nation-State*, grounded surprisingly not in Aristotle's *Politics* or *Nicomachean Ethics*, but in his *Metaphysics*. The *Just Mind* is asserted to be the *democratic consciousness*, and across fourteen stages of development, is traced up from the initial *dependent consciousness*. *Just Rule Theory* culminates in the genealogical development of the *democratic constitution*, and synthesizes the political philosophies of Locke, Rawls, Habermas, and Dworkin. *Just Environment Theory* transcends the ubiquitous manichaean conflict between imperialism and indigeneity by proffering the *democratic universal safe space*, and, again, theorizes solutions to the Habermasianly identified social pathologies. *Just Economy Theory* functions as an *a priori* ethical critique of Capitalism — contra Marx's arguably outdated, albeit Hegelian, *das Kapital* — and asserts that any democracy must possess a *democratic economy*. The *Just World* is argued to be the *democratic world*, which is, that world that exists at the end of the teleological development of world history, after all twenty-three of its stages and processes have taken place, which is, a world defined by its international *harmony*. *Dialectical harmonism* is revealed to be the method for the work, and it is argued to replace Hegelian-Marxian *Dialectical materialism*; *Dialectical harmonism* is inspired by Gottfried Leibniz's metaphilosophical and metaphysical emphasis on *harmony*. Whiteheadian-Derridean *Process Epistemology* and *Process Ethics* develop into a *Process Politics* and a *Process Theory of Law*. Furthermore, a *Darwinian Theory of Ideological Natural Selection* is employed to explain why some ideas and sets of ideas are more *fit* and *persistent* than others, etc. So much for a thematic overview of the work and its three segments, *Anthropoepistemology, Anthropocognitivity*, and *Metapoliticality*.

Now comes the time for a tour of Hegelian dialectics, which is to be sublated into a coinage of your author: Leibnizian dialectics. If you'll just buckle in your seatbelts, we'll rev up the existentialist motorcycle and take the royal road into the jungle that is Hegelianism: just as Joseph Conrad's Charles Marlow in *Heart of Darkness* journeyed into the imperialist abyss that was the Congo, we'll set out to find the dark heart of this historied system. What is so special about Hegel? First thing's first: how do we grapple with Karl Marx, Hegel's right-hand man, whose legacy in the West, as articulated in Jacques Derrida's *Specters of Marx*, is almost as profound as Hegel's? Any serious liberal must contend with Marx, unless, of course, like most liberals, they dismiss him and *das Kapital* out of hand: irrelevant and refuted, they say! That would make sense were it not for the fact that Marx is grounded in Hegel, and no one today would say: *incontestably*, Hegel is irrelevant, for, his specter haunts on: *ooga booga booga!* To get rid of Marx, you have to go for his Hegelian jugular. Unfortunately, in the absence of any such Hegelian arteries, all we have to grapple with, instead, is a hypercomplex Quinean *web of belief*, encoded in abstruse and fundamentally *eccentric* language. Thus, there is no easy refutation to be had here. Overcoming Marx and his liege lord, Hegel, is not an easy feat to accomplish. First, the merits of their respective systems must be concretely identified and measured against the whetstone of *perfection*, in order to expose their weaknesses. From there, antitheses must be procured, and applied, in order to effect a series of syntheses, which turns out to be a Hegelian move itself, if one is paying attention to the dialectics of it all. Thus, there is a turn, here, a *Dialectical turn*, wherein the dialectic shifts not to the contents of any of Marx or Hegel's respective philosophical views, but instead, to the metaphilosophical concept of *dialectics* itself. It is only in this headspace that one can begin to gain headway in the subversion of Hegelianism, for, the *Science of Logic* — the mature expoundation of Hegelian dialectics itself, the core of the Hegelian system — is the nigh impenetrable fortress within which the specter of Hegel and his vassals hide, grimacing at their detractors. If their very system is grounded in dialectics, perhaps that is the way to overcome them, as Derrida and Žižek identify as a possible aspiration for the philosophical literatures — one wonders why neither of them ever attempted to do it!

But, there is a caveat here: dialectics cannot merely be replaced, for it is the lifeblood of all philosophical praxis, for, dialectics is essentially *performative*: which is to say, there is no such thing as the Aristotelian *analytic*, for, a performance even performed by oneself still has the audience of oneself, and therefore all modalities of *analytics* are merely *self-Dialectical*, or self-discursive: this is to say that *Analytic* philosophy is really *Dialectical* philosophy. Instead of worrying about refuting the Hegelian Dialectical method, then, it is the *manner* of dialectics that must be, not refuted, but replaced: so, no matter what move we make here, we are still going to be stuck with a theory of dialectics: is that so bad? Famously, *Dialectical materialism* is the view espoused by Marx, and implicitly attributed to Hegel, despite those who repeat and repeat the view that Hegel was 'turned on his head' by Marx. Yet, Hegel was arguing for a *Philosophy of History* the whole time: could there be a history, without a modality of materialism, or its recent theoretical friend, Lewisian physicalism? Of course not. Thus, *Dialectical materialism* was always itself a Hegelian view — or at least that is the Marxian view on the matter, shared by your author. Straight to the point: the chief methodology of this work will employ, not *Dialectical materialism*, but *Dialectical harmonism*. A *harmonism* of the dialectic argues that the infamous Hegelian aufhebung — or the overcoming-synthesis — may emerge not merely from matter, but any *source of influence*, and, most *influences* are sourced from phenomenological consciousness: hence the view, *phenomenological constructivism*, which argues that phenomenological consciousness is the root *base* to any conceivable Marxian or Althusserian *superstructural* Kantian-Searlean *social constructs*.

Harmonism, therefore, traces any possible movement on the Dialectical chessboard: *harmonism* is the resolvement of any imaginary conflict, inherently. This dialectic, taken to its teleological endpoint, results in international *harmony*: nothing more, and nothing less. Thus, dialectics is not about *negation*, but *temporal blocking*: the resolvement of the conflict is not accomplished due to the negation of one term from another, but instead, is grounded upon the phenomenological realization that there is no conflict at all, and that there always existed a certain *harmony* between the two terms in the dialectic. Until the *temporal blocking* is superseded, the *realization* of the inherent harmony between the terms is not conceivable. Thus, the improvement beyond Hegelianism lies not in *negation*, but in *harmony*. In social matters, there obviously exists a certain *polynomial* dialectics, wherein there are multiple, if not innumerable, terms inherent to the Dialectical process. The source of this work's merits rest in its employment of *Dialectical harmonism* as a method — as a methodologically necessary development in Dialectical theory that takes us beyond the contributions of Hegel and Marx. In the division of this work labeled *Ethics*, even justice is defined as Leibnizian *harmony*, contra Rawls. The whole of the natural procession of the world accords to *Dialectical harmonism*: should international *harmony* truly be an aspiration of the human race. Firstly, *Dialectical harmonism* must become the *applicative dialectic*, in order to truly instigate the liberal dream of *progress*. *Harmony* is like gravity, where the dominant forces of the dialectic will always triumph: until human beings manifest the appropriate conditions for international *harmony*, there is no concrete way of knowing whether or not the teleological end of history shall be reached: the answer to that question is noumenal. In order to transcend difference, we must actively seek out the points of *harmony* shared among the terms in a given Dialectical equation. This work attempts at an optimal application of Dialectical *harmony* to philosophical matters, and, according to the logic of that aspiration, provides a system of philosophy that may be referred to as *American Idealism*, for, with its emergence, the legacy of *German Idealism* may finally be challenged on its own terms, in an attempt to replace it with a fresh modality of performing dialectics. Hegel was right about innumerable things, one of those being that America was the place wherein dialectics would accomplish the greatest possible degree of human freedom. This freedom involves the freedom from Hegelian dialectics, however. With the advent of *American Idealism*, truly are demonstrated to now be merely *historical*, rather than *contributive* to any contemporary debates on dialectics.

Besides, although this is not the place for an *a priori* ethical critique of Hegelian dialectics, it goes without saying, that the Hegelian emphasis on *negation* contrasted with the Leibnizian emphasis on *harmony* — is inherently *sadistic* insofar as it is inherently *combative* to the extent that Hegelian Dialectical *negation* is built atop the *logic* of the master / servant dialectic, with entities engaging in an infamous Hegelian "battle for the death," as articulated in Hegel's famous *Phenomenology of Mind*. If Hegel and Marx have been philosophically dissected and discarded by means of Leibnizian *Dialectical harmonism*, which other Hegelians are next in line for the philosophical guillotine? Let us now turn to Jacques Derrida, whose *deconstructive* method is none other than applied Hegelian dialectics, according to your author's own reading and reconstruction of Derrida's *Of Grammatology*: what could be more fundamental to Derridean deconstruction than the negation of binary oppositions toward a perpetual process of synthesis? If deconstruction really is applied Hegelian dialectics, then it too is centered on *negation* rather than *harmony*; and, to turn now to another philosopher whose Hegelian roots show like none other, Martin Heidegger in his *Being and Time* touted the Hegelian line through-and-through. Indeed, Hegel was engaging in phenomenological research long before the birth of Heidegger. To return to our interrogation of Derridean *deconstruction*: the name of Derrida's very deconstructive method came to him not whimsically, but instead from Heidegger's own philosophical method of *destruktion*: it's all there, in black and white, clear as crystal: *deconstruction* is itself based on *negative dialectics*, to the extent it is rooted in Hegelianism and also to the extent that it borrows from Heidegger's own arguably Nazi method of *destruktion*; and need we even mention the political philosophy of the infamous Paul de Man? Therefore, to whatever extent Hegel and Marx can be successfully critiqued via Leibnizian *Dialectical harmonism*, so too can Derrida, and his entire project of deconstruction.

To ask Lenin's question: *what is to be done?* We cannot merely deconstruct deconstruction itself, for that would be to employ the same *sadistic* and *combative* form of Dialectical logic that Hegel championed in his magnum opus, the *Science of Logic*; it should here be noted that the Dialectical method of Hegel bears great semblance to the friend / foe dialectic espoused in Carl Schmitt's *The Concept of the Political*, with entities coming into conflict with one another in manner where one negates the other, not altogether unlike the Hegelian master / servant dialectic; what's more, Alain Badiou in his dialogue on German Philosophy with Jean-Luc Nancy, insists that Hegelian *negative dialectics* is too heavy in its approach — Badiou goes so far as to refer to Stalinist policies as being in accord with the method of *negative dialectics* itself. To *reconstruct* Hegelian *negative dialectics* we must again turn to Leibniz: and, may also play the Hegel card on Hegel, by sifting the wheat from the chaff inherent both to Hegelianism and deconstructivism. To turn to Leibniz here, is not to even remotely consider negating either Hegelianism or deconstructivism: instead, Leibnizian *Dialectical harmonism* mandates that we appropriate, synthesize, and *harmonize* as much as possible. Thus, *deconstruction* as a method must be replaced by *reconstruction*, or, a method by means of which entities are analyzed for their constituent Dialectical parts, and then conceptually *reconstructed* in order to effect a *harmonious* synthesis among the terms involved in the given Dialectical equation. Again, this is to assert the existence of a *polynomial dialectics*, wherein even an infinite amount of terms could be involved in a given Dialectical equation. For yet another substantive critique of deconstruction: binary — nay, *polynomial* — so-called oppositions — which deconstruction claims to deconstruct — are inherent to the very praxis of deconstruction itself. In deconstructing any given positivist structure, or merely identifying its limits, even, one enters into an oppositional relation to the positivist structure under scrutiny — to whatsoever extent oppositional relations exist at all and are not merely imaginary constructs rooted in our cognitive capacities — therefore, deconstruction in entering into relations of scrutiny, itself perpetuates so-called binary and polynomial oppositions: between the structure and the deconstructionist. The key here is not to oppose the structure, but to reimagine and replace said structure by means of Leibnizian imaginative dialectics: hence, the key is to reconstruct, not to deconstruct. Furthermore, the key is to reconstruct positivist structures ad infinitum, according to the logic of Hegelian-Whiteheadian process epistemology and process metaphysics; the perpetual reconstructive positivism of structures inaugurates a new Project of Being: *the perpetual encyclopedification of the world, eternally revised, eternally reconstructed, and perpetually re-posited: toward the ultimate aspiration of a perpetually improved applied methodology of praxis itself.* Just as Hegel and Marx met their philosophical fates at the hands of Leibnizian *Dialectical harmonism*, so too have Heidegger and Derrida. There is a call, here, to seek out *negative* dialectics wherever they emerge, and then pull them up out of the ground that nourishes them: *and plant new seeds!* In this way, Hegel, Marx, Heidegger, Schmitt, and Derrida — *The Combative Metaphysicians* — have been uprooted, and now have only to be replaced by precocious scholars both at the senior and junior levels of academia. Leibnizian *Dialectical harmonism*, and *reconstruction* may be employed in any number of fields in the humanities ranging from: Anthropology, Sociology, History, Cultural Studies, English, Comparative Literature, and especially in Philosophy.

Now that *reconstruction* is on the table, and its methodology of Leibnizian *Dialectical harmonism* has been established, might we turn to the most pressing philosophical debate of our times, namely, the tension between the *Analytic-Modernists* and the *Continental Continental-Postmoderns*? The *Analytic-Modernists* implicitly or explicitly hold dear the tenets espoused in Habermas's *The Philosophical Discourse of Modernity*, and respect and cherish so-called Enlightenment values — these folks are inherently *logocentric*, and a lot of them are Neo-Kantians for exactly this reason, and are shrewd and mathematically-oriented; all analytic philosophers except for the Brandomites are *Analytic-Modernists*. On the other hand, the *Continental-Postmoderns* counter *logocentrism* with the infamous charge that it is not merely *logocentric*, but instead, too, *phallogocentric*, or the belief that the history of civilization has been dominated both by *men* and by *reason*. Nothing could be more false than the claim that history has been dominated by reason, which, ultimately, is a Hegelian claim, made in his *Lectures on the Philosophy of History*. To whatever extent women have been dominated throughout history — which truly is an egregious fact of history — have we forgotten one of the most basic of all the *Continental-Postmodern* claims? Namely, that the master / servant dialectic entails that the servant in fact triumphs over the master by becoming more intimate with themselves, etc., and, as Nietzsche famously argues, *what does not kill me makes me stronger*. Thus, the *Continental-Postmoderns* ignore this basic fact of the Hegelian corpus, famously written in Hegel's *Phenomenology of Mind*; therefore, the *Continental-Postmodern* claim that *phallogocentrism* is the case is based upon an inconsistent internal logic. The *Continental-Postmoderns* must choose between Derrida's critique of *phallogocentrism* on the one hand and Hegel's master / servant dialectic on the other on the other hand — *a Sophie's Choice par excellence*. Here, Leibniz smiles: *surely you have heard of my Law of Non-Contradiction?* We need not like a cat toy with the *Continental-Postmodern* mice: to return to the inherent tension between the *Analytic-Modernists* and the *Continental-Postmoderns*: might there be a Leibnizian aufhebung between the two opposing camps of thought? Let us now discuss where *Dialectical harmonism* sees fit to take us: *ontological harmonism* — a harmony of all entities, not necessarily pre-established, but capable of being established — just as the Aristotelian dialectic goes on how the tree exists within the acorn, etc.

Here, to digress, the infamous problem of evil may be dismissed out of hand, for, the mere possibility of utopia's emergence justifies any conceivable and so-called evil: thus, both with and against Leibniz: pre-established *harmony* does not exist per se. It is certainly the case, however, that it is possible for this world to accomplish *international harmony*. Therefore the problem of evil is null and void;

instead of being a *vulgar consequentialist view*, this proposition that the permanent manifestation of utopia justifies any so-called evil may be understood to be in line with your author's own *Leibnizian General Theory of Ethics*, i.e., *Virtue Cycological Speculative Optimalism*. *Universal Harmony* is the ideal aim of any conceivable effort, and certainly is the telos of Being. As mentioned before, there is no such thing as *Analytic* Philosophy — the word *analytic* philosophically originates in Aristotle's *Organon* — because every act of *reconstruction* is self-performative, self-discursive, and hence *Dialectical* etc., thus, there is only *Dialectical* Philosophy. This work seeks to eviscerate *Continental-Postmodernism* via Leibnizian *Dialectical harmonism*, however, it also — just as Leibniz stole Spinoza's philosophy — steals the best philosophies from every other competing philosophical program, most of all *Continental-Postmodernism* itself. People say that Hegel's system incorporates other systems and that it is kraken-esque, however Leibniz indubitably stole Spinoza's philosophical program just about in its entirety, but, made it so much better, and made it idealist. Here, to go one step further down the ladder rung, everyone knows that Hegel is believed to be a pantheist — as was Spinoza. Thus, this tension between Leibnizianism and Hegelianism did not just materialize out of thin air: it has been in the background of the dialectic for centuries now. If this work hopes to accomplish anything at all, that something would be the demonstration of the triumph of the Leibnizian philosophical program against the joint philosophical program that is Spinozist-Hegelianism.

To return to *Universal Harmony*: it and nothing else is the true telos of history, as is argued in the last subchapter of this work: *Just World Theory: or, Of the Genealogical Development of Leibnizian International Harmony*. Thus, *Leibnizian Harmonism* itself may replace both Analytic-Modernisms and Continental-Postmodernisms. Just as David Hume's billiard balls trigger other billiard balls, it is the aspiration of the author that this work will trigger its reader into the *Revolutionary Consciousness*, guided by *die Unterfrau*. So much for the introduction to this work, the system of *American-Idealism*, and its Leibnizian method, *Dialectical harmonism*, its telos of history, *international harmonism*, as well as its Leibnizian philosophical modality: *reconstruction*.

iv. OF THE INTRODUCTORY REMARKS II

Of Philosophy For Wittgensteinian Duckrabbits: Beyond Berlin and Dworkin

FAMOUS philosophers Isaiah Berlin and Ronald Dworkin pondered the Ancient Greek question of whether or not it was better for a philosopher to be a fox or a hedgehog.[1] "The fox knows many things, but the hedgehog knows one big thing," the ancient Greek saying goes. How might that apply to philosophy, though? Late in Dworkin's career, he produced yet another excellent book: *Justice for Hedgehogs*. In the book, Dworkin delves into whether or not it is better to have many nuanced theories of ethics — microethics — or whether or not it is better to have one central keystone of an ethical theory — macroethics. Suppose we took a step back — for we are nowhere near the division of this work to be distinguished as *Ethics* yet — and instead asked: might this dichotomy between fox and hedgehog apply, generally speaking, to all of philosophy itself? Now we are beginning to tackle what about this dichotomy is so important for philosophy, especially as practiced in the twenty-first century. Nowadays, nowhere can a philosophical system be found; and yet, for the entire history of philosophy, philosophical systems abound — left and right, as it were — they are ubiquitous. The tendency to be a fox toward philosophical matters — to focus on minute issues rather than grandeur issues — is the contemporary modality of philosophy, perhaps despite the tendency toward grand theory inherent to the writings of Jürgen Habermas and the Frankfurt School philosophers. Philosophical systems did not merely go out of fashion due to the critiques of the so-called *masters of suspicion* — Karl Marx, Friedrich Nietzsche, and Sigmund Freud — instead, this author would rather assess the cultural phenomenon of Fox-like modalities of production — speech, acts, and thought — by asking Cicero's question: *who benefits?*

With the hegemony of neo-liberal capitalism strangling our modalities of production — our very expressions of being — it has become hard to be a hedgehog during our times. For, once a hedgehog has finished their system — what remains

---

[1] Berlin, Isaiah. 1967. *The hedgehog and the fox.* London: Weidenfeld & Nicolson; Dworkin, Ronald M. 2011. *Justice for hedgehogs.* Cambridge (Massachusetts): Belknap Press of Harvard University Press.

but implementation? With Marx, the point of philosophy is not to describe the world, but to change it. While foxes may change the world with their bit-sized, nuanced critiques, the reality of the Hegelian-Lacanian *Linguistic Superstructure* — as the more mature Ludwig Wittgenstein so well understood — is that the limits of meaning can go on infinitely.[2] Thus, foxes, if they lived forever, would forever be inching along with their little projects. Hedgehogs, on the other hand, are thankful for the work of the foxes, because the atomistic views of the foxes are the units of a grand philosophical system. Therefore, the hedgehogs need the foxes in order to produce their great works, whereas, the foxes need the hedgehogs to give them direction: how many scholars these days devote their careers to the ideologies of one hedgehog or another? Systemization is important: in fact, considering how the Mind works, it automatically systematizes. The Mind is not altogether a fox, for, it is always integrating and synthesizing information on a subliminal level, and therefore resembles a hedgehog. However, the phenomenological program of Mind is very fox-like, because the witnessant — or the entity that witnesses phenomena that exists within us — can only focus on a few minute phenomena at once. Mind, as shall be discussed later on in this work, has two central programs: the *automatic program*, and the *phenomenological program*. The automatic program best represents the modality of the hedgehog, whereas the phenomenological program best represents the modality of the fox. How, then, might the two programs work together, and what modality of form are they together best represented by? Let us now consider the modality of the duckrabbit, a Wittgensteinian fictional creature that, because of its versatile makeup, could be considered either a duck or a rabbit — hence the name, duckrabbit — so its modality was inherently versatile depending on the context of who was looking at it, and how.[3] The duckrabbit in essence can be many things to many different people, while all the same retaining its oneness, differing from the fox in that it retains a hedgehog-esque oneness. However, Mind deals with hypercomplex ideals and phenomena all of the time, and is forced to translate these hypercomplex phenomena into minute atoms of content that are ready for weaving into thoughts, speech, and actions.[4] Worse yet, when one considers, for example, the nothing — how might human Minds compute that? Or any other noumenal concept that escapes our grasp?

Our Minds must apply both an overarching principle of reconstruction and also consider at the same time all fox-like, atomistic, and nuanced phenomena that are relevant to the hedgehog-like hermeneutical principle of reconstruction.

---

[2]   Hegel, Georg Wilhelm Friedrich. 2004. *Hegel's Science of logic*. Amherst, N.Y.: Humanity Books; Lacan, Jacques, Jacques-Alain Miller, and Alan Sheridan. 2019. *The four fundamental concepts of psycho-analysis*; *Wittgenstein, Ludwig, and Peter M. S. Hacker*. 2010. P*hilosophische Untersuchungen = Philosophical investigations*. Oxford [u.a.]: Wiley-Blackwell.

[3]   Wittgenstein, Ludwig, and Peter M. S. Hacker. 2010. *Philosophische Untersuchungen = Philosophical investigations*. Oxford [u.a.]: Wiley-Blackwell.

[4]   Fodor, Jerry Alan. 2014. *The modularity of mind: an essay on faculty psychology*. Cambridge (Mass.): The MIT Press.

And, a lot of the times, these overarching principles and atomistic phenomena are *noumenal* in nature, and hence, instead of being comprehended, must merely be *intuited* using our faculty of *intuitive assessment*. In order to legitimize and objectify our views, we must hold them against the whetstone of the *Imaginary Graph of Being*, or the total set of perfect Platonic forms that consists of all axes of critique.[5] By imagining the noumenal *Imaginary Graph of Being*, we can get our assessments to be as close to *justice* as possible. Thus, this incredible undertaking, that occurs all the time, both automatically — subliminally — and phenomenologically, is the way that we can get closest to *just assessments*. How can we assume that there is such a thing as a *perfect, absolute essence*, as plotted on the *Imaginary Graph of Being*? Here we must borrow the logic of Saint Anselm's ontological argument for the existence of God: if regular perspectives can exist, then a perfect perspective does exist, because it is greater than can be conceived — and is, hence, noumenal.[6] If the Mind is constantly comparing its views to the perfect Platonic forms plotted on the *Imaginary Graph of Being*, then what kind of modality is that? Surely not the modality of the fox, and not the modality of the hedgehog, but instead, the modality of the duckrabbit. Thus, philosophical systemization involves both the modalities of the fox and of the hedgehog, but, ultimately, must be represented by the modal versatility of the duckrabbit. It is not merely to say that Minds must behave with the versatility of duckrabbits, but instead, it is to say that Minds already behave like duckrabbits. This human ponderance of whether or not to be either a fox or a hedgehog is both unnatural and extremist: instead, the aufhebung of the two, the duckrabbit, is the natural modality of Mind under whose reign human beings flourish the most. Thus, we must both systemize and be nuanced at the same time: we must have a *nuanced systemology*. Why systemize? While Mind systemizes automatically, and most resembles the hedgehog, the phenomenological program of Mind most resembles the fox, but, with the two working together in mutual harmony, Mind most resembles the modality of the duckrabbit. To have a nuanced system allows us to apply the principles of *coherency* and *consistency* to said system; even though Ralph Waldo Emerson complained, "consistency is the hobgoblin of fools," we can reject his complaint by arguing instead: consistency helps us root out problems in our conceptions of nature. What is the ultimate project of the duckrabbit[7]? Nothing other than the systematic encyclopedification of the world: nothing more, and nothing less. We must have a systematic philosophy that grounds the world, like the hedgehog, and then, atomistically like the fox, produces nuanced critiques of the world where it may be atomized. Thus, so much for philosophy from the modality of the ontologically versatile duckrabbit.

---

[5]   Plato, and John M. Cooper. 2009. *Complete works*. Indianapolis: Hackett.

[6]   Anselm, Brian Davies, and G. R. Evans. 1998. *The major works Anselm of Canterbury*. Oxford; New York: Oxford University Press.

[7]   Emerson, Ralph Waldo. 2016. *Self reliance & other essays.*

CHAPTER

I

OF ANTHROPOEPISTEMOLOGY

ANTHROPOEPISTEMOLOGY is nothing less than the science of human understanding. Contrast it with for example, the understanding of a cat or of a dog. To claim that there is a science of specifically human understanding is to realize that human beings evolved a certain way, and that their way of evolving has dire consequences for the lived practice of understanding and communicating in the world today — such is famous philosopher Alvin Plantinga's thesis.[8] Even before tackling the science of human understanding, we must first lay the groundwork for how human beings think in general. Indeed, humans produce many entities from their Minds, chief among these being all modalities of speech, action, and thought. Thus, in the coming subchapters, we shall see how human beings *practice* epistemology. Moreover, we shall see how human beings grapple with the basic categories of existence, such as being and nothing. What could be more realistic and helpful than a science of human understanding? Because we are all human beings, such a science will lighten up the world for us in ways perhaps never seen before. First, this chapter shall explore the concept of Noumenality, and how it closely relates to the concept of nothing. Then, the *Imaginary Graph of Being* will be posited as the total set of Plato's ideal forms; the Imaginary Graph of Being will also be discussed as the chief tool that human beings have at their disposal for arriving at *perfect views*. All of the world may be analyzed according to the set of forms composite to the Imaginary Graph of Being, and the world may be divided into entities insofar as they can be distinguished and plotted on the Imaginary Graph of Being: the distinguishment of entities one from the other shall be discussed to occur due to the *Axes of Being* that exist on the Imaginary Graph of Being. Then, Heideggerian being-in-the-world shall be discussed, alongside a bipartite theory of information that concludes there are two modalities of information: *aesthetic information* and *banal information.*[9] Aesthetic information is information that is relevant to an individual's core identity, whereas banal information is that information that lacks any bearing to an individual's

---

[8]   Plantinga, Alvin. 2011. *Where the conflict really lies: science, religion, and naturalism.* New York: Oxford University Press.

[9]   Heidegger, Martin, John Macquarrie, and Edward S. Robinson. 2019. *Being and time.*

core identity, e.g., that towel that is hanging up over there on the rack. After that, the phenomenology of time will be discussed, in particular, the durational theory of consciousness as proposed by famous philosopher and Nobel laureate Henri Bergson.[10] Then, measurable time will be analyzed, and what the author refers to as *Nietzsche's Wager* will be commented upon. *Nietzsche's Wager* is the idea that Being repeats itself ad infinitum, and this view greatly resembles the Hindu and Buddhist notions of the karmic cycle, except that for Nietzsche, there is no hope for release from this cycle, whereas the Hindu and Buddhist philosophers argue for a release referred to as *nirvana*.[11]

Following that discussion, there will be an analysis of the metaphysics of informativity, which involves the neuroscientific *General Theory of Procession* that processes information as realized in the world, and then makes it available to the phenomenological consciousness. After that, will follow, a discourse around the notion of *absolute* and *perfect essences* — two concepts that form the bedrock of any sophisticated theory of a transcendental epistemology. Following that discussion will be another discussion on *social constructs*, i.e., *metaphysical hypotheticals* that are grounded both through projectional essentialism and political rapportionality — two notions that will be discussed at greater length toward the latter half of this work. Then, modalities of determining which entities are in fact metaphysically hypothetical, will be addressed, and, will be put into conversation with the epistemological theories of two famous epistemologists, namely, Alvin Goldman and Ernest Sosa.[12] The view that will be synthesized out of their two views, will be referred to as *idiosyncratic constructivism*, or the idea that each individual has their own unique set of ways of forming knowledge: ultimately the realization of a true justified belief will be argued to be most probable to attain should the phenomenology of the individual resemble the *Pragmatic-Cognitivist Consciousness*, or that modality of consciousness that weighs epistemic beliefs based on their virtue, reliability, and transcendentality. Then, the emergence of hypothetical *social constructs* will be discussed as a critique of anthropomodal servility toward their own creations: human beings let their own hypothetical *social constructs* come to dominate their lives in unchecked ways; true, the boon of *social constructs* is that they reinforce human lives and scaffold them in ways never imagined by our ancestors who existed before civilization did, however, these entities sometimes have a tendency to get out of hand, and thus must be limited with checks and balances.

---

[10] Bergson, Henri. 2002. *Time and free will: an essay on the immediate data of consciousness*. London: Routledge.

[11] Nietzsche, Friedrich Wilhelm, Walter Arnold Kaufmann, and R. J. Hollingdale. 1968. *The will to power: a new translation*. New York: Vintage Books.

[12] Goldman, Alvin and Bob Beddor, "Reliabilist Epistemology", *The Stanford Encyclopedia of Philosophy* (Summer 2021 Edition), Edward N. Zalta (ed.), URL = <https://plato.stanford.edu/archives/sum2021/entries/reliabilism/>; Sosa, Ernest. 2009. *A virtue epistemology: apt belief and reflective knowledge*. Volume 1 Volume 1. Oxford: Oxford University Press.

Next, the concept of indebtion will be discussed, which is a peculiar way that language ensnares human beings into all modalities of debt and so on. Then, questions themselves will be interrogated, because questions form the bedrock of any serious philosophical or political-theoretical endeavor. Then, the science of *trajectorics* will be discussed, or the general way in which entities move across the temporal timeline; becoming shall also be discussed immediately after the subchapter on trajectorics. Then, the concept of the *witnessant* shall be addressed and interrogated, as that entity which perceives all phenomena in the Mind; the concept of the *witnessant* is meant to replace René Descartes's *cogito ergo sum* argument.[13] After that, will be discussed, a *General Theory of Focalization*, or the specific limits that are set upon a conceptual entity that make it that entity and that entity alone: focalization allows for specification and distinguishment of that entity being focalized from all other entities. Then, a quick reconstruction of the Set Theoretical Logic of Books in general will be discussed, on account of books and journal articles being the predominant mode of academic communication. Finally, the last subchapter before the commencement of the division of this work entitled *Anthropocognitivity* shall be a discussion of *productive imprint*, or that resemblance a product of Mind bears that links it to its producer or author. So much then, for the prefatory remarks on the division of this work labeled *Anthropoepistemology*.

1. Of the Noumenality of Being: Plato, Kant, and Hegel; or, Of the Doctrine of the Unfalsifiability of Being

The philosophical usage of the term noumenon pre-dates even the ancient figure Plato.[14] A philosophical issue is just something that encourages us to think about the issue in a complex way rather than in a simple way. Famous philosopher G.W.F. Hegel actually wrote an article about abstraction — in which he claims that abstraction is a modality of thought that involves oversimplification — wherein he warns us that thinking about matters in a simple way can be both dangerous and irresponsible; nevertheless, most people think abstractly, because it is far easier than thinking about issues in a complex manner.[15] So, following Hegel, the stakes are high, here, to be sure. Thus, we must attempt to think complexly about complex issues, and simply about simple issues; furthermore, we must seek the wisdom to know the difference between when to think simply and complexly. Unfortunately, Noumenality is a very complex issue. It is usually contrasted with the word phenomenality, which is a word that is used to talk about all of the various

---

[13]   Descartes, Rene, and F. Sutcliffe. 2005. *Discourse on Method and the Meditations*. https://www.vlebooks.com/vleweb/product/openreader?id=none&isbn=9780141944203.

[14]   Honderich, Ted. 2005. *The Oxford guide to philosophy*.

[15]   Hegel, Georg Wilhelm Friedrich, and Stephen Houlgate. 1998. *The Hegel reader*. Oxford, UK: Blackwell Publishers.

experiences that we perceive through our senses. Now, Noumenality is something altogether different. Noumenality is a word used to talk about both simple and complex things, and these things are usually things that resist sense perception. Which is to say, that we cannot perceive noumenal entities in themselves. Rather, we must imagine them. This entire work will be about noumenal entities, because from a certain point of view, the most extraordinary and practical questions, either have noumenal answers — which means that the answers to these questions resist our understanding in some way — or they involve noumenal things in the answering of other questions. In some cases, the word noumena may also refer to the most basic and fundamental parts of reality. Let us now consider an example, to prove a point: following the materialists, famous philosopher David Lewis argued for physicalism, or that idea that metaphysics fundamentally is physics.[16]

Yet, what is physics? Lewis here appears to fall prey to the pitfalls of the early Wittgensteinian and the Vienna Circle's *verificationist* philosophy, or that philosophy that celebrated mere assertion more than anything else.[17] To tell the story: famous philosopher Karl Popper put an end to their verificationist ideations with his equally famous work, *The Logic of Scientific Discovery*.[18] In that work, Popper argued that the chief principle of any scientific epistemology must be its ability to be falsifiable. Yet, when this logic turns upon the verificationist *assertion* that is Lewisian physicalism, it is clear that merely asserting physics as a metaphysical reality is not exactly on the table, for, there may well be a refutation of physics lurking somewhere in the future, as of yet undiscovered. Thus, the question of a First Philosophy — of a fundamental metaphysics — ultimately has a noumenal answer: for, it cannot be asserted one way or the other whether or not physics exists, without running into the same woes that the early Wittgenstein and the Vienna Circle encountered when first confronted with Popper's *theory of falsificationism*: hence we can only be *agnostic* about physical fundamentalities. Thus, if the question of the fundamental reality of the world is noumenal, what other examples of Noumenality are to be found across philosophy? An aim of this work is to elucidate these areas of philosophy that have noumenal answers, and, as shall be seen, many such noumenal answers are not only identified, but are exposited, in this work. As this work carries along, and as more and more examples of noumenal entities are demonstrated, the essence of Noumenality will become clearer and clearer. So much, then, for the notion of Noumenality.

[16] Hall, Ned, Brian Rabern, and Wolfgang Schwarz, "David Lewis's Metaphysics", *The Stanford Encyclopedia of Philosophy* (Fall 2021 Edition), Edward N. Zalta (ed.), URL = <https://plato.stanford.edu/archives/fall2021/entries/lewis-metaphysics/>.

[17] Wittgenstein, Ludwig. 2022. *Tractatus Logico-Philosophicus*. [S.l.]: Penguin Books.

[18] Popper, Karl Raimund. 2014. *The logic of scientific discovery*.

2. *Of the Noumenality of Nothing: Hegel, Heidegger, and Sartre*

Many famous philosophers have held the concept of the nothing to be central to their works and writings. Two of these philosophers were Jean Paul Sartre and Martin Heidegger.[19] Returning to the nothing, in fact, on page two of Hegel's masterpiece, *The Science of Logic*, he claims to refute the existence of the nothing.[20] Yet, this author would instead argue that the issue of the nothing is more complex than Hegel gives it credit for. While on the one hand it would be tempting to say that the nothing does not exist, at the same time, there are many examples today in mathematics and physics that would appear to point toward the existence of nothing. Take for example imaginary numbers in mathematics, which are made up entities that, once imagined to be real, help us to understand mathematics in a better light. So, there are certainly some reasons to believe that the nothing could exist. However, ultimately, the answer to this question escapes us, because it is so complex, and therefore, because the answers lie outside of our sense perception, we could actually claim that the answer to the question is *noumenal.* The answer would be noumenal to the extent that the matter is simply too hard to grasp for us human beings and our science of understanding. We are, after all, limited as human beings in our capacities to understand hypercomplex issues such as the nothing. Therefore, in our first assessment of the work, we shall declare the nothing to be noumenal, which means that it is impossible to solve for human beings. On the other hand, even though we have declared the issue of nothing to be noumenal, that does not mean that we cannot experiment with our phenomenological imaginations to *imagine* what noumenal entities may be like. In fact, crucial to this work, will be the idea that in fact, noumenal entities, may be imagined via the faculty of intuition: such is the basis for any of famous philosopher John Searle's *social constructs.*[21]

Human beings have a webwork of beliefs and emotions — Quinean *webs of belief* — that are both intertwined with each other — and this webwork may be referred to as their *subliminal prioritization*s, each of which is unique to a given human being.[22] Thus, by making good use of our faculty of intuition, human beings may come as close to the noumenal as possible — the goal is to arrive precisely on the limit between the phenomenal and the noumenal. How might we intuit the ontology of nothing, using our phenomenological imaginations? The nothing might best resemble *the absence of anything*, or might resemble *pure absence.* Now, while it was not too difficult to infer and intuit that basic and simple assessment about the concept of nothing, and even though we have come as close to we can

[19] Sartre, Jean-Paul, and Sarah Richmond. 2021. *Being and nothingness: an essay on phenomenological ontology; Heidegger, Martin, John Macquarrie, and Edward S. Robinson. 2019. Being and time.*

[20] Hegel, Georg Wilhelm Friedrich. 2004. *Hegel's Science of logic.* Amherst, N.Y.: Humanity Books.

[21] Searle, John Rogers. 1996. *The construction of social reality.* London: Penguin Books.

[22] Quine, Willard Van Orman, and J. S. Ullian. 1970. *The web of belief.* Quine. New York: Random House.

to the concept of nothing, we nevertheless cannot proceed any further, for, it is ultimately a noumenal question that will never have any sufficient answering. Yet, how can we tell that the concept of nothing is for us a noumenal issue, instead of a phenomenal issue? For one, the concept of nothing resists representation, as has been demonstrated by famous philosopher Rudolf Carnap, and, secondly, the concept of nothing resists the cognitive faculties of human beings, for, as an issue, human beings have never progressed all that far with it, and, hence, given that miserable track record, it seems fair here to lay rest to the issue and argue instead that it is simply a noumenal issue that resists our understandings as human beings.[23] So much for the concept of nothing.

3. Of the Platonic Imaginary Graph of Being: Parfit, Butler, and Sider

In Philosophy, identity is a central concern and lies at the heart of many issues. Some of the most famous of these issues involve theories and arguments about gender and personal identity. Is gender a part of someone's basic identity? Is an individual's personality real or merely an illusion based upon our faulty human understanding of reality? Two famous philosophers who focus on these issues are none other than Judith Butler and Derek Parfit, separately and distinctly, of course.[24] Because the noumenal may refer either to the most basic and real things in the world, but also, to those things that resist our sense perception, Noumenality becomes important to the philosophical issue of identity. An identity is merely a set of parts put together in a certain way, for simple and physical objects. For more complex things — for example consciousness — an identity can likewise be more complex than a mere arrangement of parts. Famous philosopher Theodore Sider argues that personal identity consists of temporal parts — or the arrangement of parts in such and such a way that a specific identity exists because of the arrangement of those parts.[25] It is not immediately clear whether or not consciousness resists the argument about temporal parts, therefore, we must interrogate the issue further. Some philosophers would argue that the nature of consciousness is so complex that its identity could not merely be a matter of physical parts arranged in a certain way across time. Instead, they would argue against that sort of reductionism — a reduction of consciousness down to its basic parts — and would champion an argument more holistic in nature. A more mental kind of argument might be called idealism, or

---

[23] Heidegger, Martin, and David Farrell Krell. 1993. *Basic writings: from being and time (1927) to the task of thinking (1964)*. New York: Harper Collins College.

[24] Parfit, Derek. 2007. *Reasons and persons*. Oxford: Clarendon Press; Butler, Judith. 2006. *Gender trouble*. New York, London: Routledge.

[25] Hawley, Katherine, "Temporal Parts", *The Stanford Encyclopedia of Philosophy* (Summer 2020 Edition), Edward N. Zalta (ed.), URL = <https://plato.stanford.edu/archives/sum2020/entries/temporal-parts/>.

the general idea that Mind processes phenomena in complex ways that distinguish it from other parts of the world, namely, physical entities. Returning to a more holistic conception of consciousness, there is a view called holism, which basically argues that the whole of some entity is greater than the sum of its parts — which is certainly very compatible with idealisms.[26] To explain this idea further, consider all of the parts that go into making a car. Imagine them separated.

Now, imagine them all put together in the shape of a car. If the car is taken apart, can it be driven? Of course not. It is only when the car is arranged in a certain way that it can be driven. Thus, the whole that is the car is more complex than the sum of its parts, because when put together it not only becomes a thing in itself, but also it gains a new function that it did not have before, which is the ability to drive. Thus, here is where someone would be able to apply the same kind of argument to consciousness itself: put together all of the parts of the brain, and suddenly we have a new entity that we are dealing with. While identity is at the heart of this subchapter, the word essence is also important here, because some would argue that an identity is wrapped up with its essence, or its basic features. An essence is at once both a simple and a complex issue. It is the set of information relevant to a given thing that exists, and usually, is the most vital and important information about an object that helps us understand why that object is specifically itself and not another object. Because *absolute essences* are imaginary concepts that we use to understand the world, they are necessarily noumenal. Which is to say, that they cannot be perceived by our senses, but can only be imagined by our Minds and intuited by our Hearts — our total sets of integrated information, both emotionally charged and uncharged, as stored in our mental depositories. On the other hand, *partial* and *limited* essences exist within our Minds, which is to say, that our Minds at least partially comprehend Platonic forms, and then project them into the world in order to distinguish and identify worldly entities from other worldly entities — this view is known as *cognitivism*, and was made famous by Kant.[27] An important point to make, here, is that in order to define a thing, it must be defined in relationship both to itself and to the entire set of possible worlds — and all they contain — thus, let us now undertake a general division between *limited essences* and *absolute essences*, because, ultimately, before we can reach an *absolute epistemology*, we must employ our human means of understanding — which, may be labeled here a certain *limited* and *partial* modality of epistemology, or, put in terms more relevant to human beings, a certain *anthropoepistemology*. Thus, human understanding perceives and conceptualizes partial and *limited* essences. How can we be sure that there is a category of knowledge beyond human beings? Simple, if we imagine that human beings did not exist, would the world still fundamentally be a basin of information? The answer here is that, of course,

---

[26] Healey, Richard and Henrique Gomes, "Holism and Nonseparability in Physics", *The Stanford Encyclopedia of Philosophy* (Spring 2022 Edition), Edward N. Zalta (ed.), URL = <https://plato.stanford.edu/archives/spr2022/entries/physics-holism/>.

[27] Kant, Immanuel, and Paul Guyer. 2009. *Critique of pure reason*. Cambridge: Cambridge Univ. Press.

there would still be information contained in the world, and hence, there may be an epistemology outside of the existence of our frail and human epistemologies — that is to say, outside of our *anthropoepistemologies*. Furthermore, how can we know that our views are *just*, or, as famous philosopher Ernest Sosa calls them, *virtuous*?

Firstly, we cannot know whether or not our views are just — such an inquiry is noumenal from the start. However, let us now consider an ontological argument from famous philosopher Saint Anselm, for the existence of God, except, let us remove it from its context, and apply it to epistemology. Saint Anselm argues: if there is a being that is greater than can be conceived, then it exists, and so on.[28] Imagine there was a *perfect assessment*, greater than could be conceived: it would have to be hypercomplex, and would involve information from every existing set of possible worlds, in order for it to be the most just, reliable, and accurate assessment in the total set of all possible worlds. Now, certainly, before we even get started, we must limit this inquiry: without a doubt, it is a noumenal thought experiment from the beginning. However, even though it is a noumenal entity — an *absolute, perfect assessment* — we may still *intuit* and *infer* around it, and doing so will yield great fruits for our inquiry. Here, *speculative reason* becomes vital for the practice of any epistemology, or, reason that involves noumenal entities or noumenal issues. Because the *perfect assessment* itself must exist in relation to all other possible assessments across the total set of worlds — both real and imaginary — there must be a set of assessments existing on what we might call an *Imaginary Graph of Being*. Here, it would be useful to distinguish between two kinds of graphs fundamental to epistemology in general: firstly, to the *Imaginary Graph of Being*, and secondly, to the *Ontological Graph of Being*, or, the graph that consists of the set of all existing entities across the total set of all possible worlds. Our world exists plotted on the axes of the *Ontological Graph of Being*, whereas the worlds of *The Golden Ass* or *Silas Marner* exist plotted on the *Imaginary Graph of Being*. Now, the difference between these two graphs may at times be *noumenal*, however, that does not mean that we should disregard the *Imaginary Graph of Being* as useless, for, it is absolutely useful in innumerable ways. As a thought experiment — and as a way to ontologize imaginary entities such as fictional plots, and so on — it is the very realm of thought itself — it is the realm of Plato's *perfect* and *absolute* forms. How might this pertain to epistemology or identity? Simple. While human beings have their *anthropoepistemologies* that are limited in infinitely many respects, the *perfect epistemology* instead consists of a complete and total knowledge of Plato's realm of forms — of the *Imaginary Graph of Being*. In fact, the only way to improve our knowledge consisting of *partial* and *limited essences* is to imagine and then intuit how our limited views compare with the *perfect viewpoints* as plotted on the *Imaginary Graph of Being*. The *Imaginary Graph of Being* will be discussed and interrogated at greater length during the division of this work labeled *Aesthetics*.

---

[28]   Anselm, Brian Davies, and G. R. Evans. 1998. *The major works Anselm of Canterbury*. Oxford; New York: Oxford University Press.

4. Of Conforming the Lewisian Ontological Graph of Being to the Platonic Imaginary Graph of Being

Distinct from the *Platonic Imaginary Graph of Being*, the *Lewisian Ontological Graph of Being* is a concept that involves the total set of all entities across the total set of all possible worlds. Where the Imaginary Graph of Being either involves *perfect*, *metaphysical*, or *fictional* entities, instead, the Ontological Graph of Being involves entities of a more concrete and real nature. This is not to say that the Imaginary Graph of Being contains no entities that are real, rather, it is to say that those entities are either hypothetical, metaphysical, or noumenal. Let us now consider what might happen should these two graphs overlap on a specific coordinate set series. Such an overlapping is not necessarily — as may be expected — the ultimate aim of any scientific epistemology, because, a conspiracy theory, for example, could be plotted on both graphs, but, one immediately sees why such an emplotment is ethically malefic: for, even though conspiracy theories may exist on the Imaginary Graph of Being — because they are inherently fictitious — it is ethically unconscionable for a conspiracy theory to exist within the internal, *Idiosyncratic Cognitive Graph of Being* that is contained within a Mind. For, all of Mind may be plotted on a Graph of Being, and such a graph allows us to, in theory, perfectly distinguish between one Mind and another Mind. Yet, because the Imaginary Graph of Being contains Plato's *perfect forms*, the goal of any scientific epistemology is to *justly overlap* the Imaginary Graph of Being with the Ontological Graph of Being. Because the Imaginary Graph of Being is inherently noumenal, because it involves Plato's perfect forms, the ability to know for certain when there is an overlapping between the two graphs is impossible — it is a *noumenal endeavor*, or an endeavor that will never yield *absolute* and *perfect* knowledge. However, because of the human faculty of intuition, which itself is a mode of thought, human beings may transcend their own anthropoepistemologies in their attempt to overlap their *partial* and *limited* assessments with the *absolute* and *perfect* assessments plotted on the Imaginary Graph of Being. When there is a discord between the two graphs — such as in the case of conspiracy theories — that is when a malefic thought has occurred. Yet, in the case of realpolitik and utopia, there exists a very real status of discord: for, the current emplotment of the practice of politics on the Ontological Graph of Being, is far removed from the coordinate set series that is utopian on the Imaginary Graph of Being. Thus, supposing we were aiming for utopia, the ideal here would be for the two graphs to benefically *align*. Hence, any practice of scientific epistemology that seeks to transcend the limits of Anthropoepistemology, must seek to unify the Ontological Graph of Being — the real and total set of worlds — with the *perfect* and *absolute* set of ideal forms that exist along the axes of the Imaginary Graph of Being.

    Why must we conform the Ontological Graph of Being — the *descriptive* Graph of Being — within the confines of what is the *prescriptive* Imaginary Graph of Being? Because the Imaginary Graph of Being is more *perfect* and *elegant*, and reflects the *best possible essence* of any given entity, the very practice of any scientific and species transcendent epistemology must aim not merely for truth, but for *axic alignment* between the two main Graphs of Being: the Ontological Graph and the Imaginary Graph. Here, the subterranean argument is: *perfection* is the ultimate aim of any endeavor. Unfortunately, in the *Nicomachean Ethics*, Aristotle gets this point wrong: every action must not be directed toward some good, but rather instead, every action must be directed toward *perfection* itself.[29] This shall be the universal argument of this work, and it will be applied to epistemology, aesthetics, ethics, and politics. Why not just assume Aristotle's position? Because the good is fundamentally *imperfect*, and furthermore, because the good is a notion wrought up by human beings: it is anthropoepistemological in nature. Thus, for any epistemology to shed the yoke of its anthropological bearings, it must turn to the ideal of *perfection*, which itself is the chief ideal as represented on the *Imaginary Graph of Being*. Now, Alvin Platinga has a very serious argument on this point: if human beings evolved merely to survive, then they did not evolve to know *justly*, which is to say, to know *perfectly*. While this may be a controversial argument, no philosopher would deny that human beings — and their anthropoepistemologies — are limited, finite, and fundamentally *imperfect*. Existing epistemologies of our day Alvin Goldman's *reliabilism* and Ernest Sosa's *virtue epistemology*, are inherently anthropoepistemological, for, reliabilism is grounded on the human ideal of utility, whereas virtue epistemology is grounded upon the human notion of *production*, or the emergence of thought, speech, or action.

How might the Imaginary Graph of Being counteract the limits of Anthropoepistemology, and Anthropocognitivity in general? The Imaginary Graph of Being — Plato's set of *ideal* and *perfect* forms — indeed, that even consists of *ontological fictions*, because it involves *perfect entities* — automatically transcends the limits of any anthropoepistemology. But, because the Imaginary Graph of Being is noumenal, and hence resists anthropoepistemology, we have but one escape route, as it were: the faculty of phenomenological imagination which itself is a submodality of thought. Thus, through the faculty of phenomenological imagination, human beings may transcend themselves. Phenomenological imagination itself was extended to allow for this process of transcendentalization through the autodiversifcation of the Linguistic Superstructure that evolved the human race out of nature and into society, by means of the reflexivity equation. Let the Linguistic Superstructure be known as the total set of the uses of sign systems in the human Anthropocognitivity, akin to famous psychoanalyst Jacques Lacan's symbolic register; the Linguistic Superstructure's process of autodiversification occurs naturally across time, as human beings develop more and more signs and referents during the process that itself is civilization.[30] Let the reflexivity equation

---

[29]   Aristotlelēs, and C. D. C. Reeve. 2014. *Nicomachean Ethics*. Indianapolis: Hackett.

[30]   Johnston, Adrian, "Jacques Lacan", *The Stanford Encyclopedia of Philosophy* (Fall 2018 Edition), Edward N. Zalta (ed.), URL = <https://plato.stanford.edu/archives/fall2018/entries/lacan/>.

be known as an anthropomodal mechanism for considering two things: how information relates to an individual *descriptively*, and how information ought to relate to an individual *prescriptively*. Fundamentally, the Imaginary Graph of Being must be made to confine to the Ontological Graph of Being *descriptively* — this is the process of any scientific epistemology or aesthetics — but, also, the Ontological Graph of Being must be made to conform itself to the Imaginary Graph of Being *prescriptively* — this is the process of any scientific undertaking of ethics. So much for the Imaginary Graph of Being.

5. Of the Axes of Being

Once we have understood the two Graphs of Being — namely, the Lewisian Ontological Graph of Being and the Platonic Imaginary Graph of Being — we ought now extend our interrogation of these issues to the logical nature of both graphs; first, we shall look at the *Axes of Being*. An axis is merely a certain plottable modality on a particular graph. Because we believe agnostically in the Ontological Graph of Being, which is a simple and not complex concept at all, the next step to take to the matter is: how many dimensions or axes are there on the Ontological Graph of Being? Or, on the Imaginary Graph of Being? The answer could be infinitely many, or there could only be a certain number of axes on the graph. Some philosophers argue for fourth dimensionalism, a belief that implies that the fourth dimension is apparently quite influential in our day to day affairs.[31] An axis of Being might be depth for example, or color, or weight, or density. Here, to be conserative, it would make sense to argue that there are infinitely many axes of Being, because language or thought could be arranged in certain sets that privilege uniqueness across an infinite trajectory. Recollecting from our grammar school days how to plot a graph, what happens when there are coordinates to plot? Let an identity be understood as a set of coordinates on the Imaginary Graph of Being; we say Imaginary Graph of Being here, instead of the Ontological Graph of Being, because many philosophers today debate the existence of identities and essences, and, because such inquiries around those issues are fundamentally noumenal, it is up in the air whether or not they actually exist; hence, we can at least take the philosophically conservative route and argue that essences and identities exist on the Imaginary Graph of Being. The Ontological Graph of Being, however, represents the entire world and also all of the other possible worlds that definitively exist, or about whose existence we may at least be agnostics, following the logic of Popper's falsificationism.[32] Therefore, what could not be plotted either upon the Ontological Graph of Being or upon the Imaginary Graph of being? These two graphs can even plot themselves upon themselves, to be sure. It should be noted

---

[31]   Sider, Theodore. 2013. *Four-dimensionalism: an ontology of persistence and time.*

[32]   Popper, Karl Raimund. 2014. *The logic of scientific discovery.*

that the Imaginary Graph of Being drastically improves our understanding of the world, but does not necessarily exist.

Conservatively, we can argue that the Imaginary Graph of Being exists chiefly in the Mind, as a tool of the phenomenological imagination. Because the existence of the Imaginary Graph of Being is itself controversial, how might we go about categorizing it? Perhaps it should be called a noumenal concept, to the extent that its parameters can be imagined, but that it cannot be perceived in the world. Even the Ontological Graph of Being exists only on the Imaginary Graph of Being, for, there is no such entity in the world that links all existing entities in quite the same way that it accomplishes to do so. Returning to axic cross-sectionalism, try to imagine what would happen when, say, five hundred axes of being intersected — or met — on a single point on the Imaginary Graph of Being. While it is probably true that any complex thing such as a cat or dog could have a huge set of coordinates, we could imagine for this example's sake that it only takes five hundred facets of an identity to make up a dog or a cat. Hence, we are all capable of being plotted on both the Ontological Graph of Being and the Imaginary Graph of Being. Identity therefore is the cross section of a set of coordinates of information that altogether make up the existence of a given entity or an organic subject, akin perhaps to Kimberle Crenshaw's theory of *intersectionality*.[33] While some might argue that monism is the case, and that hence the Ontological Graph of Being has an existence outside of the Imaginary Graph of Being, it is not this work's motive to argue one way or the other for that issue; instead, we ought to be content to declare that specific issue noumenal and therefore unanswerable. So much for the two graphs of being; however, it is central to note that the Lewisian Ontological Graph of Being is itself an imaginary concept, for, it is only a thought experiment that better helps us to understand the world. So much for the two graphs of being and axic cross-sectionalism.

6. Of Heideggerian Being-in-the-World and a Bipartite Theory of Informativity; or, Of Aesthetic Informativity Versus Banal Informativity

Being-in-the-World is a complex phenomenon, to be sure. If we can say anything basic about the world, first and foremost, there are entities. Secondly, there is a category of entities that also possess some level of consciousness. While it is possible for there to be consciousness without perception, all of consciousness involves phenomenality, or the perception of entities, and, judging conseravtive, at the very least, mere thoughts internal to the Mind. So, we can confidently say a few things about being-in-the-world as perceptive human beings. We know that

---

[33]   Crenshaw, Kimberle. 2012. *On Intersectionality The Seminal Essays*. New Pr.

the world contains objects, and the nature of an object is that it protrudes into the world. What does that mean? It means that an object forces the rest of the world to consider that object and its own nature. Basically, an object gives off information that other objects are made to feel the forces of, and that animal subjects may come to form concepts about. The very words on this page take up space on the page and provide information about the color of the text and so on. Thus, informativity, or the science of information, will become vital to the pursuit of human knowledge. Because knowledge necessarily involves information, it makes sense that this theory of being-in-the-world focuses on information. This is an eccentric move to make in philosophy, but it is the view of the author that such a position enables us to arrive at an understanding of the functionalities of the world. Objects and subjects are constantly protruding in the world, which is to say, exerting their influence on the world and on animal subjects. Furthermore, consciousness is constantly projected into the world, as is essence, from Mind itself; this is to agree with David Chalmers's views on *extended consciousness*, or the idea that consciousness can come to inhabit certain entities in the world.[34] As consciousness projects its witnessant — its locus of attention — into the world, the witnessant is both confined and limited by the information protruding out of its surroundings.

Then, this limited set of information in turn limits the modality of phenomenological consciousness that is witnessed by an individual. As consciousness is projected into the world, so is essence, for, as many philosophers will argue today, *essences have gone out of fashion*, yet, have essences departed from our Minds? Certainly not. Here, it will become useful to describe a third kind of imaginary graph that enables us to understand the reality of worldly and phenomenological matters in a better light: this third graph is the *Idiosyncratic Graph* that maps an individual's idiosyncratic modality of Mind, including both its *phenomenological* part, and its *automatic* parts. Thus, when a person projects essence into the world, they are in fact projecting from their internal set of concepts that in total makes up their systematic set of information, both emotionally charged and uncharged. Thus, the Idiosyncratic Graph becomes important for imagining what an individual's modality of consciousness is like: which axes of critique and which axes of being do they gravitate toward, as it were, in their practice of Heideggerian average everydayness?[35] An Idiosyncratic Graph allows us to map out a person's *Core Script*, which is a serious component of their personal identity. Not all of the information that an individual knows goes into the fashioning of their Core Script, however, for there are two sets of information that the mind contains: banal information and aesthetic information. *Banal* information — such as that there is a towel hanging on the rack over yonder — does not have any meaningfulness to my Core Script, and hence is just stored in the mental depository in a dull way. *Aesthetic* information, however, is relevant to the

---

[34] Chalmers, David John, and Tim Peacock. 2022. *Reality+: virtual worlds and the problems of philosophy.*

[35] Heidegger, Martin, and David Farrell Krell. 1993. *Basic writings: from being and time (1927) to the task of thinking (1964).* New York: Harper Collins College.

fashioning of our Core Script, which is our personal identity; *aesthetic* information is information that affects our Core Script one way or another, and usually, affects metanoia — or change of personality — in the individual. Thus, this last major point allows for a *Bipartite Theory of Informativity*, or a theory of the banal and of the aesthetic. More on these issues in the division of this work labeled *Aesthetics*.

7. Of the Augustinian-Bergsonian Phenomenology of Time

For some philosophers, time is non-physical, while for most philosophers, time is physical. To be clear: physics is not a complete science, and we are far from a completed Science. What then can we say of time? Two famous philosophers become relevant to our discussion, in the view of your author. These two philosophers are Saint Augustine and Henri Bergson. What is so distinctive about their respective theories of time that they need to be mentioned here? To be sure, they both have very unique theories of consciousness that incorporate theories of the experience of time, not necessarily of physical time. For Saint Augustine, time was merely an illusion grounded in the Mind — his view is not in vogue so much today, but Bergson's is set to be all the rage, because, for many, consciousness is something that is so mysterious — so noumenal — that it cannot be explained.[36] The view that consciousness cannot be understood through our anthropoepistemologies is called *new mysterianism*, and was made famous by philosophers, one such being Colin McGinn. While consciousness certainly is mysterious — which is to say, noumenal — there are many things we can definitively know about consciousness, as shall be discussed in the division of this work labeled *Anthropocognitivity*.[37] Returning to Bergson — for him — the experience of time was separate and distinct from the concept of time as employed by physicists and their acolytes.

Bergson referred to the mental experience of time duration, which could best be related perhaps to cinema, for which there was a continuous flow of information presented to the witnessant — to the perceiver. For Bergson, the phenomenology of time was qualitative rather than quantitative, and hence could not be measured in any sophisticated kind of way, perhaps as the physicists and their acolytes would like to do to consciousness, if they could only figure it out. Although we have not yet begun to discuss semantics and meaning in this work, some basic treatment of these issues will be necessary to complement the discussion on temporal identity. If meaning is projected into the world from the Mind, then it is important to consider Saint Augustine's line of thought: that the experience of time may in fact be entirely in our heads. Yet, that view no longer has traction today, however interesting and unique it is; still, the mental experience of time is

---

[36] Augustine, and R. S. Pine-Coffin. 2003. *Confessions*; Bergson, Henri. 2002. *Time and free will: an essay on the immediate data of consciousness*. London: Routledge.

[37] McGinn, Colin. 2000. *The mysterious flame: conscious minds in a material world*. New York: BasicBooks.

relevant to us because, if meaning is contained within the brain and processed by consciousness, then we have a concept of time within a depository that is in our brains. This concept of time is also processed by our animal consciousness.

Because essences exist within our Minds in the form of concepts, and perhaps outside of our Minds on the Imaginary Graph of Being, the identity of time is itself contained within human understanding, in addition to both forms of time being represented on the Imaginary Graph of Being: phenomenological time and physical time. Yet, this conception of time is unfortunately a very human one, limited by our anthropoepistemologies. While the true essence of time may be totally different from the concept of time as humans understand it, the case is nevertheless that human beings have their own understanding of time which directly impacts human civilization and human relationships. Thus, Saint Augustine is right to point toward the phenomenology of time, because it is such a vital force in our own human lives. Bergson's conception of time is even more astute because, it is not just time that is durational and qualitative, it is concepts themselves as experienced by the Mind. These concepts that we project onto the world are mostly qualitative, which means that they do not necessarily involve numbers or quantity, and even the concepts involving numbers that we project into the world, involve qualities of quantities, and not quantities themselves. In this work, the phenomenology of time will be considered more important than the actual nature of so-called physical time, because this is a work about human beings and the concomitant concept of civilization. Extra-physical time is time as processed by the consciousness, and is what Bergson referred to as duration in his early work, *Time and Free Will*. Because this is chiefly a work involving human elements, it makes sense to be more focused on non-physical time rather than physical time.

8. Of Bergsonian Durational Consciousness and the Zeitgeistal Jungian Collective Consciousness

Bergson's phenomenological reconstruction of time is helpful to this research program for a number of reasons. It is the most glaring and famous contention in Western Philosophy that accuses the phenomenological faculty of Mind to be qualitative rather than quantitative and extensional, perhaps only rivaled by René Descartes's dualism.[38] It is not controversial at all to differentiate between the duration of time experienced by a fruit fly and by a human being: for the fly, a day is a lifetime, and must carry on for ages. While complex mammals may have concepts of time, perhaps the fruit fly has no such conception of time. What would it be like to be a fruit fry? Famous philosopher Tom Nagel wrote a journal article

---

[38] Descartes, Rene, and F. Sutcliffe. 2005. Discourse on Method and the Meditations. https://www.vlebooks.com/vleweb/product/openreader?id=none&isbn=9780141944203.

called *What is it like to be a bat?*[39] In this piece, he discusses the limitations of bat consciousness. Whether what we are considering is a human, a bat, or a fruit fly, it is clear that distinct organisms have distinct conceptions of time. What's more, distinct human beings have distinct conceptions of time. And, as noted before, the concept of time is only one concept employed by human beings, which means that there are infinitely many more concepts employed by human beings in their anthropoepistemologies, for example: color, car, truck, duck, or Shakespeare.

To understand that there are differences in consciousness is to understand that there are personal differences in human beings — differences of thought, speech, action, and perception. Thus, Bergson's theory of duration is an excellent example to demonstrate the complexity of human consciousness. Here, it would be relevant to consider: what of a collective holism of the phenomenological experience of time, is such a thing possible? While, using the Imaginary Graph of Being, we may imagine the total set of all phenomenological experiences of time — even a set of interspecies phenomenological experiences of time — but, what could we do with this conception? Is there such a thing as a *social witnessant*, or a collective set of phenomenological experiences? May one be a holist about this set of witnessants, and allow for the existence of a social witnessant? Whether or not there is a social witnessant, is a matter of great speculation, which, ultimately is noumenal at this time: perhaps even one might apply the view of the new mysterians here, and argue, that we cannot at this time know whether or not there is such a thing as a social witnessant — here, we might argue that such an inquiry is fundamentally from the beginning a noumenal inquiry. However, a social witnessant, or a collective entity that perceives the total set of phenomenological experiences, might be inferred if we are holists and take the gamble as did psychologist Carl Jung that there is such a thing as a *collective subconsciousness*.[40]

Especially if we believe in body politic and the ontology of nation-states; these issues shall be analyzed at greater length in the division of this work labeled *Politics*. However, some species do employ mechanisms of *collective modality*, where ants will all function in certain ways to accomplish certain collective tasks. If a species as minute as ants could accomplish so great a feat, we must ask the question: is such a holism of the human race *descriptive* of the human race, and, if it is not, ought it to be *prescriptive* for the human race? Ought we all to be cogs in a grand political mechanism perhaps of Plato's design, envisioned in his *The Republic?*[41] Again such issues will be delved into further in the division of this work labeled *Politics*. Bergson is right to emphasize that the phenomenological reconstruction of time is more relevant to anthropoepistemology than is the physical explanation of time, because human beings, as Martin Heidegger wrote,

---

[39]　Nagel, Thomas. 1997. "What is it like to be a bat?" *Nature of Consciousness : Philosophical Debats / Edited by Ned Block, Owen Flanagan, and Güven Güzeldere.*

[40]　Jung, C. G., and Joseph Campbell. 1971. *The portable Jung.*

[41]　Plato, and John M. Cooper. 2009. *Complete works.* Indianapolis: Hackett.

experience time in a very real and consequential way: human beings are, according to Heidegger, *beings-toward-death*, which is to say, that human beings exist along a temporal axis, at the end of which, is their demise.[42] So much for Bergsonian durational consciousness.

9. Of the Cyclicality of Being, or, Of Nietzsche's Wager

Cycles are one of the most fascinating of all natural phenomena, and, as shall be delved into in the division of this work labeled *Anthropocognitivity*, cycles quite literally play a predominant role in the goings on of Mind. Yet, the cyclology of Being is a different kind of cycle altogether, because its referent is none other than the total set of all beings across Being. The argument of the cyclology of Being is simple: that the universe is part of a grander, cyclical trajectory across time that expands then declines and back and forth again for an infinity. Famous philosopher Friedrich Nietzsche reflected upon this concept later on in his career. The idea of the *Eternal Return* is that everything has already existed before, in the history of the multiverse, and that we are doomed to repeat ourselves over and over again.[43] While Nietzsche did not believe in reincarnation, this theory of the Eternal Return certainly gives off reincarnational vibes. Thus, is Being itself cyclical? Perhaps. If it is true, then we ought to live our lives according to what Nietzsche referred to as *amor fati*, or the love of fate and destiny. Here it would be helpful to bring in the arguments of famous philosopher Blaise Pascal on what is called Pascal's Wager.[44] Pascal argues, heaven and hell may exist, thus we ought to believe and behave as Christians in order to take the chance that there is a heaven, so that we may have a chance to earn admission into it. Take Pascal's argument and apply it to the Eternal Return: it could be the case that the Eternal Return is true, in which case, we ought to take the gamble and live our lives as though we will have to live them the same way forever: boldly, uniquely, and passionately.

Thus, we could call this argument Nietzsche's Wager, because his discussions of the Eternal Return are profound and original. However, there is both a malefic conception of *amor fati* and a benefic conception of *amor fati*: on the one hand, we might feel ourselves inclined to give up all hope, should the Eternal Return be the case, which is the malefic conception of this matter; and, on the other hand, there is a certain conception, that, because we are called to live our lives over and over again, that we may as well live them optimally, in such a way that we are living the best possible modality compatible with Anthropocognitivity.

---

[42] Heidegger, Martin, and David Farrell Krell. 1993. *Basic writings: from being and time (1927) to the task of thinking (1964)*. New York: Harper Collins College.

[43] Nietzsche, Friedrich Wilhelm, Walter Arnold Kaufmann, and R. J. Hollingdale. 1968. *The will to power: a new translation*. New York: Vintage Books.

[44] Pascal, Blaise, and A. J. Krailsheimer. 1986. *Pascal Pensées*. Harmondsworth: Penguin.

Clearly, the benefic conception is to live optimally, as will be explored later on in the division of this work labeled *Metapolitics*, wherein we will analyze to what extent the conception of *optimality* may be applied to ethics and politics. As we have seen before, the concept of *perfection* figures largely in any epistemology that seeks to transcendentalize its knowledge by weighing it against the universal truths contained in the Imaginary Graph of Being. Similarly, the concept of *perfection* will both drive and ground the theories of ethics and politics to be expounded in this work. Returning to the Eternal Return, let us suppose that we accept Nietzsche's Wager, or the idea of the cyclicality of Being, what then? Furthermore, what relevance might the Eternal Return have upon our conceptions and practices of any future epistemology? First, if we accept Nietzsche's Wager, then we ought also to accept the postulate of perfection, or, namely, the idea that *perfection* is the ultimate aim of any action, contra Aristotle's view that the aim of any action is mere goodness. At any rate, we ought to be called to live our lives optimally as best we may derive our vocations and contributions to the ongoing *process* of civilization, which itself is another *perpetual endeavor* that human beings engage in. Returning to transcendental epistemology, it must be the case that epistemology must ultimately *encyclopedify Being*, in such a way that is a *perfect* replica of the Imaginary Graph of Being. However, encyclopedification is itself another *perpetual endeavor* that must be carried out infinitely. To whatever extent that we are *concerned* with the pursuit of knowledge in itself, *attemptive perfectional encyclopedification* is the ultimate aim of any future practice of epistemology. So much for the cyclicality of Being and of Nietzsche's Wager.

10. Of the Metaphysics of Informativity: Beyond Young Wittgenstein

Informativity is the science of information and the world's defining characteristic: the world may be described as a collective set of information. Then, why ought we disagree with the early writings of famous philosopher Ludwig Wittgenstein, who argued that the world is the sum total of all the facts about the world, in his *Tractatus Logico Philosophicus?*[45] Because, once consciousness becomes involved in the equation, it can perceive forms in nature, and also can interpret the world in multiple ways. Thus, we can employ the concept of holism, once again: to argue that the world is holistic, is to argue that the world is more than merely the sum of all its facts. There are metafacts, or facts that transcend nature or are more important than regular facts. And, again, once consciousness becomes interactive with the world, it fundamentally troubles the early Wittgenstein's position, because it allows for a science of hermeneutics and interpretation. In terms of information, and, to return to the Imaginary Graph of Being: an entity that does not occupy many

---

[45]   Wittgenstein, Ludwig. 2022. *Tractatus Logico-Philosophicus.* [S.l.]: Penguin Books.

coordinates on the Imaginary Graph of Being may be referred to as a simple entity. Here, it is reasonable to argue that the concept of a simple entity will be therefore a simple concept. One also hears the phrase "simple-Minded," and this calls to Mind Hegel's essay *Who Thinks Abstractly?*, wherein he argues that to think abstractly is to think in a very simplistic manner. Instead, one should think concretely, which is to say, to not isolate the thought from its referent in the world; and to make sure that the thought is itself complicated and not simple; on the other hand, the mere idea of a simple thought is purely anthropoepistemological, for, thoughts are only made simple, based upon the logic of the *Theory of Anthropological Parsimony*, wherein it is argued that human beings naturally attempt to simplify their modalities of thought wherever possible: through simplification, the Mind is naturally inclined to *essentialization*, or the reduction of an entity's nature into its essence.[46] Some occasions do, however, merit for simple usages of thought, speech, and action: chit chat, yes or no questions, certain kinds of analytic reasoning, or the type of reasoning that aims to break down concepts into their basic qualities and then consider how the components all relate to each other.

As we shall see later on, the concept of quality will also become quite important for this work. A quality is an abstract facet of identity for either a concept or a thing, except that a quality has nothing to do with measurement or quantitative reasoning. Returning to Bergson, who, for example, believed that consciousness was qualitative and not capable of being measured using quantitative methods, Bergson can be deconstructed to have an argument involving holistic consciousness, which would argue that consciousness transcends the kind of physical monads that calculus is able to calculate. It might be said to challenge calculus: can there be a calculus of the Mind? Of course not. However, such a question is at the present moment merely noumenal, or existing outside the bounds of human understanding and perception — which is to say, that your author is a McGinnian *New Mysterian* — or, a *noumenalist* about consciousness. On the other hand, there is the conception of quantity: quantity as a concept infects the Mind and causes it to behave, think, and speak in some truly animalistic modalities. Quantity is a concept that hopefully humankind will transcend, sometime in the future. In a utopian world — from the perspective of a *Just World Theory* — could it really be the case that quantity will survive as a concept? Measurement instills the need for comparison and limitation. Quality on the other hand is more abstract and utopian, because it does not hierarchize — or cause unjust hierarchies among humans. Because dehierarchalization is one of the eighteen ideal principles of the *Benefic Speculative Formulation* — as we shall see later on in the division of this work labeled *Ethics* — we must unequivocally condemn and harangue most quantitative modalities of reasoning. Returning to the Imaginary Graph of Being: what is complex is what is plotted with many coordinates along the axes of Being on the Imaginary Graph of Being.

---

[46] Hegel, Georg Wilhelm Friedrich, and Stephen Houlgate. 1998. *The Hegel reader*. Oxford, UK: Blackwell Publishers.

Take for example the concept of New York City: could we define even the *partial* essence and nature of New York City in only five minutes? Such a feat could not be done in a second, let alone a year, and probably not even in a lifetime. First and foremost, because all entities are subject to temporal flux and change, especially a huge city like New York, such a feat is almost impossible to accomplish — certainly the inquiry is noumenal. Thus, complex things may be defined as those things which resist simplification. Here it will make sense to comment that anthropoepistemology is really the aufhebung — the synthesis — between the complex and the simple. Human Beings are constantly trying to simplify their language and speak as directly as possible — this is the *Anthropological Theory of Mental Parsimony*, or the theory that argues for the idea that Human Beings are finite, limited, and thus must produce actions, thoughts, and speech reflective of that limitation and finitude — and hence must simplify wherever possible; this is akin to the *Pragmatic Theory of Essence*. There is a limit to how complex human language can become, and we can clearly see that with the hypercomplexity of Schizophrenic behavior, thought, and speech — it simply cannot be understood by our limited brains. The *Theory of Procession* will not work for decoding it — and it is a variety of code, Schizophrenic language — it is not however meaningless babble; instead, it is merely hypercomplex and idiosyncratic. In fact, Schizophrenic language is a proof of the *General Theory of Semantic Projectionalism*, because it goes to show to what extent the Mind is working to assign meaning to everything it sees, whether internal thought or external stimuli. So much for the metaphysics of informativity.

11. Toward a Hegelian-Derridean General Theory of Procession

Now comes the *General Theory of Procession*, or the mechanisms by which the processing of phenomena may occur. It is not necessarily the case that this theory will map *exactly* onto the world; rather, it is the case that this theory describes the logical steps inherent to any theory of phenomenological experience, and it will describe the logical steps involved in processing phenomena; because of Bergson's theory of durational consciousness, it is not necessarily the case that a physicalist theory of procession would greatly improve our understanding of these matters. The first step in the theory of procession is emergence (1), which is the emergence of any act, speech, or thought coming from either another person, or it could also be that inanimate objects emerge into the phenomenal domain or perceptual field of a given person or sentient animal. The second step is interaction (2), and involves the interaction of the given phenomenal object with the sensory receptors (monads) of a given subject. The third step in the logic process is called sensory procession (3) and involves the sensory processing of the phenomena into the brain and so on and so forth. The fourth step (4) is identification; during this step, the brain makes sense of the phenomena and assigns identifying predicates to the given phenomena at hand. In this way, the brain internally labels the phenomena. The fifth step is sorting (5), and involves the brain sorting the information into logical and coherent structures.

The sixth step is deconstruction (6), which involves the deconstruction of the identified and sorted units of information into atoms of content, or the most fundamental units of computation. Then, the seventh step is deposition (7), which involves the depositing of these units of information into the brain's depository for such entities, i.e., where memories are stored. Step eight is derivation (8) which is when meaning is finally derived from the deconstructed phenomena. The ninth step is the triggeral enmeshment with receptors (9), which inaugurates either novel trajectories or cyclical trajectories; any trajectory that repeats or has repeated in the past becomes a cycle. Thus ends the *General Theory of Procession*. It should be noted here — as it will be in the section on *Metalinguistics* — that meaning is something that is internal to the Mind; if there were meaning in a word, one would be able to reach in and grab it out; but there is not meaning in objects, speech, acts, or behavior, rather, there is only information. What is going on here is a sort of *semantic projectionalism*, where the Mind projects meaning into the words only after the fact of having internally derived information from the phenomena. It should be said that underneath the phenomena there are atoms of content, which are micro-units of information. These units ground phenomena, and the logic of these atoms of content provides the information that makes our day-to-day affairs possible. Furthermore, the process of *deconstruction* — which resembles Jacques Derrida's deconstructive method, a form of applied Hegelian dialectics — is an automatic process that occurs within the Mind perpetually.[47] Thus, *autodeconstruction* is a natural, automatic process that everyone — *including Analytic philosophers!* — conducts on an immediate basis everyday.

12. Toward a Perfectional Theory of Absolute Essence: Plato and Saint Anselm

One may be able to perceive a house, for example, but can one phenomenologically experience its essence? Can one perceive it in its *totality*, which is to say, in its relationship both to itself and to every other existing entity in every logically possible world? Or, may we perceive an entity and its relations to every *perfect* and *imaginary* entity on the Imaginary Graph of Being? Certainly not. Now, one might say: well, on the Imaginary Graph of Being, we do not need to know everything about a given entity, in order to derive its *partial* essence. Yet, in order

---

[47]   Spivak, Gayatri Chakravorty, and Jacques Derrida. 1998. *Of grammatology*. Baltimore: The Johns Hopkins University Press; Hegel, Georg Wilhelm Friedrich. 2004. *Hegel's Science of logic*. Amherst, N.Y.: Humanity Books.

to differentiate this thing from every other thing, it is imperative to keep close to the first *General Theory of Differentiation*: that we need to imagine how this entity compares to every other entity, and also to itself, for, therein lies the noumenal reality of its difference — that component of the entity that makes it unique and special. Digressionally, every entity, whether animate or inanimate, is unique in its own way. Returning to the noumenal: it is that which cannot be perceived, but which can be imagined. If we accept the *General Theory of Differentiation*, then we ought to understand that whatever feeble entities we have in our Minds are in no way perfect, in fact, they are anthropoepistemological *partial essences*, or *functional essences*. Here, there is a certain *Pragmatic Theory of Essences* lurking in the background of this reconstruction, for, if human beings have a *functional* grasp of essence, do they need any further, extra-functional information about the essence? A *Pragmatic Theory of Essence* argues that anthropoepistemological essences are *partial* and *limited*, but that this is a satisfactory arrangement of affairs. For, so long as the *process* of civilization may persist, then all that is required of our essences is that they be *pragmatic, functional,* and *limited* — which is to say, that they be *partial essences*. Now, the issue with *partial essences* is that they are not *absolute, perfect,* and *unlimited essences* — they are not perfect, as it were, as are Plato's forms, or the totals set of coordinates as plotted on the Imaginary Graph of Being.[48]

In order for human beings to transcend the limits of their anthropoepistemologies, they must allow their knowledge to undergo a certain *process* of *transcendental universalization*, or that is to say, that our *partial essences* must be made to *align* as much as possible, and become parallel to, their *perfect* manifestations as represented on the Imaginary Graph of Being. Thus, the essential features and structures of concepts — and concepts are really only representations of forms — may only be perceived hazily — impressionistically — and may not be perceived in their purer, noumenal form as represented on the Imaginary Graph of Being. Thus, *noumenology* is the science of the noumena, of mysterious things, of things which cannot be known, and of things which either resist our perception or understanding, and lastly, of things which we merely perceive impressionistically. To perceive an entity impressionistically is to not be able to grasp it in its entirety, i.e., there must exist some barrier between human beings and *absolute, perfect* knowledge. While human beings may have their limitations, they do have one faculty of Mind that may be counted up to release them from the shackles of their own anthropoepistemology: the powers of their *intuitive imagination*. Through their faculty of imagination, human beings may intuit the *absolute* and *perfect essences* of entities, which is to say, human beings may proceed up out of their anthropoepistemologies via the royal road of their imaginations. Even if essences do not exist in the world — which is ultimately a noumenal question, so it is inconclusive — the Mind nevertheless functions as though there

---

48   Plato, and John M. Cooper. 2009. *Complete works*. Indianapolis: Hackett.

were essences, so while the descriptive reality bends toward a *Pragmatic Theory of Essence*, the prescriptive imaginary bends toward a *Perfectional Theory of Absolute Essence*. Because essence and meaning are such interchangeable concepts, and, as discussed earlier, because the Mind projects meaning into words or objects after it perceives said entity as a phenomena, this means too, that meaning is projected into the world, in addition to essence, from the Mind: call this view *semantic projectionalism*, which is an advancement in the dialectic compared with Kant's *cognitivist* theory of Mind.[49]

Thus, even if essences may not exist external to the mind, they do — very much so — exist within the Mind, furthermore, they do exist in the imaginary along the axes of the *Imaginary Graph of Being*. Even though *perfection* is a noumenal concept, it nevertheless is the grounding *ideal* as represented as the *ideal of ideals* on the Imaginary Graph of Being, and henceforth, must drive any practice of Anthropoepistemology that aims to *attemptively* transcendentalize its knowledge. Hence, human beings must aim for the noumenal concept of *perfection* in all their endeavors, so as best to *transcendentalize* themselves: their anthropoepistemologies, their anthropomodalities, and their practice of metapolitics, or, their practice of aesthetics, ethics, and politics. Thus, while the *Pragmatic Theory of Essence* may be the *descriptive* case for any anthropoepistemology, it must be the case, that in order to effect a *universalized transcendentalization* of our knowledge, that it must be imagined *as if* parallel to the *absolute* and *perfect* forms as represented on the Imaginary Graph of Being: which is to say, that we must *perpetually* make the *attempt* to attain a knowledge consistent with the *Perfectional Theory of Absolute Essence*, to whatever extent we value our knowledge to be *just*, *absolute*, and *perfect*. Here, we must take what Soren Kierkegaard referred to as a *leap of faith*: we must have faith in Saint Anselm's ontological argument, that there is such a modality of entity known as a *perfect* and *absolute essence*, and furthermore, we must have faith that through the powers of the human imagination, we may overcome the limits of our anthropoepistemologies and hence affect a *transcendentalization* of our forms of knowledge.[50] So much for a *Perfectional Theory of Absolute Essence*.

13. Of the Metaphysics of Kantian-Searlean Social Constructs

Metaphysics: the science of non-physical entities and their relationship to physical entities. Now, then, what is a *social construct*, i.e., a metaphysical hypothetical? How does it relate to the concept of the noumenal? *Noumenology* — as mentioned above — has a few different definitions, a few of which are noumenal themselves.

[49]   Kant, Immanuel, and Paul Guyer. 2009. *Critique of pure reason*. Cambridge: Cambridge Univ. Press.

[50]   Kierkegaard, Søren, Walter Lowrie, and Søren Kierkegaard. 2013. *Fear and trembling, and: the sickness unto death*. Princeton, N.J.: Princeton University Press; Anselm, Brian Davies, and G. R. Evans. 1998. *The major works Anselm of Canterbury*. Oxford; New York: Oxford University Press.

Noumenality could be considered the most fundamental kind of reality, or it could be considered a form of mysticism that surrounds an entity, or it could be considered that which resists sensory perception. Ultimately, the noumena play powerful roles in the world and society at large. Let us take for example the case of merely one form of Kantian-Searlean social constructs: perhaps a corporation.[51] Let us ask some questions: imagine if we took all of the human beings away from Earth, and then visited some corporation's headquarters. Is it still a corporation, or is temporal rapportionality — the quality of a rapport's being inherent to some set of relationships between entities across the temporal timeline — inherent to the concept of a corporation? Intuition informs us that, yes, without people, there would be no such entity as a corporation. How so? It may be useful here to ask: what is the meaning of a corporation? If meaning is involved, then we can answer: well, it depends on who is projecting that meaning onto the corporation, from their Mind. Yet, what happens when a great number of people are all projecting meaning into the allegedly same entity, for each person's understanding of the corporation is necessarily distinct, unique, and projectional? While we have not yet arrived at the division of this work labeled *Ethics*, it may nevertheless be worthwhile to discuss the nature of temporal rapportionality at greater length. Rapportionality is the quality of indigenous — which is to say natural and organic — rapports with other humans; it is both the rapport itself and all of its concomitant implications, duties, and responsibilities. The corporation is grounded upon two things: first and foremost, the collective projectionalism of all of its employees, and all of its customers, and all civilians who know of it; secondly, it is grounded upon the rapportionality of all of its employees, customers, and the civilians who know of it.

The corporation is born of those two human elements. However, just because the corporation is grounded upon projectionalism and temporal rapportionality, does not mean that the corporation actually exists. Instead, it makes sense to argue that the corporation is a *social construct,* i.e., a metaphysical hypothetical — humans *accord* their behavior *as if* the corporation existed, but when push comes to shove, the corporation does not exist in itself, nor for itself, but instead, it exists *as if*: this is to say, that the corporation is a *fictional* entity that exists along the axes of the Imaginary Graph of Being, and is merely imagined in the Minds of human beings, and projected into the world through their Minds, and then *concretionalized* in the world through human temporal rapportionality. Thus, the corporation has a functioning and pragmatic hypothetical existence. Human beings birth it into being through their rapportionality and projectionalism of essence: nothing more, and nothing less. Is therefore the corporation itself noumenal, as in, it cannot be perceived? Without a doubt, the corporation *in itself* is noumenal. Now, when this logic is applied to the rest of human civilization, one might argue that doing so illuminates one to the fact of the hypothetical existence of so many social constructs.

---

[51]   Kant, Immanuel, and Paul Guyer. 2009. *Critique of pure reason*. Cambridge: Cambridge Univ. Press; Searle, John Rogers. 1996. *The construction of social reality*. London: Penguin Books.

Here enters Martin Heidegger and his discussion of tools in *Being and Time*: a pen, a hammer, a suitcase — all of these are anthropomorphic, ergonomic tools that we use as equipment to supplement our being.[52] The supplement, without the metaphysics of *essential projectionalism*, would revert to its quality of being mere object. Thus, human beings transform their worlds by supplementing them with Siderian *temporal parts* on top of which essences may be projected. Human beings arrange matter in such and such a way to complement their internal worlds.[53] While these entities have no existence apart from human beings, nevertheless, Minds imbue entities in the world into a mode of *formal* and *hypothetical* existence. Thus, while the corporation exists only because of essential projectionalism and temporal rapportionality, it nevertheless takes on a formal kind of existence — in which case it exists then as a noumenal entity insofar as its form accords with an abstract concept from off the Imaginary Graph of Being. Thus, these entities exist as metaphysical hypotheticals, and resemble what famous philosopher John Searle referred to as *social constructs* in his book, *The Construction of Social Reality*.[54] So much for the ontology of entities whose existence can only be explained by reference to the imagination, and its *perfectional abstraction*, the Imaginary Graph of Being.

14. Of Two Modes of Ascertaining Kantian-Searlean Social Constructs

Now, how will we be able to discern the noumenal from the phenomenal? Here, there are two ways both to ground and discover noumenal entities. Firstly, if the hypothetical noumenal entity improves our understanding of some given concept, then the noumenal relationship between physical entities ought to be acknowledged to exist, albeit, as a noumenal, abstract form, which nevertheless has some *physical influence*, but is not actually a part of physics, because it is merely an abstract relationship that merely better explains physical matters. Secondly, if the entity in question has a pragmatic impact — if the entity in question explains a natural *function* that occurs within the realm of physics, then we ought to admit that the noumenal relationship in question exists as a noumenal relationship between physical entities, because it can be verified empirically as a pragmatic and functional relationship between entities that occurs in the realm of physics, e.g., the noumenal metaphysics of a corporation. To expand upon the noumenal: a *noumenal truth* is some relationship within the world that an abstract entity possesses that resists our perception, and also that is inherently mysterious insofar

---

52 Heidegger, Martin, John Macquarrie, and Edward S. Robinson. 2019. *Being and time*.

53 Hawley, Katherine, "Temporal Parts", *The Stanford Encyclopedia of Philosophy* (Summer 2020 Edition), Edward N. Zalta (ed.), URL = <https://plato.stanford.edu/archives/sum2020/entries/temporal-parts/>.

54 Searle, John Rogers. 1996. *The construction of social reality*. London: Penguin Books.

as it also resists our understanding. Yet, as much as the noumena is mysterious, our imaginations can still attempt to project essences onto the noumena. How to aptly apply these essences is a serious inquiry that demands much attention: it involves both of the leading theories of famous anthropoepistemologists — Alvin Goldman's *reliabilism* and Ernest Sosa'a *virtue epistemology*.[55]

To synthesize their two projectional modalities of Anthropoepistemology: the Kantian-Cognitivist Projectional Categories projected by Mind must be aptly applied in such a way that our knowledge of them becomes reliable and consistent — this was also the view of the philosophical pragmatists, e.g. Charles S. Peirce — but the aim is also to make sure that the method of categorical application is sufficient — one might say, virtuous.[56] However, what both of these theories of epistemology do not consider is that the method and function of belief can never confirm for certain noumenal truths. Furthermore, these theories do not take into account the logic of the projection of essences and meaning. More than reliabilism, virtue epistemology attempts to ensure the method of belief is justly apt; however, even that view has its limits when it comes to the application of essences to noumenal concepts. Here, the anthropoepistemological reality is nothing other than that every individual has their own idiosyncratic method for arriving at what they believe to be true conclusions or beliefs. Call this view *idiosyncratic constructivism*, or the idea that each individual has their own unique and pragmatic way of arriving at what they perceive to be true beliefs. Again, here it is important to recollect that, because the *absolute* essences of concepts are noumenal — or out of bounds to our sense perception — noumenal or ultimate truths are unavailable to us. Even Descartes realizes that mathematical truths cannot guarantee noumenal truth, because our anthropoepistemological understanding is all too finite and could always be wrong — this is also called the *Gettier Problem* in Analytic Philosophy.[57] Returning to the notion of *idiosyncratic constructivism*, this view may be simplified along the following lines: our phenomenological worlds are full of subliminally cherry-picked beliefs of our own automatic-systematic design.

To be sure, the structure of our modality of Anthropoepistemology may be intentionally or subliminally sculpted, and hence the sculpture of our anthropoepistemologies is both willed by us, and affected subliminally by the entities we empirically occur within the world. Hence, instead of being concerned about how to arrive at true beliefs — which we cannot arrive at because the answer to that question is noumenal — we ought to be focusing on *projective cognitivism*,

---

[55]   Goldman, Alvin and Bob Beddor, "Reliabilist Epistemology", *The Stanford Encyclopedia of Philosophy* (Summer 2021 Edition), Edward N. Zalta (ed.), URL = <https://plato.stanford.edu/archives/sum2021/entries/reliabilism/>; Sosa, Ernest. 2009. *A virtue epistemology: apt belief and reflective knowledge*. Volume 1 Volume 1. Oxford: Oxford University Press.

[56]   Kant, Immanuel, and Paul Guyer. 2009. *Critique of pure reason*. Cambridge: Cambridge Univ. Press; Peirce, Charles S., and Edward C. Moore. 1998. *Charles S. Peirce: the essential writings*. Amherst, N.Y.: Prometheus Books.

[57]   Gettier, Edmund L., and Marc Andree Weber. 2019. *Is Justified True Belief Knowledge?/ Ist gerechtfertigte, wahre Überzeugung Wissen?*: Englisch/Deutsch.

or the view that our Minds project our consciousnesses and its concomitant tools into the world, e.g., essences. Furthermore, these projections from our Mind supplement our worlds, and become, as it were, tools for navigating the world. Take for example a sailor who has sailed the Sargasso Sea her entire life: she no longer needs a map to navigate it. Her Mind supplements the world with her concept of the sea and hence she navigates the sea with true mastery. Thus, Heideggerian equipment — as discussed earlier — may also be a *supplement* to our day to day navigation of the world.[58] Furthermore, let it be understood that the world *complements* our Minds. Here there is an aufhebung to be had between dualism: between the idea that the Mind is separate from the body; the aufhebung here is that human beings live in a world embodied with consciousness, as was Deleuze and Hegel's view on this issue.[59]

15. Of the Emergence of Kantian-Searlean Social Constructs

While human beings have the power to birth into existence many hypothetical entities, through their projectional consciousness and collective rapportionalities, they frequently forget that they have this temporally intrinsic power. Hence, as a result, these hypothetical entities — these *social constructs* — then dominate their originators — human beings. This forgetting takes place due to the overwhelming nature of what Heidgger called *average everydayness* in his magnum opus, *Being and Time*.[60] Average everydayness colonizes lived human time and causes this forgetting of which we speak. Idleness, says Bertrand Russell,[61] is the root of all creativity and inspiration. Unfortunately, lived human time is colonized by the forces at work in civilization: namely, capital, imperialism, and even natural human distractions, e.g., the phenomenologies of lust, avarice, envy, competition, etc. As discussed before, the concept of holism means that the whole is more significant than the parts of any given thing. Recall the example of the car and its parts: only when the parts are arranged in such and such a way may the car function, that is to say, drive. Imagine, then, the concept of holism applied to human civilization itself. This idea has been labeled the *superstructure* by philosophers such as Karl Marx and Louis Althusser.[62] The way that the holistic superstructure functions is

---

[58]   Heidegger, Martin, and David Farrell Krell. 1993. *Basic writings: from being and time (1927) to the task of thinking (1964)*. New York: Harper Collins College.

[59]   Deleuze, Gilles, Félix Guattari, and Brian Massumi. 2019. *A thousand plateaus: capitalism and schizophrenia*; Hegel, Georg Wilhelm Friedrich, and Terry P. Pinkard. 2018. *Georg Wilhelm Friedrich Hegel: the phenomenology of spirit*.

[60]   Heidegger, Martin, John Macquarrie, and Edward S. Robinson. 2019. *Being and time*.

[61]   Russell, Bertrand. 2017. *In praise of idleness*.

[62]   Marx, Karl, Ben Fowkes, and David Fernbach. 1990. *Capital: a critique of political economy*; v.1. London: Penguin Books in association with New Left Review; Althuser, L., and Etienne Balibar. 1990. *Reading capital*. London: Verso.

dependent upon human forgetfulness: forgetfulness of the human right to imagine and project essence into the world. When the truth is forgotten about the nature of social institutions — for example corporations — these entities take on a dominant existence of their own. It is a metaphysical existence to the extent that it has no real grounding outside of human rapportionality and projectionalism of consciousness and essence.

And yet, we feel the influence of these institutions on our day to day lives, because other human beings act, think, and speak as though these institutions were real. Once however, humans grant these entities existence due to their forgetfulness, these hypotheticals take on a certain metaphysical existence. Then, the world *functions* much differently than it did prior to these metaphysical entities. Because these institutions do not exist in the world proper, they cannot be facts; however, because they are metaphysical entities, they may be considered to be metafacts. Thus, the metafactuality of the superstructure is such that it influences human lives only because humans think, act, and speak as if these institutions existed. As mentioned earlier, famous philosopher John Searle argued for the social construction of reality, and it is fair to pluralize reality into hypothetical entities entitled *social constructs*.[63] But that is only part of the equation: it is not merely the temporal rapportionality of humans that births into existence these metafactual, metaphysical superstructures, it is also the essential projectionalism of human beings that *assumes* certain information about factual, worldly entities. These metafactual superstructures exist contingent on the whims of human civilization: what happens to a corporation when it goes out of business, and dissolves, as it were? Here we must provide a *General Theory of Mental Inflation and Mental Deflation*.

Mental inflation is what happens when humans project information onto a set of facts within the real world, and, on top of those facts, create metafactual entities such as corporations. Mental deflation is what happens when humans deflate the metafactual by withdrawing their life-giving information from the superstructure; thus, consciousness projects and withdraws information both onto and away from certain monads within the world. Once these metafactual, metaphysical superstructures gain traction, then they start to influence human affairs. This is also a *General Theory of Human Institutions*. Until human beings dislodge or deflate these metaphysical superstructures, they will continue to be dominated by them. So much for the emergence of *social constructs*, i.e., metaphysical hypotheticals.

---

[63]   Searle, John Rogers. 1996. *The construction of social reality*. London: Penguin Books.

16. Of Whiteheadian-Derridean Process Epistemology, Goldman, Sosa, and the Pragmatic-Cognitivist Consciousness

Here the question arises, following both the lines of thought of Goldman and Sosa, what is the appropriate approach to take to the acquisition of knowledge[64]? Certainly, it has been observed that many phenomena in the lifeworld are dependent upon human consciousness for their existences, and, secondarily, upon human rapportionality to ground their existences. Yet, there is another facet of social epistemology at play here, and, is more of a *social phenomenology* than it is a Goldmanian *social epistemology*.[65] Thus, instead of worrying about which abstract approach to knowledge allows us to best arrive at true justified beliefs, as it were, the approach taken in this work will be that of a Husserlian sort of *social phenomenological* approach.[66] Or, namely, that approach that takes the phenomenology of persons to be vital to both the acquisition and the discernment of what constitutes knowledge. Here, there are two modalities of consciousness for the acquisition of knowledge that shall be argued to be the inverses of each other. Both, in their own way, are involved in any formation either of *just knowledge* or *unjust knowledge*, and, being extreme modalities of consciousness, cannot for very long function in the lifeworld without running into or causing any trouble. The first extreme modality of epistemological consciousness is the *gullible consciousness*, or that consciousness that believes everything it encounters in the lifeworld, whether these be sensations, illusions, statements, lies, etc. Its inverse modality of consciousness is none other than the *skeptical consciousness*, or that consciousness that casts doubts upon everything it encounters in the lifeworld, and most resembles the Cartesian skeptic who cannot quite justify whether anything exists in the lifeworld. To be sure, both of these modalities of consciousness are foolish, but both, when fine tuned, result in more nuanced versions of themselves.

Firstly, expanding upon the philosophy of Alfred North Whitehead, it is to be argued that the proper approach to abstract epistemology is none other than a *process epistemology*, wherein epistemology and the pursuit of knowledge are defined as those endeavors that are *perpetual, noumenal, and incomplete*.[67] Once *process epistemology* has been adopted by both the *gullible* and the *skeptical* consciousnesses, each blossoms into a new manifestational

---

[64]   Goldman, Alvin and Bob Beddor, "Reliabilist Epistemology", *The Stanford Encyclopedia of Philosophy* (Summer 2021 Edition), Edward N. Zalta (ed.), URL = <https://plato.stanford.edu/archives/sum2021/entries/reliabilism/>; Sosa, Ernest. 2009. *A virtue epistemology: apt belief and reflective knowledge*. Volume 1 Volume 1. Oxford: Oxford University Press.

[65]   Goldman, Alvin I., and Dennis Whitcomb. 2011. *Social epistemology essential readings*. Oxford: Oxford University Press.

[66]   Husserl, Edmund, Ingo Farin, James G. Hart, and Edmund Husserl. 2006. *The basic problems of phenomenology from the lectures*, winter semester, 1910-1911. Dordrecht, the Netherlands: Springer.

[67]   Whitehead, Alfred North. 1990. *Process and reality: an essay in cosmology*; Gifford Lectures delivered in the University of Edinburgh during the session 1927-28. New York: Free Press u.a.

mode of phenomenology: the *gullible consciousness* becomes the *conspiratorial consciousness*, and the *skeptical consciousness* becomes the *Pragmatic-Cognitivist Consciousness*. Now, the *conspiratorial consciousness* is that consciousness that gullibly accepts far fetched information without grounding it either virtuously or reliably — as Sosa and Goldman would call for — whereas the *Pragmatic-Cognitivist Consciousness* is that consciousness that meditates all information it encounters in the lifeworld with a general sense of detachment and skepticism — in short, it is a consciousness involving the process of detached, scientific inquiry. Detachment is key here due to what may be referred to as the *reflexivity equation*, or that mechanism of Mind that weighs how certain information pertains to the agent who is weighing that information and making assessments about the information based on their own concept of themselves — on their own Core Script. Thus, which consciousness reigns superior to the other, especially where concerns epistemology and the process of the acquisition of knowledge? Surely, the *Pragmatic-Cognitivist Consciousness* reigns superior to the *conspiratorial consciousness*, because it does not allow its animal nature — its animal phenomenology — to dominate its existence. By this, is meant, none other than that the *conspiratorial consciousness* is dominated by the vices of its animal phenomenology — xenophobia, hysteria, racism, sexism, and fascism. All of those vices of the *conspiratorial consciousness* are caused by the animal natures of human beings, and must be limited, overcome, and transcended wherever possible.

Here, the *Pragmatic-Cognitivist Consciousness* employs their Habermasian capacity for rationality to overcome their animalistic nature and phenomenology, and thereby proves itself to be both more reliable and virtuous according to Sosa and Goldman, and hence, superior to the *conspiratorial consciousness*.[68] Later, in the division of this work labeled *Ethics*, there will be a discussion of the ideal of *hope* and its inverse ideal, *doubt*, but here it is important to clarify, that the *Pragmatic-Cognitivist Consciousness* is not immoral because it is *skeptical*, instead, it is much more moral than the *conspiratorial consciousness* that wreaks havoc throughout the lifeworld through its inflated metaphysicals and its lies. Censorship of the *conspiratorial consciousness* must for this reason become a social norm, for, the *conspiratorial consciousness* gives rise to xenophobia, hysteria, sexism, racism, fascism, etc., inasmuch as it is fueled by human animal instincts. Here, famous philosopher Alvin Plantinga's views on evolutionary epistemology become relevant: Plantinga argues that because human beings evolved to survive, instead of to know, they consequently are not the best equipped to arrive at true justified belief.[69] Thus, true justified belief must overcome the animal instincts of human beings, in addition to overcoming the perspectivisms of Friedrich Nietzsche,

---

[68]   Habermas, Jürgen. 2007. *The theory of communicative action.* 1, 1. Boston, Mass: Beacon Press.

[69]   Plantinga, Alvin. 2011. *Where the conflict really lies: science, religion, and naturalism.* New York: Oxford University Press.

Ronald Dworkin, and Stanley Fish.[70] Therefore, true justified belief is that belief which is virtuously arrived at, pragmatically reliable, which overcomes animal instinctivism, and which overcomes mere perspectivism: such is the view of the Whiteheadian and Derridean *process epistemologist*.[71] So much then, for *process epistemology*, the *Pragmatic-Cognitivist Consciousness*, and the *conspiratorial consciousness*.

17. Of the Nietzschean Metaphysics of Indebtion: Speech Act Par Excellence I

At the root of the question itself is the concept of indebtion. The metaphysics of this phenomenon are fascinating, indeed. Take for example even just a simple question: Antigone asks you what your name is — what are the metaphysics of that question? The conversation Antigone engages in with you will proceed one of two ways: either you answer her question, or you reject it. What does it mean to reject a question, and, what indeed is one rejecting? When Antigone asks you for your name, using language, she is placing a debt upon your consciousness. How does that figure? When she asks you the question, she acknowledges that she has a void of information, and then formulates her question such that she requests from you a specific set of information relevant to the void of information she has. Either you will provide her this information or you will not, but nevertheless, she has attempted to indebt you — to put you into debt — by asking a question. Thus, the metaphysics of the question involves a certain *metaphysics of usury* — of putting people into debt through mere language.

We will investigate this phenomenon at greater length later on in the work, when we discuss the obligations of civilization and metapolitics, in the division of this work labeled *Metapolitics*. This inquiry ought to frighten and shock one to their very Core Script: to think that human beings can be put into metaphysical debt through *mere* wordplay, as it were, is egregious. Imagine the extent to which such wordplay could be malicious: a jealous partner who questions and questions his lover about her whereabouts: where were you? Thus, by projecting into the world our own voids of information, we indebt other humans to us if and only if they feel obligated in some way to respond — to fill in our void of information with a set of information that can be projected into words, speech, or action and transmissioned from one person to another. Unfortunately, more often than not, individual's accept to incur this modality of debt from other individuals: and,

---

[70]   Kaufmann, Walter Arnold, and Friedrich Nietzsche. 2011. *Beyond good and evil: prelude to a philosophy of the future*. New York: Vintage Books; Dworkin, Ronald. 1986. *Law's empire*. Cambridge, Mass. u.a: Belknap Pr. of Harvard Univ. Pr; Fish, Stanley Eugene. 2003. *Is there a text in this class?: the authority of interpretive communities*. Cambridge, Mass: Harvard Univ. Press.

[71]   Cornell, Drucilla, Michel Rosenfeld, and David Carlson. 2016. *Deconstruction and the possibility of justice*.

perhaps the worst part is, that most of this occurs on a subliminal level. While indebtedness mostly may be viewed as a challenge for those attempting to live life in an uninhibited and independent manner, it is also the case that autoindebtion occurs upon birth: one is signs the autocontract that is the *social contract* immediately upon their emergence into the community; therefore, as founding father Alexander Hamilton realized in *The Federalist Papers*,[72] not all debt is bad debt, for, it may incur morality in an individual, as does the autodebt incurred by the *social contract*. So much for prefatory remarks on the *metaphysics of indebtion*, a most frightening and fearful webwork of certain interactions between different consciousnesses, and, indeed, sometimes between a consciousness and itself; had Nietzsche been alive to read J.L. Austin's *How To Do Things With Words*, he would no doubt have considered indebtion to be a speech act, only, only imbued with the power to cast others into one's debt, e.g., *priestcraft* — which Nietzsche lambastes in his seminal *On The Genealogy of Morals*.[73]

18. Of the Metaphysics of the Question

The *metaphysics of the question* concern the specific metaphysical situations that questions frequently draw human beings into. Now, we will undertake a general survey of the metaphysics of the basic words used in questions, at least in the English language. To start, the word "who" projects into the world a void of information concerning a subject. This subject could be a human, a cat, or a ghost, for example. Who knocked over the table? Etc. Consciousness is directly involved in any question using the word who. Next, we will discuss the nature and function of the word "what." This word concerns any object but may also refer to metafactual superstructures. It is a bit early in this work to be discussing the *metaphysics of groups*, however, take for example the metaphysics of an army. When we ask about "what" caused the sacking of Byzantium, we acknowledge that the word "what" is not only referring to objects, but also to abstract entities such as metafactual superstructures — such as a holistic group known as the Ottoman Turkish army. Or when we ask, "what is wrong with you," we may call into question a person's virtue and moral upbringing. Next, we shall discuss the word "why," an elusive and mysterious word to be sure. When we ask the word why, we are asking for a thing's efficient cause, to bring Aristotle into the mix.[74] An efficient cause is something that is responsible for bringing about a phenomenon. Your author is the efficient cause of this very text that is currently being read by you right now. Why is more

---

[72]   Wootton, David. 2003. *The essential Federalist and anti-Federalist papers*. Indianapolis: Hackett publ. co.

[73]   Austin, J. L., J. O. Urmson, and Marina Sbisà. 2009. *How to do things with words: the William James lectures delivered at Harvard University in 1955*. Oxford: Oxford University Press; Nietzsche, Friedrich, and Walter Arnold Kaufmann. 2011. *On the genealogy of morals*. New York: Vintage Books.

[74]   Aristotle. 1990. *Aristotle: Metaphysics*.

of a metaphysical, abstract questionologistic, and it should be contrasted with the more worldly and factualist word "how." To begin to discuss the word "how," it asks from a person the details that made possible some event. "How could you do this to me," we can imagine someone asking. It could call into question someone's morals, for example, and could involve a strict disapprobation.

Next, we will approach the modal questionologistics, or the words involving logical possibilities. First, we will discuss the word "could." "Could you make me a mimosa, Antigone?" The indebtion here is more subtle, it involves logical possibilities. By using could, the indebtion is indirect — it does not command a person to do anything, but instead asks if such a thing is possible. In a way, this questionologistic could be manipulative — it could be an indirect way of getting someone to do something for you. Next, is the word "would." This word too involves modalities and possibilities except here it sometimes involves a request: "would you grab the telephone for me?" Or, it could be speculative, "would Caesar have been assassinated if he decided not to visit the senate?" Lastly, we shall investigate the word "when." This is the most fascinating of all the questionologistics, because it involves time. Here we must distinguish between measured time and phenomenological time, with Bergson — or, between objective time and subjective time.[75] It can also speak to the future, "when we go to Orleans," for example. So much for questionologistics. Let it be understood that indebtion infests language, writing, thought, speech, and action — it is ubiquitous. Hopefully this brief analytical subchapter will have illuminated the reality that all products of the human Mind come into regular contact with this concept of indebtion. A metafactual entity, indebtedness can be used to colonize the lives of human beings. Nietszsche blames the feeling of indebted guilt for the emergence of Christianity, for example. *Indebtion*, to be sure, is at the root of guilt — and so many other emotions.[76]

18. Of the Pragmatic-Newtonian Science of Trajectorics

What do we know of the world? We know that there is both time and monads, and that these monads move according to a temporal timeline: thus goes the logic of Siderian *temporal parts*. Thus, the very existence of movement allows for a metafactual science: the science of trajectorics. For a monad to be in motion, it must have an originpoint and an endpoint. Thus, we have the science of trajectorics — or, the science of trajectories. Recalling the Imaginary Graph of Being, monads are constantly in flux as represented on the graph: we humans are

[75]   Bergson, Henri. 2002. *Time and free will: an essay on the immediate data of consciousness.* https://search.ebscohost.com/login.aspx?direct=true&scope=site&db=nlebk&db=nlabk&AN=790187.

[76]   Nietzsche, Friedrich, and Walter Arnold Kaufmann. 2011. *On the genealogy of morals.* New York: Vintage Books.

a constellation of monads, ourselves; in human beings, there are both dominant and submissive monads. Monads may be either physical or metaphysical, factual or metafactual. An *absolute* alcoholic may be dominated by his core's emotional complications, and thus his emotivics which consist of monads, when, conceived of as a single, dominant monad, take control over this person's life. Without monads, there would be no world. Yet, whether or not monads are the most fundamental substance or not remains at this time a noumenal question. For all we know, there could be infinitely many dimensions and layers of the world. Some even propose that the world is dappled, for example, such as famous philosopher Nancy Cartwright.[77] Such concerns are not ours in this work, because the focus of this work is on the metaphysics of the process of civilization itself. Now, both facts and metafacts, e.g., superstructures, may be conceived of on the Imaginary Graph of Being. And, because of time, all entities are in motion. Thus all entities are on trajectories. Thus, the science of trajectories is a ubiquitous science — it simply involves everything in our world. Perhaps even everything in all of the logically possible worlds. As monads follow their trajectories, their physical components can become dislodged from the whole in question that forms certain objects or subjects. A tree is chopped down by a lumberjack, for example, and the monads making up the tree divide into two sets of monads. Likewise, if the factual is always shifting because of time, on what grounds is the metafactual? What is the nature of the metaphysical or the metafactual? The metafactual is much more resilient than its factual and physical counterparts. One may cut down a tree, but it is impossible to erase from the temporal timeline the metaphysical trajectory of the tree.

A metaphysical trajectory is a constellation of points as represented on the Imaginary Graph of Being spread out across the temporal timeline. Might the metafactual be immune to deterioration? While the metafactual is dependent upon consciousness — the projection of essence into the world — and also dependent upon rapportionality — the metaphysics of rapports between conscious agents and even between themselves, self-reflexively — it may nevertheless decline in prominence. Who now believes in the Ottoman Empire? To be sure, it used to be a force to be reckoned with. Yet, will it ever be erased from history? Never. It still exists in history and its trajectory will forever be graphed onto the temporal timeline as represented on the Imaginary Graph of Being. And, because the Ottoman Empire was only ever a projected essence — albeit a holistic group — it is more immune to deterioration than factual entities. Furthermore — although this discussion will be premature — personal identity is another of these metafactual entities that we store in our Minds as an essence, and also project into the world through our own Minds. Thus, contra Derek Parfit, the *Phenomenological Constructivist Theory of Identity* argues that we are for the most part, the sum total of what we think of ourselves consciously and subliminally, and what everyone else thinks of us, consciously and subliminally: however, it is also the case that the form of ourselves

---

[77] Cartwright, Nancy. 2010. *The dappled world: a study of the boundaries of science.* Cambridge: Cambridge Univ. Press.

is best represented on the Imaginary Graph of Being — in Plato's realm of forms — and hence, even though we access these forms through our phenomenological imagination, personal identity has a dual existence: in the Minds of human beings, as John Locke thought in his *Essay Concerning Human Understanding*, and plotted upon the Imaginary Graph of Being itself.[78] The concepts of our personal identities as represented on the Imaginary Graph of Being are both *perfectly partial* and *perfectly absolute*. This is to say, that even the *imperfect* versions of ourselves are capable of being represented on the graph — as *perfectly partial* versions of our identities — however, it is also the case that the *perfect* version of ourselves is capable of being represented on the graph, too.

Therefore, the Imaginary Graph of Being contains innumerable modal sets of our possible personal identities: it is up to human beings which they choose to identify with; it is a moral imperative, though, that human beings ought to pursue the *democratic consciousness* and the version of themselves as represented on the Imaginary Graph of Being that is *perfect*. Returning to *personal essence*, how might *personal essence* deteriorate across the temporal timeline? The components or Siderian temporal parts of an individual may be gradually reduced to the minimum required to keep an individual alive. However, if we are holistic about Mind — if we believe the whole is greater than the sum of its parts — then we must reject the Siderian hypothesis that personal identity is a matter of parts rather than of holistic wholes.[79] In this case, the whole is the entire psychosomatic — the Mind, emotive, and bodily — composition of the person in question. For now, we must wonder: what happens when the flame of consciousness burns out? To be sure, every night we go to sleep, our locus of attention — the part of the Mind that witnesses events mental and worldly, referred to as the *witnessant* — rests and focuses on dreams and so on. Famous philosopher Derek Parfit argued that teleporters, for example, could dislodge a theory of personal identity, because once a person is duplicated, they lack the same material parts.[80] However, based upon *phenomenological constructivism*, we can respond to the Parfitians — it is not the continuity of consciousness that keeps a person alive, but the projected essence that human beings store in their Minds and project into their worlds. Thus, we may refute the teleporters example: just because you can duplicate an individual, does not mean that they are no longer a person; rather, the person becomes two persons, just as cells divide and share the same DNA.

Later, we shall argue for the existence of *scripts*, or the fundamental units of information, and will discuss how the essence of personal identity as stored in the Mind takes the form of a script, which is something quite akin to the DNA

---

[78]   Parfit, Derek. 2007. *Reasons and persons*. Oxford: Clarendon Press; Plato, and John M. Cooper. 2009. Complete works. Indianapolis: Hackett; Locke, John. 2011. *Essay concerning human understanding ... the twentieth edition, etc.* [Place of publication not identified]: British Library, Historic.

[79]   Hawley, Katherine, "Temporal Parts", *The Stanford Encyclopedia of Philosophy* (Summer 2020 Edition), Edward N. Zalta (ed.), URL = <https://plato.stanford.edu/archives/sum2020/entries/temporal-parts/>.

[80]   Parfit, Derek. 2007. *Reasons and persons*. Oxford: Clarendon Press.

found in all living organisms, except it is stored in the Mind as a concept of essence. Furthermore, believing in the *phenomenological constructivist* view, it would be prudent, here, to comment upon famous philosopher Jacques Derrida's concept of *hauntology*.[81] For Derrida, hauntology is the ontology — the existence — of ghosts and specters. For us Idealists of Personal Identity, we may find that even though the parts of a person become disassembled, their personal essence still thrives and flourishes within our Minds. This is an explanation of why we mourn: because, we still are intimate with the essence of a person, even though that person no longer is no longer manifested in the world as a personage. However, this person still haunts the Minds of their loved ones because they maintain an existence in the Minds and hearts of other human beings. Thus, a person does not truly experience death until they are forgotten by every single living human being. This is why so many cultures worship their ancestors: to keep their memories fresh and alive in the lived human ecosystem. More on personal identity in the division of this work labeled *Politics*.

19. Of Vagueness Explained By An Appeal to the Idiosyncratic Qualitative Cognitive Graph of Being; or, Of Temporal Cognitive Idiosyncrasy Across the Temporal Timeline

The metaphysics of vagueness and becoming involve trajectories as represented on the Platonic Imaginary Graph of Being, but which attempt to trace actuality, as plotted on the Lewisian Ontological Graph of Being. The exact moment when a person begins to corrupt rather than become is itself noumenal, however. This is the question of vagueness in philosophy. Many famous philosophers, such as Kit Fine, gnash their teeth over this very concept.[82] How might we respond to it? Following Bergson, if consciousness is qualitative, then the concepts and concepts of essence that we use in our Minds are likewise qualitative.[83] Therefore, it is a non-sequitur to ask: at what point does a heap evolve from a mere few grains of sand into a heap; or, at which precise loss of hair does a person become bald? The answer is that because concepts are qualitative, such as baldness and so on, that it makes no kind of sense at all to ask: when does this qualitative concept become quantitative? Again, we answer: cognitive holism is the case. Underneath the information provided by the metafacts — labels, signs, language — are atoms of content — these small particles serve chiefly to construct concepts within the Mind.

---

[81]   Derrida, Jacques. 2011. *Specters of Marx: the state of the debt, the work of mourning, and the new international.* New York: Routledge.

[82]   Fine, Kit. 2020. *Vagueness: a global approach.*

[83]   Bergson, Henri. 2002. *Time and free will: an essay on the immediate data of consciousness.* https://search. ebscohost.com/login.aspx?direct=true&scope=site&db=nlebk&db=nlabk&AN=790187.

Human beings project Temporal Categories, a la the logic of Kant's cognitivism espoused within his *Critique of Pure Reason*, onto the physical entities laid out in front of us. Therefore, there is no vagueness external to mind — vagueness is inherently a cognitive issue and not an issue that exists external to cognition itself; this line of argument puts Kant's categories into conversation with Whitehead's process philosophy, yielding, as it were, a *Temporal Category*, akin to a *Temporal Platonic Form*.[84] For human beings to label a bunch of physical matter *a heap of sand*, we must respect that Kantian-Cognitivist Projectional Categories are necessarily qualitative and not quantitative. Therefore, the myriad debates on vagueness are merely language games that have no correlation to the world: if there were no cognition, there would be no vagueness. However, we can pragmatically identify when a person is becoming, or when an acorn is growing rather than rotting; and when a tree is flourishing rather than declining. Suddenly these qualities become apparent to us — all of a sudden the whole takes on a new, fresh quality that it did not have before: call this view the *Sudden Realization Theory of Vagueness*. It will take a while for the whole to become impacted by new qualities: we see the same issue in personal identity, when a person is trying to change their mode-of-life, because such changes take a long time to fructify and manifest in the qualities of the whole. The process of *metanoia* — or the change of heart and Mind — occurs as part of natural development — the natural process of *metanoia* may be referred to as *autometanoia*. The modality of metanoia shall be discussed later on in the work. So much for the becoming and corruption of wholes.

Even if vagueness has been argued to be merely cognitive rather than non-cognitive, or Mind-external, let us now attempt to explain why vagueness has been such an enduring problematic across so many domains of philosophy and thought itself. First and foremost, why does Antigone conclude that Mercutio is bald with four thousand hairs atop his head on Monday, but on Friday articulates that Mercutio, having actually grown more hairs since the past day — unbeknownst to Antigone — still looks just as bald as he did the day before? Or, take for example, that in September Antigone remarks that baldness is the quality of having 5,000 hairs atop one's head, but in December, remarks that baldness is the quality of having a mere 3,000 hairs atop one's head? Let us now reel in the concept of the *Idiosyncratic Qualitative Cognitive Graph of Being*: Antigone is Antigone(X) in September, but is Antigone(Y) in December, on account of process metaphysics and the general flux of time itself: hence, Antigone is a different person on those two days, and this disjuncture of temporality may be applied even one moment after Antigone first remarks her comment, meaning that she could full well have another entirely different view on the matter, conceivably, even just a few moments after her initial remark. Here, the *Idiosyncratic Qualitative Cognitive Graph*

---

[84]   Kant, Immanuel, and Paul Guyer. 2009. *Critique of pure reason*. Cambridge: Cambridge Univ. Press; Whitehead, Alfred North. 1990. *Process and reality: an essay in cosmology* ; Gifford Lectures delivered in the University of Edinburgh during the session 1927-28. New York: Free Press u.a.; Plato, and John M. Cooper. 2009. *Complete works*. Indianapolis: Hackett.

of Being accounts for the fact that Antigone is a process-Being, or a being who changes over time. What's more, because personality is itself a Kantian temporal category, projected into the world through our faculties of cognition, the very notion of personhood, with the Buddhists, may be found, metaphysically, to be empty; but this is not to say that personality may not have a projectional, cognitive, and pragmatic definition, too, in which case, even though personal identity is a mere cognitive concept, projected into the world, and rooted in Mind more than anything else, nevertheless, personal identity may serve a pragmatic function in the world. At any rate, what explains the logic of the difference between Antigone(X) and Antigone(Y), both of whom have two differing opinions on the definition of vagueness?

Simple: there must therefore be, fluctuating mechanisms, within of faculties of cognition, that are imperfect, not constant, contingent upon the context, and so on and so forth: basically: even though human cognition is standardly reliable, nevertheless, the mechanisms and modules inherent to Mind may fluctuate concerning their functionalities across time. Indeed, here, it will be useful, to introduce the concept of *Epistemic Releventia*, for which there is an innate faculty within the mind that sorts information based on whether it is *relevant* to the inquiry or situation at hand: to explain why the two Antigones have differing views on the notion of vagueness, one may argue that: it was not merely that the mechanisms for identifying the relevantia — the relevant set of information given some input focused on by the Mind — are imperfect and do not function the same ways across all times and all contexts, but it is also worthy here to assess that: if two different people cannot agree on what makes a concept vague or not, then the issue of vagueness clearly must be rooted in their respective cognitions; what's more, the same pragmatic (but not metaphysical) person can even contradict themselves when it comes to asserting whether an entity is vague or not: hence, the idiosyncratic disagreements on vagueness, clearly show that vagueness is a fundamentally cognitivist Wittgensteinian language game, rooted in the idiosyncratic cognition and cognitive capacities of the agent in question.[85] So much for the *metaphysics of vagueness and becoming*.

20. Of Cartesianly Witnessing Concepts in the Mind

A concept is the mental set of information relevant to a specific concept, but is composed of intertwound atoms of content within the Mind; these concepts are also linked to the emotions. These concepts are noumenal to the extent that their essence and totality is alienated from us, because they are subliminal, and because we cannot perceive *absolute* essences in the first place. Some will say: are

---

[85] Wittgenstein, Ludwig, G. E. M. Anscombe, Peter M. S. Hacker, and Joachim Schulte. 2010. *Philosophische Untersuchungen = Philosophical investigations*. Chichester, West Sussex, U.K: Wiley-Blackwell.

not concepts perceptual, and cannot one perceive the concept of myself or of the number seven in my head? Our answer would be: no, for, even while there may be an impression within the Mind of said phenomena, such phenomena are finite and limited and are therefore incomplete. We merely perceive the projection of the phenomena too, but this is merely a mirage compared to its real, noumenal existence. Again, essences may exist in reality — as Plato thought — but that is a noumenal question — it cannot be answered — however essences for sure exist within the Mind — as was thought by Kant, his view being, nothing other than *cognitivism*.[86] We can know that essences exist within the Mind because we project them into the world on a daily basis. The locus of attention is such that when we are paying attention to a person's words, for example, the process of *procession* may take place; however, if one is not paying attention, as it were, then the concept of *procession* may not take place. Against Descartes, human beings cannot claim that they know for sure we are thinking: for, more fundamental than thinking is *witnessing* phenomena within the Mind: thus the fundamental motto ought to be: *I witness, therefore I am*.[87] We may refer to the Mind's eye going forward as the *witnessant*. The witnessant perceives phenomena in the Mind all day long, and these phenomena are composed of thoughts that are projected from the subliminal Mind — what famous philosopher Jerry Fodor referred to as the *Language of Thought* — into the conscious Mind.[88] The emergence of thought, action, and speech will be later defined as *production*, or the quality of being products of Mind, and will become important later on in our philosophical interrogations.

22. Of the Focalization of Concepts in the Mind: Plato and Derrida

Every concept must have some focalization, to the extent that it is a meaningful concept. An empty concept may still inform the world as to its own physicality: the text *beep bop doo bop* still takes up space and has an existence within the world, to be sure. Necessarily, every meaningful script has a set of coordinates on the internal Graph of Being, and these are directly linked to the logic of its production. Call these sets of coordinates the *focalization* of the production: of the thought, speech, or action. A focalization is the specific set of information that limits the concept and differentiates it from all other concepts. What is the focalization of the concept of my cat Buffy Anne Marie Summers, for example? Too innumerable to illustrate, here, but it is every single thing that makes Buffy Anne herself and no one else. Take for example the focalization of the concept for the word coffee: it

---

[86] Kant, Immanuel, and Paul Guyer. 2009. *Critique of pure reason*. Cambridge: Cambridge Univ. Press.

[87] Descartes, Rene, and F. Sutcliffe. 2005. *Discourse on Method and the Meditations*. https://www.vlebooks.com/vleweb/product/openreader?id=none&isbn=9780141944203.

[88] Fodor, Jerry A. 2010. *The language of thought*.

denotes a liquid entity with caffeine that is black without milk, etc. The focalization of an entity is precisely the limiting factor of semantics: a focalization limits and plots concepts on the Idiosyncratic Cognitive Graph of Being in order to differentiate the entity from all other entities. Without focalization, there could be no such thing as meaning, to be sure. Human beings are focused on focalization: but defocalization allows us to understand each other better because it allows us to understand with greater nuance the innermost mechanisms of the logic of projection and production — speech, acts, and thought.

Thus, to *defocalize* is to *deconstruct* in the sense of Jacques Derrida's deconstruction — it is to deconstruct an entity and feel out its innermost nuances in order to understand it better.[89] Thus, defocalization ought to be an imperative: what grounds a given production of Mind? Again, production may be taken to mean any emergence of thought, action, and speech from an individual. A focalization may be considered the essence of a given thing, whether that be a word, a sentence, a person, etc. The focalization of personal identity is what differentiates us from other human beings — it is what makes us unique and different. Thus, although such a statement is premature — for we have not arrived at ethics division of this work yet — we may argue: *defocalization* is a component of the *Benefic Categorical Imperative*, or the set of moral duties and ideals that mandate our behavior based on our pursuit of perfection in this world, for, *perfection* is the beauty to which all art must aspire, and, morality may be considered an art in itself: therefore the science of morality is the pursuit of *perfection*, as Plato thought.[90]

23. *Marxian Exposition:*
Of False Consciousness and Conspiracy Theories

A Marxian exposition is in order, because conspiracy theories haunt our age. A conspiracy theory is a concept set series that departs from reality, but yet is very persuasive for some reason. This may extend to all ideologies in general. Either conspiracies are inflated or deflated. To inflate a conspiracy theory is to birth it into being through a production of Mind — through a speech, act, or thought — and these may emerge intentionally or unintentionally. An inflation may be a co-worker whispering in one's ear: "did you hear what Antigone did, it must mean that she…" In that sentence, the conspiracy theory begins to bloom as a concept in the Mind of another; but, there is a reciprocal effect here, also, in that the one uttering the theory is also reinforcing it in his or her own Mind. To deflate a conspiracy theory is to refute it with facts. Conspiracy theories are frequently metafactual though, chiefly because they involve thought and language, and hence are born of

---

[89]   Derrida, Jacques. 2017. *Writing and difference.*

[90]   Plato, and John M. Cooper. 2009. *Complete works.* Indianapolis: Hackett.

consciousness. For example, the European fascists inflated conspiracy theories in the Minds of many of their citizens, and in so doing, caused a disastrous scenario and even a world war. Vitriolic conspiracy theories in general must be limited wherever possible, and should even be made illegal, so as to prevent another disaster the likes of which has never been seen before. Relevant here is the Marxian critique of false consciousness as elucidated in Marx's *Das Kapital.*[91] So much for conspiracy theories.

24. Of the Set Theoretical Logic of Books

Because this is a book, your author can justify a quick discourse on the nature and essence of the concept of the book itself. A book is a set of concepts, piled on top of atoms of content — the letters themselves and the paper that it is printed upon. A book is a set of these concept chains that were produced by an author or authors. Although, when one thinks about it: one is a different person at each moment in time, therefore there is a plurality of authors even when there is only one author, because, a book is not written in a moment, and therefore, multiple consciousnesses are involved in the production of the entire set of scripts produced for the book. My consciousness now as I am typing this sentence will be different in five minutes from now, therefore, when I am writing up the next section, I will be the same person, because personal identity is qualitative and not quantitative, however, my consciousness will have a different focalization at that point and time. Where does a book fall on the Imaginary Graph of Being? It is a product of Mind that was produced by either a person or a machine, for now, even machines can be programmed to produce signs that have a logic to them.

It is not clear — *it is noumenal* — whether computers may project meaning into their words, but this is not the work wherein your author will discourse around such matters. Instead, a book must be considered to be a set of products from a Mind. Ultimately, there is a logic to certain sets of information that are projected onto the book. There may be infinitely many logics affiliated with the text of a book, however. What grounds the work? What questions does the author focalize on? What is the focalization of the book on the Imaginary Graph of Being, and how do those coordinates differ from the set of coordinates to be found in the internal, Idiosyncratic Cognitive Graph of Being? Such questions are reasonable to ask, here. The work must be grounded in its efficient cause to be sure, but there are also other causes involved. The formal cause, or the modality of its being; the teleological cause, or the purpose of the work; and the material cause, or the physical stuff that the book is made up of.[92] So much for the logic of the book.

---

[91]   Marx, Karl, Ben Fowkes, and David Fernbach. 1990. *Capital: a critique of political economy*; v.1. London: Penguin Books in association with New Left Review.

[92]   Aristotle. 1990. *Aristotle: Metaphysics.*

25. Aufhebung: Theory of the Hegelian-Freudian Productive Imprint; or, Of the Recentering of the Notion of the Author

If the General Theory of Focalization is accepted, then there is more business to discuss around it. While we have not yet tackled the nature of *production*, nevertheless, we may begin to discuss it insofar as it is germane to the issues raised above. Of all the issues discussed above, the aufhebung — or the synthesis — of them all, is nothing other than the concept of a *productive imprint*. A person produces across time a book — what is the relationship between that person's Mind and heart and the product that was produced? Your author claims that each product of the Mind and heart — each psychosomatic product — bears an imprint of the Idiosyncratic Cognitive Graph of Being of the producer. This means that a product is imprinted with the consciousness and subconsciousness of its producer. How else may we explain the focalization of the psychosomatic product? Why is that product exactly the way it is and no other way? What is the logic of the product? Here, we may answer: the psychosomatic mode of production is a function, and has inputs and outputs. The best way to analyze a person's identity is to take the set of all the products of their Mind — actions, speech, and thoughts — from the day they were born — and derive the functionalities of that said Mind and heart based upon the logic of their productions.

This is because, when a product is produced, there is a mode of production that ensures it is produced in a certain way. Thus, in a feat of reverse-engineering, if a product is engineered, then there must be an engine that produced it. Because the product was filtered through this engine, it bears the logic of this engine. Thus, the *Imprintational Theory of Production* argues that the products of Mind reflect a logical imprint from the Mind and heart that produced it. An example: if God sculpted human beings, then human beings are products of God, in which case, the logical modality of human beings is such that it bears an imprint from the consciousness and subconsciousness of God. This text that your author is writing at the present moment: it is structured in such and such a way according to the logical modality of my consciousness and subconsciousness. Why is my prose different from Marcel Proust's, for example? Because we have two separate and distinct — and idiosyncratic — logical modalities about us that directly impact our prose styles, and, indeed, any product of the Mind or heart. The *Imprintational Theory of Production* stems not merely from the implications Hegel's dialectic of the master and servant — found, of course, in his Phenomenology of Mind — but also from a generalist's reading of Freud's *Basic Writings*, especially his case studies.[93] Thus, the *Imprintational Theory of Production*.

---

[93]   Hegel, Georg Wilhelm Friedrich, and Terry P. Pinkard. 2018. *The phenomenology of spirit*; Freud, Sigmund, and Abraham A. Brill. 1938. *The basic writings*.

Chapter
II

OF ANTHROPOCOGNITIVITY

ANTHROPOCOGNITIVITY is the science of human modality, or the way in which human beings *are* within the world. Thus, in this section, we shall investigate general theories of how human beings are in the world. However, we shall also interrogate the Mind and its ecosystem. Where there have been metafacts earlier in the work, there shall be metafacts in this section of the work, also. Again, proof of the existence of metafacts is twofold: firstly, metafacts will improve our understanding of the world; secondly, metafacts will display some functionality in the world. Thus, even though they cannot be perceived — even though metafacts are noumenal — they may be derived from speculative empirical observation and speculative reason. In this section, we shall discuss production and language; recall that production is the process by which thoughts, speech, and actions emerge from the individual. Language, Martin Heidegger called it, is the house of being: it is the science of the metafactual, for, language is a superstructure built overtop the world — built overtop the atoms of content that inform the world.[94] As a metafactual superstructure, language is a production of Mind and a referent to items within the domain of consciousness. While language is not noumenal itself, instead, the projected essence that informs all language is; therefore, language is intricately tied up with the noumenal — as we shall see in the section on metalinguistics. How may we ground a science of Anthropocognitivity? Because some facets of the human identity are metafactual, we will have to employ speculative reason — a mechanism of the imagination. Without the imagination, such a project would be hopeless from the very beginning. However, because human beings exist across the temporal timeline, and are a set of coordinates on the fluctuating Imaginary Graph of Being, they do leave traces on the world in a very real, physical sense.

To start, the *programmatologies of Mind* shall be discussed: these being, the *automatic* and *phenomenological* faculties of Mind. Following that discussion, an analysis of the concept of the *trigger* shall be performed; then, the *trigger* will be identified as the fundamental unit of historical progression. Inherent to the *automatic* programmatology of Mind will be the concept of *cyclology*, or the study

---

[94] Heidegger, Martin. 2009. *On the way to language*. San Francisco: HarperOne.

of cycles. For, certainly the *automatic* processes of Mind are cyclical at least in part; indeed, it is perhaps the case that most processes of Mind are cyclical rather than novel in character. The process of *production* will be discussed, wherein our Minds produce thoughts, actions, and speech. After that, a discussion of the *polyintentionality* of the Will shall be discussed, which is a novel approach to the concept of the Will. Then, the *systematic* faculty of Mind shall be discussed, which too falls under the umbrella of the *automatic* programmatology of Mind. Then, the Cartesian *witnessant* will be discussed; this discussion shall be followed by an exposition of the so-called *liberated consciousness*.[95] Then, animalistic and linguistic phenomenologies shall be discussed, and criticized, each in their own way: especially the concept of *instinct* shall be criticized and exposed. Following those analyses, the *narrativity of Heart* will emerge as an important feature of the *systematic* faculty of Mind.

Then, a Heideggerian discussion of *Mood* will follow, that will culminate in a *General Theory of Productive Vibes*.[96] Next, will follow a small subdivision of the work on *metalinguistics*. A *Leibnizian General Theory of Projectional Optimalism* will be the first philosophical gambit of the *metalinguistics* subdivision, which is the theory that human consciousness *automatically* attempts to understand a given situation in the best possible light that suits their needs and instincts. Importantly, the dialectic will progress into the ballpark of the Hegelian-Lacanian *Linguistic Superstructure* itself, which is responsible for the elevation of human beings up out of nature and into society, contra the views of Hobbes, Locke, and Rousseau.[97] After that, the concept of *indebtion* will be discussed as an explanation for *guilt* and what Kant and Nietzsche both referred to as *priestcraft*, or the deliberate manipulation of other human beings grounded in modalities of debt.[98] Then, the arguments of Saint Anselm shall be brought into the dialectic in order to progress it into the terrain of *Temporal Projective Categoricism* and *objective essentiality*; three figures

---

[95]   Descartes, Rene, and F. Sutcliffe. 2005. *Discourse on Method and the Meditations.* https://www.vlebooks.com/vleweb/product/openreader?id=none&isbn=9780141944203.

[96]   Heidegger, Martin, John Macquarrie, and Edward S. Robinson. 2019. *Being and time.*

[97]   Hegel, Georg Wilhelm Friedrich. 2004. *Hegel's Science of logic.* Amherst, N.Y.: Humanity Books; Lacan, Jacques, Jacques-Alain Miller, and Alan Sheridan. 2019. *The four fundamental concepts of psycho-analysis*; Hobbes, Thomas, and Ian Shapiro. 2010. *Leviathan: or, The matter, forme and power of a commonwealth ecclesiasticall and civil.* New Haven, Conn: Yale University Press; Locke, John, Mark Goldie, John Locke, and John Locke. 2016. *Second treatise of government; and a letter concerning toleration*; Rousseau, Jean-Jacques, Quintin Hoare, and Christopher Bertram. 2012. *Of the social contract and other political writings.* London: Penguin Books.

[98]   Kant, Immanuel, Theodore M. (Theodore Meyer) Greene, and Hoyt H. Hudson. 1960. *Religion within limits or reason alone*; Nietzsche, Friedrich, and Walter Arnold Kaufmann. 2011. *On the genealogy of morals.* New York: Vintage Books.

will complement this discussion: Nietzsche, Fish, and Dworkin.[99] Lastly will follow a critique of Fodor's *Language of Thought*, which will function more as a revision of his inaccurate terminology instead of a direct refutation; the Fodorian *Language of Thought* will be described as noumenal, which is to say, that the process of mental *production* is alienated from our understandings, and is, too, noumenal.[100] So much for the prefatory remarks on the division of this work labeled *Anthropocognitivity*.

1. Grounding of the Derridean-Fodorian Programmatology of Mind

It is to be argued that there are two basic and fundamental programs of Mind. These two programs that the Mind runs may qualitatively be described as, first, the Automaticity of Mind, or the automatic functions and cycles that the Mind operates regularly, and secondly, the phenomenology of Mind, or the experience of consciousness. Important to consider is that the phenomenology of Mind — or consciousness — may directly interact with and alter the automatic functions and cycles of Mind. A function is an entity that occurs once, but if it repeats, such repetition is grounds to identify it as a cycle. A cycle is any repeating function that has a trigger that activates a receptor, and that also has a receptor that initiates either a function or a cycle. What is a cycle? Imagine that Antigone calls her ex-boyfriend Mercutio, except that she calls Mercutio thirty-five times. Thus, we may derive using our phenomenological imaginations, the existence of a drive and a cycle within her psyche: thus, all actions, speech, or thoughts that occur once may be conceived of as mental functions, but as soon as they repeat — even just once — they may be conceived of as cycles. Hence, Antigone has a drive and a cycle — some atavistic urge-toward-intimacy with Mercutio, which itself is not as important as the proof of a general existence of cycles that the example provides. The automaticity of Mind, or the sets of functions of Mind that repeat automatically — including the production of novel emergences of actions, thoughts, and speech — has two main subprograms: these are *Production*, or the process of speaking, acting, and thinking; and *Systemization*, or the integration and disintegration of information into the mental depository of information, and also, the narritivation of this information. For *Production*, especially of the production of thought, we will enter into an analysis of what intuition is; intuition, basically, involves *subliminal probabilitism*, or the subliminal calculation of information relevant to a given subject that produces an intuition based on the probability calculation that

[99]   Anselm, Brian Davies, and G. R. Evans. 1998. *The major works Anselm of Canterbury*. Oxford; New York: Oxford University Press; Kaufmann, Walter Arnold, and Friedrich Nietzsche. 2011. *Beyond good and evil: prelude to a philosophy of the future*. New York: Vintage Books; Dworkin, Ronald. 1986. *Law's empire*. Cambridge, Mass. u.a: Belknap Pr. of Harvard Univ. Pr; Fish, Stanley Eugene. 2003. *Is there a text in this class?: the authority of interpretive communities*. Cambridge, Mass: Harvard Univ. Press.

[100]   Fodor, Jerry A. 2010. *The language of thought*.

occurs subliminally. For *Systemization*, one of its most important of all the cycles within its domain, is the *Affect Cycle*. It is one thing for information to be neutral — that a towel hangs on a towel rack is basically neutral information for me; but, the information that my loved one is sick in the hospital is not neutral information to me, to be sure: instead, it is emotionally charged information.

What determines whether or not information that is being integrated into the mental depository is either neutral or emotional is precisely the *reflexivity equation*; the *reflexivity equation* is an internal mechanism that filters information during the process of systemization to ascertain whether or not said information is pertinent to the internal concept of oneself. The internal concept of oneself has two components: firstly, the descriptive component — or the information about *what* we are and were; and secondly, the prescriptive component — or the information about *how* we should be or should have been. Thus, this reconstruction argues for the existence of a Core Script that contains a set of information pertinent to the overarching concept of the self. While it is a noumenal question whether or not essences exist in the world, it is without a doubt that essences exist within the Mind and are projected into the world via *idealistic projectionalism*, akin to Kant's *cognitivist* view formed due to the problem of universals, that states, the Platonic forms exist not in the external world somewhere, but merely in the Minds of human beings as concepts — such is the *cognitivist* view of Kant.[101] Thus, the concept of the Core Script exists within the Minds of human beings, and especially the concept of the Core Script exists within the Mind of the individual; yet, as mentioned above, human beings have not only a Core Script for ourselves, but also for every other person we know; only, our very own Core Script is the most developed and intricate of them all, because we have the most information about ourselves. In some cases of self-ignorance, others may perceive us more aptly than we perceive ourselves, however. So much for a grounding of the Derridean-Fodorian *programmatology of Mind*, which expands upon Fodor's modularity of mind, in conjunction with Derrida's concept of grammatology itself, weaving the two strands of thought into a complex synthesis in order to account indeed for the gargantuan — perhaps noumenal — complexity of Mind.[102]

2. Of the Pragmatic-Newtonian Trajectorics of the Trigger

There are two basic units in the *programmatology of Mind*, these being, triggers and receptors. In order for a trigger to accomplish anything, it must meet with a corresponding receptor. A receptor is an entity which, when stimulated by the presence of a trigger, initiates either a novel trajectory or a cyclical trajectory. As

---

[101] Kant, Immanuel, and Paul Guyer. 2009. *Critique of pure reason*. Cambridge: Cambridge Univ. Press.

[102] Derrida, Jacques. 1998. *Of grammatology*. Baltimore: Johns Hopkins University Press; Fodor, Jerry Alan. 2014. *The modularity of mind: an essay on faculty psychology*. Cambridge (Mass.): The MIT Press.

discussed earlier in the work, a trajectory is any motion across the temporal timeline that occurs on the Axes of Being as may be plotted on the Imaginary Graph of Being. Because Mind has two fundamental components — the *Phenomenological* component, and the *Automatic* component, they are to be plotted on the Imaginary Graph of Being separately. Because the phenomenological component of Mind is qualitative — to return to Bergson's qualitative theory of durational consciousness — it is merely plotted on the Imaginary Graph of Being as qualitative, and not quantitative or extensional in the Cartesian sense.[103] On the other hand, the Automatic component of Mind may be plotted on the Imaginary Graph of Being with much more ease, because it is quantitative and extensional, which is to say that it involves physical components. Now, this means that there may be trajectories of the automatic and physical kind, but that there may not be phenomenological trajectories, just because the Phenomenology of Mind is qualitative and resists engraphment on the Imaginary Graph of Being. All that can be graphed of the *phenomenology of Mind* is that it is qualitative. Yet, to be sure, there are different modalities of phenomenology — as has been discussed in Hegel's *Phenomenology of Mind* — but, because these modes are qualitative and durational — which is to say they are fundamentally temporal entities — they resist complex, quantitative engraphment on the Imaginary Graph of Being. Now, triggers may occur in the phenomenological realm, or they may be subliminal — which is to say, *automatic.* Take for example the issue of, if one has a kidney ailment during one's youth, and if one later in life has another kidney ailment — and the ailment itself — the physicality of the pain in the same location as before — triggers all number of childhood memories to resurface. Phenomenological triggers have been discussed at great length in Marcel Proust's masterpiece, *In Search of Lost Time*, to be sure.[104] However, subliminal triggers occur on the physical level, and are trajectories as may be plotted on the Imaginary Graph of Being; an example of a subliminal trigger would be, the various operations that a cell undergoes during replication, and so on — the entire process is dependent on triggers that inform the cell as to how to operate during the procedure of cell replication.

While subliminal triggers occur naturally and physically, phenomenological triggers occur in a more simple manner; while subliminal triggers function as do billiard balls striking one another, phenomenological triggers function more impressionistically, according to the *General Theory of Procession* discussed earlier. Thus, triggers emerge, interact, are processed into the brain, are identified in the brain, are sorted in the brain, are deconstructed for information, are deposited into the informational depository, and finally, are derived for their essential influence — then, there is a ninth step: triggers then

---

[103]   Bergson, Henri. 2002. *Time and free will: an essay on the immediate data of consciousness*. https://search. ebscohost.com/login.aspx?direct=true&scope=site&db=nlebk&db=nlabk&AN=790187;   Descartes,   Rene, and F. Sutcliffe. 2005. *Discourse on Method and the Meditations*. https://www.vlebooks.com/vleweb/product/ openreader?id=none&isbn=9780141944203.

[104]   Proust, Marcel. 2002. *In search of lost time boxed set*. London: Allen Lane.

interact with receptors underground the phenomenology, the doing so of which inaugurates either novel trajectories or cyclical trajectories in the *automatistic* brain; in the phenomenology of Mind — or the consciousness of Mind — triggers are more impressionistic than they are causal, because, each repetition of the *General Theory of Procession's* Procession Cycle represents a fundamentally interpretive moment. Thus, there are two modes of triggers, automatic and phenomenological; and, phenomenological triggers are more hermeneutic and impressionistic, whereas, automatic triggers are more granular, quantitative, and causal. In general, there is such a thing as the *trigger cycle*, because — in an abstract manner — every time that a trigger meets with a receptor, it repeats an abstract trajectory, which is to say, the repetition of the process of triggering, becomes a cycle, insofar as it repeats. Pragmatic because triggers occur within the realm of phenomenological praxis, and Newtonian because they involve causality, both phenomenological and physicalist, trigger theory therefore settles pragmatically for a Newtonian explanation of the phenomena on account of Einsteinian and Quantum Mechanistic explanations being anything but firmly rooted in the scientific community; this is to say, that physics and physicalism as discussed in the first section of the *Anthropoepistemology* are very much so noumenal concepts, not being able to be grasped one way or the other — therefore, any conclusion regarding higher philosophical matters such as physics of physicalism must be made pragmatically; hence, a merely *Newtonian Theory of the Trigger*.[105] So much for triggers and receptors.

3. Of the Trigger as the Fundamental Unit of History: Of Autosystemization and the Reflexivity Equation

There has been great controversy over what the fundamental unit of world history and history is — and one can see why — for to have answered the question aptly would be a great laurel atop the head of the philosopher in question who did the answering. After the most recent discussions of the trigger, it would be easy to see why we are about to claim that the fundamental unit of history — the unit which drives history — is the trigger. How could the fundamental unit of history be anything other than the trigger? Take for example Martin Luther and his dynamic personality — was not he profoundly triggered by the Catholic Church and its foolishness around the issue of indulgences?[106] Certainly there were more triggers involved in the triggering of Luther than merely that one, to be sure. How may we explain why some triggers impact a Mind more profoundly than others? The answer to this question lies in the automatic domain of the Mind. The process of

---

[105]   Newton, Isaac, C. R. Leedham-Green, and Isaac Newton. 2021. *The mathematical principles of natural philosophy.*

[106]   Mullett, Michael A. 2015. *Martin Luther.*

systemization — or rather — of *autosystemization* — occurs naturally and on a regular basis, indeed, on an immediate basis all of the time. Constantly, the Mind is at work integrating and deintegrating atomistic monads of information. Yet, the *reflexivity equation* becomes prominent again in our reconstruction — for, emotions are grounded in emotionally charged information, and thus, emotions are born of either integrations or disintegrations of information.

The information that my partner just proposed to me elevates my love for them, when integrated into my mental system of information. However, when I have not seen my partner in over forty years, eventually, the love for them will disintegrate just as the memories do, and so, it is clear to see that information and emotions are bound at the hip. It is the reflexivity equation that determines whether or not information deserves or qualifies for emotional charge. Emotional charge may be either positive, neutral, or negative — all emotions are variants of those three elements. When the information is being derived in my Mind, and when the trigger meets with the appropriate receptors — all those receptors deemed by the Mind to be relevant to the trigger in question — this itself is a *screening process* — then the reflexivity equation weighs the information to judge two things: whether this information is relevant to its host either prescriptively or descriptively, i.e., whether this information pertains to how a person should be or should have been, or how said person is or was. Thus, when Luther was triggered by all the various stimuli, the triggers were like dynamite within him, due to his pre-existing systematics of Mind — which is to say — due to the pre-existing set of integrated and emotionally charged information he had within the automatic domain of his Mind. That is to say, Luther's *subliminal prioritization*, or pre-existing set of emotionally charged and neutral information, was exactly of the mode that it would strongly interact with the triggers when presented with them. So much for the trigger as the fundamental unit of history; but what could be more truthful, when analyzed, that the trigger is responsible for all actions, speech, and thoughts? This is not to say that there cannot be an *autonomy of the will* cycle, as indeed will be exposed within no time at all in this work.

4. Of the Automatic Faculty of Mind: Of Production and Systemization

As mentioned earlier, the automaticity of Mind has two submodules: these being, the *cycle of production* and the *cycle of systemization*. These two cycles all take place automatically, mostly on a subliminal level; but as shall been seen, the production of thought, action, and speech, occurs simultaneously to its construction — to its logical and modal assembly, and thus, production simultaneously occurs jointly on a subliminal and phenomenological level. The production cycle involves the emergence of all thought, action, and speech. The systemization cycle is by far the most intricate and complex: it involves the systemizing of information — whether integrating or disintegrating information from the system — and, due to the *reflexivity equation*, the systemization cycle employs the very same as a mechanism to filter out which information is relevant to the modal Core Script that is one's *logic-of-the-self*; furthermore, the mechanism that is the reflexivity equation, filters the recently processed information twofoldly: prescriptively and descriptively; which is to say, that the information is weighed on the scale of: how does this information pertain to who a person should have been, and how said person should be, and, how does this information pertain to what said person has been, and what said person should be? Let it also be known that the reflexivity equation is the root cause of the human emotional matrix. For, as information is assessed by the reflexivity equation —that is to say, integrated or disintegrated from our depositories of information — if the information is weighed to be relevant either to our modal Core Script — prescriptively or descriptively — said information then becomes emotionally charged information, and hence, the *reflexivity equation* is the grounding of an emotion. Without the reflexivity component of the process of systemization, there could be no such thing as an emotion, let alone an emotivics — a science of the emotions. So much for the automaticity of Mind.

5. Of the Freudian-Lacanian Cyclology of Mind; or, Of the Oligarchy of the Dominant Cycles

Let cyclology be known as the study of cycles. Any trajectory that repeats becomes a cycle. Repetition must be considered in the abstract, because, due to the difference in time, no two trajectories may technically be considered the same; Freud's dichotomy of repetition and compulsion grounds cyclology, but so too does Lacan's analysis of repetition.[107] However, when the logical form of the trajectory — when the metafactuality of the trajectory — bears a semblance to another logical form of a separate trajectory, thus, the second trajectory may be considered a repetition of the first. Hence, the existence of cycles. Let cycles be understood as a more rigorous theory of Aristotelian habit, that is not merely behaviorist a la B.F. Skinner, but also mentalist in the Cartesian sense.[108] Therefore, human habits must be understood to be cycles. Because triggers cause both novel and repetitive trajectories — trajectories that repeat are cycles — and because of the earlier reconstruction of triggers and their relationship to triggeral receptors,

---

[107]   Freud, Sigmund, and James Strachey. 2001. *Beyond the pleasure principle: group psychology and other works; (1920-1922)*. London: Vintage; Lacan, Jacques, Jacques-Alain Miller, and Alan Sheridan. 2019. *The four fundamental concepts of psycho-analysis*.

[108]   Aristotle, and Charles David Chanel Reeve. 2014. *Nicomachean ethics*. Indianapolis: Hackett Publishing Co.; Skinner, B. F. 2008. *About behaviorism*. [Bridgewater, NJ]: Distributed by Paw Prints/Baker & Taylor; Descartes, Rene, and F. Sutcliffe. 2005. *Discourse on Method and the Meditations*. https://www.vlebooks.com/vleweb/product/openreader?id=none&isbn=9780141944203.

it must be understood that cycles — both mental and behavioral — may be interrupted. Indeed, receptors may also be inhibited to prevent triggers from triggering them and causing trajectories and cycles to occur. Let it be understood that there are dominant and submissive cycles within any given human program. When Immanuel Kant's schedule is dominated by his daily walk, he has a dominant cycle that figures prominently in his psychosomatic composition.

A submissive cycle is one that may be considered recessive: it will not occur if a more dominant cycle is active or activated during such time as the trigger hits the receptor for that given submissive cycle. Because so much of human programmatology is repetitive, it must be understood that there is an *oligarchy of the cycles* that, aggregately, dominate a given human programmatology.[109] How may freedom occur, then? Simple: there is such a thing as an *autonomy cycle*, wherein the dominant cycles may be interrupted firstly, and then inhibited — all of this is very surgical — then, during a process of *metanoia*, the concept of the Core Script may be revised and edited. It should be noted that the process of metanoia is automatic and measurably occurs across the temporal timeline: for, all of us will agree that personal changes take place quite automatically and naturally: thus, *autometanoia* is a very real and serious process that, when analyzed, shows how metanoia may occur *intentionally* — which is to say — *phenomenologically*. Thus, through the process of internal reflection and interrogation, whether personally or with the help of a psychoanalyst, such metanoia may occur by inhibiting certain cycles of behavior, thought, and speech; the process of inhibiting a cycle forces the emergence of a novel trajectory. Thus, metanoia may be both mentalist and behaviorist at the same time, which is to say, it must involve either a disintegration of existing cycles in order to be effective, or the insertion of a novel and dominant trajectory. This is all to say, concerning the human program, in alignment with the *Ethics* of famous philosopher Baruch Spinoza, that there are both malefic and benefic cycles; Spinoza did not acknowledge the existence of cycles, but his ethical theory was one in the same with the dichotomy between physiological maleficence and beneficence.[110] Thus, in brief, and with famous philosopher Aristotle — the science of morality is the accumulation of benefic cycles, and the mitigation and negation of malefic cycles.[111] Let therefore Aristotle's ethics be renamed *virtue cyclology*. One would write: so much for cyclology, but this is not the last time cycles will be featured in this work, to be sure.

---

[109]   Freud, Sigmund, and James Strachey. 2001. *Beyond the pleasure principle: group psychology and other works; (1920-1922)*. London: Vintage.

[110]   Spinoza, Benedictus de, and G. H. R. Parkinson. 2009. *Ethics*. Oxford: Oxford University Press.

[111]   Aristotle, and Charles David Chanel Reeve. 2014. *Nicomachean ethics*. Indianapolis: Hackett Publishing Co.

6. Of the Freudian-Lacanian Cyclology of Production; or, Of the Productive Faculty of Mind

A *Theory of Production* has haunted this work: finally comes the time to speak on production itself, or the emergence of all actions, thoughts, and speech. To argue that there is *cyclology of production,* is to claim that each emergence of an act, speech, or thought shares a form, and hence, the process of production is itself a cycle. Let us then begin to unwind precisely what occurs during the cycle of production. Firstly, we must analyze what grounds production. It must be that there is such a thing as *subliminal prioritization* — as discussed earlier — which is, the set of emotionally charged and neutral information that is systematically enmeshed within the Mind. How might one explain tendencies and cycles of production — the tendency of Samuel Johnson to write using very long sentences, frequented with semicolons and the like? Why does his writing have that *specific* modality to it? How can we explain *idiosyncratic modalities* — generally speaking — how can we explain *idiosyncraticism* — or the uniqueness of everyone — without turning to the *General Theory of Subliminal Prioritization,* or the claim, generally speaking, that the subliminal systematic set of pre-integrated information, emotionally charged and uncharged, affects any novel or cyclical productions of Mind? What are the logical limits at play during the process of production — what may a person do versus not do? One might say here, astutely, "well then there is no such thing as freedom if there is such a thing as *subliminal prioritization,*" yet, that person would be directed to read up on the earlier section of this work that discussed the *autonomy cycle,* during which, cycles may be interrupted and their receptors inhibited, thus allowing for the genesis of new trajectories and cycles. While there may be *autoproduction,* or the automatic process of production, and while even for the phenomenological Mind, there exists *subliminal prioritization,* real metanoia remains possible, because, if autometanoia is the case anyway, then certain phenomenological interruptances may without a doubt be possible.

Here, the detractors will again raise the issue: "then there is no free will, for, even the phenomenological Mind, is adjacent to *subliminal prioritization,* and hence, even so-called willed interrogations of the Core Script must be determined and limited by *subliminal prioritization.*" There, the detractors do have a point: however, our response must be: freedom is only ever the freedom to accord oneself to moral commandments — certainly freedom of the will is limited, as will be discussed later on in this work.[112] For, imagine a free will adjacent to omniscience — only then would the will be free to choose most accordantly with the axioms of its Core Script; yet, without omniscience, all freedom is a trivial and insignificant thing. All that matters in terms of freedom is that one becomes progressively more and more moral, which is to say, that their malefic cycles become negated and

---

[112] Kant, Immanuel, Jens Timmermann, Mary J. Gregor, Immanuel Kant, and Immanuel Kant. 2014. *Groundwork of the metaphysics of morals: a German-English edition.*

replaced with more benefic cycles. Now, all of that's being on the table, let us return to the cyclology of production: it is grounded firstly by *subliminal prioritization*, and secondly, the last two stages occur simultaneously: these two components of the cycle are called *simultaneous construction* and *phenomenological emergence*. Simultaneous construction is the idea that, as human beings are producing thoughts, actions, or speech, that the very same are logically constructed according to the subliminal prioritization at the same time of their phenomenological emergence, or the moment when said entities become cognizant to the consciousness of their producer. Thought, for example, is simultaneously constructed as it emerges in my Mind, and thus, there is such a thing as the *simultaneous construction* of the thought, action, or speech, because it emerges to the Mind simultaneous to its being logically assembled. So much for the cyclology of production, Freudian because Freud's work in founding Psychoanalysis laid out the groundwork for the existence of cycles and cyclology itself; what's more, Freud's optimistic views on the possibility of altering the Core Script of an individual — and hence thereby interrupting a given individual's cyclology of Mind — entail the existence of a certain Core Script — not a soul, per se — but a Core Script; likewise, Lacan's writings on repetition and drive, too, allow for the imagination of such a *cyclology of production*.[113]

7. Of the Noumenal Theory of Alienation From the Productivity of Mind: Beyond Habermas

While to be sure there may be cognizance of the modes of production, due especially to the phenomenological locus of attention being focused internally on the production itself, e.g., writing, etc., without a doubt, most of the productive process occurs subliminally — and hence noumenally: hence, if the mechanisms of production are noumenal, then, by extension, the mechanisms of discourse itself are noumenal to us: hence, a critique of Habermasian discourse theory and morality, and discursive Political Liberalisms at large.[114] Thus, the mechanisms that operate during the process of production are, for the most part, subliminal and automatic. Even when the phenomenological loci of attention is internally focused upon the construction of some production, it must be the case that the totality of forces at play in the operation of the process are concealed rather than illuminated. For, due to the mere focalization of products, all products are focused, specific, and modally uncoincidental. That is to say, that the focalization of a product in general entails that products are the manifestation of certain subliminal forces that are concealed from the consciousness underground of which they inhabit.

---

[113]   Freud, Sigmund, and Abraham A. Brill. 1938. *The basic writings*; Lacan, Jacques, Jacques-Alain Miller, and Alan Sheridan. 2019. *The four fundamental concepts of psycho-analysis*.

[114]   Habermas, Jürgen, and William Rehg. 2015. *Between facts and norms contributions to a discourse theory of law and democracy*. Cambridge: Polity Press.

These forces involve nothing other than the systematic set of information held in the subliminal depository — some of which is emotionally charged and some of which is emotionally neutral, based upon the reflexivity equation — and the given drives of an individual. A drive is a natural, automatic manifestation of certain clustered and linked sets of information that exists subliminally.[115] While memories and these sets of information may partially be accessed through the individual's phenomenology, it is largely the case that the information stored in the Mind's depository of information is obscured and subliminal to the phenomenology of said individual. Thus, the *mechanisms* of construction are obscured to the individual. Indeed, returning to the focalization of products, it must be the case that a product is the specific way it is due to all of the subliminal mechanisms at work in the brain. And, to make matters more obscure, the essence of the productions must distinguish the product from all other entities in every single possible world — how could such a feature of essence be anything but obscured to human beings, therefore? Thus, it may be concluded that the total process of the construction of products can be identified as noumenal, insofar as the total and essential means of production are obscured to human beings.

8. Of Freudian Polyintentionality and the Productivity of Mind

Worse yet than the obscurity of the means of anthropocognitive production, we now arrive at a discussion of the Will and production, for, may not we will into being certain products of Mind — certainly intentionality plays a role here, no? Here, we must reconstruct the simplistic yet traditional conception of the will: namely, the idea that the will is monointentional, which is to say, that only one intention may be willed at a time. For, when we consider the complex emotional and subliminal undergrounds of human beings — and furthermore when we take into cognizance the whole set of information that humans have stored in their mental depositories, how could it not be that all of that information — emotionally charged and neutral alike — should have no bearing on the polyintentionality of the Will — which is to say, that any *General Theory of the Will* must identify as a feature of the Will its capacity to be polyintentional. Thus, once polyintentionality is on the table, we may clearly see that the intentions involved in even a single product may be infinite. Take for example the idea that God created the world, and had foreknowledge while doing so, and so on: would not God have infinitely many intentions for nature and civilization inherent to God's plan for creation? We can only answer: certainly so!

Now, to apply polyintentionality to human products: imagine Antigone writes her ex-boyfriend a letter: what are her intentions? First and foremost she would like a date to her Junior Prom. Secondly, she feels lonely without him.

---

[115]   Freud, Sigmund, and Samuel Moyn. 2022. *Civilization and its discontents.*

Thirdly, her parents quite enjoyed Mercutio and kept nagging her to return to at least filial relations with him. This example needs no further exposition: for, the point to be made here has become blatantly obvious: that, during Willed cognition, there may be polyintentionality as demonstrated through the specific modality of the product at hand. At the same time, it follows that, when one cognizes, there may be a plurality of ideations subliminal and underground the thought: one mere sentence may have hundreds of implicit and explicit referents. How, then, given the perhaps infinite semantic chain of thought just noted, could there not be such a thing as polyintentionality, not merely of the will, but of all cognition in general? Thus, the *General Theory of the Will* is rooted and grounded in the thought of Freud, especially espoused in his case studies, which reveal anthropocognitivity to be complex in a vast way — which is to say, polyintentional.[116] So much for the polyintentionality of the product, which is, defined here as, any speech, action, or thought produced by Mind.

9. Of the Freudian General Will and Freudian Polyintentionality

Because of polyintentionality, the Will really ought to be labeled a Freudian General Will, because there are many explicit and implicit components to the Will.[117] Thus, an individual may have a General Will that encompasses all of the intentions inherent to some given production of their Mind. To probe further into what exactly a General Will is, it may be described as the manifestation of the set of drives inherent to a person's state of Mind at any given time. A drive is nothing other than an emotionally charged cluster of information that has been successfully systematized into a person's programmatology, or their modality of Mind. A drive may be derived from the modality of an individual's productive endeavors: through analyzing their products of Mind: their thoughts, speech, and actions. Because a drive is naturally repetitive, it may be considered a cycle. Thus, there is such a thing as a *constellation of cycles* — earlier identified as a certain *oligarchy of cycles* — inherent to an individual's modality of Mind. Hence, *constellationism* is the view that there is a certain set of cycles that dominate an individual's daily being or modality. This constellation of cycles may be derived, again, through a careful — perhaps psychoanalytical — reconstruction of an individual's productive endeavors — again, an analysis of a said individual's thoughts, speech, and actions. Thus, the General Will of even a single product of the Mind may involve a multiplicity of cycles that both inform and shape the product itself. How, then, if there are all of these cycles in the productive underground, may the General Will be free? Freedom must rest on the *principle of autonomy* alone.

---

[116]   Freud, Sigmund, and Louise Adey Huish. 2003. *The "wolfman" and other cases*. New York: Penguin Books.
[117]   Ibid

The principle of autonomy is merely the principle that, if one is cognizant of their limitations and cycles, and that if one's locus of attention is focused on the production of the product itself, then there is a narrow opportunity for the individual to transcend their constellation of cycles. However, an individual will never be able to transcend their systematicity of Mind, i.e., their entire integrated set of information — emotionally charged and neutral alike. Such a feat would be a priori impossible; unless the individual outsourced the General Will perhaps to a machine or supercomputer, in which case the computer could be programmed with certain axioms found desirable by the individual, and then these axioms could be applied to a hypothetical scenario that could easily be replicated in the world. Even then, the selection of these axioms would be conditioned by the integrated set of emotionally charged or neutral information inherent to the individual's systematicity of Mind. The only available option, then, to accomplish a truly unlimited and free General Will, would be to align one's modes of production and one's products alike, with certain universal, a priori ethical principles. Such a project will be further explored later on in this work. Ultimately, however, and in apparent alignment with philosopher Immanuel Kant, it is to be argued that the freedom of the General Will and whether we have it at all must itself be a noumenal inquiry.[118] Until there can be a definitive calculus of the Mind — a scientific and causal understanding of the General Will — then there can be no such refutations of the freedom of the General Will. So much for the General Will and the noumenality of either its freedom or unfreedom.

10. Of the Luhmannian Systematic Faculty of Mind

The Systematic Faculty of Mind is the part of the brain that is automatic in its processing, integration, and disintegration of information; the concept of systems here is being used in the manner of Niklas Luhmann's *Introduction to Systems Theory*.[119] While occasionally information may be handled phenomenologically — directly by the locus of attention — the lion's share of information exists and functions subliminally in human beings. Firstly, the systematicity of Mind is responsible for *subliminal prioritization*, or the information that grounds the General Will and explains the various intentions inherent to a specific product of the Mind. Values figure largely in the systematicity of Mind, because a value is a cemented combination of thoughts and feelings grounded in the needs and instincts of a given individual or group of individuals. Among the set of information existing in the mental depository, there are more than just derivative sets of emotional information. The systematic faculty of Mind narrativizes information both according to preexisting sets of values and also toward the end of forming

---

[118]   Kant, Immanuel, Jens Timmermann, Mary J. Gregor, Immanuel Kant, and Immanuel Kant. 2014. *Groundwork of the metaphysics of morals: a German-English edition.*

[119]   Luhmann, Niklas, Dirk Baecker, and Peter Gilgen. 2021. *Introduction to systems theory.* Cambridge: Polity.

new values. Thus, the systematic faculty of Mind is responsible for all value and drives. It should be noted that no one can specifically crave injustice, and that we all seek to avoid injustice wherever possible, except when there is a conflict of our values, where we prioritize certain values over other values. Deeply indebted to the reflexivity equation, values are born of our own understanding of who we should be or should have been, but also, are born of our own understanding or what we are or what we have been — thus our values are linked hand and hand with our own understandings of ourselves.

But is not the Core Script of human beings noumenal? How then may we come to an understanding of what our own values are? First, using the phenomenological imagination, and secondly, using our thoughts to produce intuitions. Thus, it is the productive faculty of Mind that allows us our intuitions, which are themselves produced through the process of *subliminal probabilitism* — a process which allows for a brief scan of the entire set of information deemed relevant to the prospective question at hand contained within the mental depository, based on a probability assessment. Of emotions, there are both simple and complex ones. During the process of the narrativization of information — during which the Mind automatically processes information from simple scripts to complex scripts, emotions in particular may be derived from the sets of integrated information — a process which produces new information in a synthetic way from pre-existing sets of information; narrative, here, may be understood in the sense of Paul Ricoeur's *Time and Narrative*.[120] For this process, the systematic faculty of Mind has a mechanism for determining which sets of information are relevant to other, merely possible sets of information. From that point, induction and derivation take place in order to synthesize this new information from pre-existing sets of information. Thus, the systematic faculty of Mind is naturally a logical process. The *Theory of Emotivic Narrativity* explains the existence of emotions both simple and complex. So much for the systematic faculty of the Mind.

11. Of Berkeleyan Cognitive-Idealistic Sensory Projectionalism: Kant Alongside Moore

We have already discussed *projectional essentialism*, or the idea that Platonic forms exist within the Mind as concepts and are projected into the world in literally meaningful ways, and have already discussed that *projectional essentialism* is not too far afield from Kant's *cognitivism*.[121] Later in this work, under the division of this work labeled *Aesthetics*, we will consider to what extent consciousness itself is projected into the world, and how it interacts with works of art: it will be discussed

---

[120]   Ricoeur, Paul. 1997. *Time and narrative*. Chicago, Ill: University of Chicago Press.

[121]   Plato, and John M. Cooper. 2009. *Complete works*. Indianapolis: Hackett; Kant, Immanuel, and Paul Guyer. 2009. *Critique of pure reason*. Cambridge: Cambridge Univ. Press.

as a *General Theory of Projectional Consciousness*, and in fact grounds the projection of essences into the logical confines — the limits — of the world.[122] What might be, then, *idealistic sensory projectionalism?* Consider the case of phantom limbs, wherein individuals who have lost either limbs or a limb, may still feel sensory activity in place of where their former limbs or limb used to exist. What might the implications of this phenomena be? If the Mind may *project* sensory feeling onto a phantom limb, that entails that the Mind is up to more than it may seem: for, with G.E. Moore, if there is one hand, then there probably is another hand. If the Mind is projecting feeling where there is no limb, then, therefore the Mind is constantly projecting sensory feeling all across the body.

This may be explained as such: rather than constantly computing all of the information that enters the senses at a given time, the Mind makes a *probability assessment* of how the feeling *should* feel in some specific part of the body. Thus, Mind is taking the place of the senses, here; and, because Mind is projecting itself into its sensory receptors, we may call this view a certain *sensory idealism*, because the senses are fundamentally triggered first by the Mind, and second by external stimuli. Thus, the Mind projects feeling all across the body in an idealistic manner; here, it would be reasonable to argue for a *General Theory of the Manufacturing of Sensory Feelings*, because, Mind here is *manufacturing senses* that are not caused by external stimuli, but instead, are grounded by Mind, and hence are idealistic. Thus, in addition to projecting consciousness and essence, Mind also projects feeling onto its own sensory receptors. In this way, Mind triggers its own modules *automatically* on a constant basis, where Mind first triggers the sensory receptors via a *probability assessment* of how the receptors *ought* to feel at the given time of perception, and then only secondarily takes into consideration any actual external stimuli interacting with the sensory receptors. So much, then, for a *General Theory of the Primacy of Mind over its Sensory Receptors*; this line of thought re-opens the door to the conceivability of George Berkeley's radical idealism espoused in his various works, for, if Mind may manufacture ghost sensations, then who is to say whether or not all sensations are in fact ghost sensations?[123]

12. *Of the Cartesian-Bergsonian Phenomenology of Mind*

Distinct from the *automaticity of mind*, the *phenomenology of mind* is that conscious domain of the Mind over which the *locus of attention* presides. Within that domain, exists the phenomenology of the *witnessant*, the phenomenology of mood, the phenomenology of vibes, and so on. In this subsection, we will also discuss how narrativity plays a role in the formation of emotions, according to the logic of the reflexivity equation. Additionally, we will discuss how consciousness

---

[122]   British Academy, and G. E. Moore. 1940. *Proof of an external world.*

[123]   Berkeley, George, and Colin Murray Turbayne. 1989. *Principles, dialogues, and philosophical correspondence.*

may be either inhibited or uninhibited, which is to say, either malefic or benefic. The discussion of both *malefic* and *benefic consciousness* will mature further in the division of the work dedicated to ethics, but, it is perhaps one of the most important and vital of all the discussions that could be had on consciousness, for, the central problematic of ethics is not the benefic life, but instead, the benefic consciousness, for, with Bergson, life occurs across moments, and, the moments of consciousness are all that human beings have at their disposal; in alignment with the philosophy of Descartes, Mind appears at the very least to be dualistic, but the inquiry remains altogether noumenal, and hence cannot be discoursed around in any kind of declarative manner.[124] Then, it will be discussed how certain moments of our phenomenologies trigger our Core Scripts, and can cause metanoia, or changes in our personal identities. Furthermore, a serious critique of personal identity will be challenged, and, hopefully, disputed, because, without personal identity — without a Core Script — how could we explain the logic of production? Mood will be described as the emotional coloring of consciousness, and vibes will be described as the general inferable sense — projected, like all other essence — that can be detected by the processional method in human beings, so long as the witnesssant is focused on them. So much for the *phenomenology of mind*.

13. Of the Cartesian-Bergsonian Witnessant

The witnessant is nothing other than the pure cognizance — the pure experience of Mind. The essence of consciousness is witnessing phenomena. Prior even to thinking — for to think is to *witness* mental phenomena — the *theory of the witnessant* is more fundamental than famous philosopher René Descartes's *cogito ergo sum*, or, I think, therefore I am.[125] Instead, the phrase must go: *I witness, therefore I am*; hence, phenomenology is the key to any First Philosophy; likewise, because Mind exists across time, it is, with Bergson, inherently durational.[126] We need not concern ourselves with solipsism in this work. If there is such a thing as a witnessant that fundamentally witnesses, it must be that it is limited in its scope and capacities. Thus, there must be a *locus of attention* — the *witnessant* — that contains the general domain of conscious witnessing; take for example, when a person is speaking to you, but your Mind is elsewhere, as it were — any information that interacts with one's sensory modules will not be processed

---

[124] Bergson, Henri. 2002. *Time and free will: an essay on the immediate data of consciousness.* https://search.ebscohost.com/login.aspx?direct=true&scope=site&db=nlebk&db=nlabk&AN=790187; Descartes, Rene, and F. Sutcliffe. 2005. *Discourse on Method and the Meditations.* https://www.vlebooks.com/vleweb/product/openreader?id=none&isbn=9780141944203.

[125] Descartes, Rene, and F. Sutcliffe. 2005. *Discourse on Method and the Meditations.* https://www.vlebooks.com/vleweb/product/openreader?id=none&isbn=9780141944203.

[126] Bergson, Henri. 2002. *Time and free will: an essay on the immediate data of consciousness.* https://search.ebscohost.com/login.aspx?direct=true&scope=site&db=nlebk&db=nlabk&AN=790187

because the mental locus of attention is not focused on it, because when one is distracted, or one's Mind is elsewhere. It may be that one overhears certain information that one is not focused on, per se, and this is because one is paying partial attention, or general attention to a number of entities at once. Perhaps I am speaking to a friend, but overhear and process a sentence from the conversation taking place behind us at the club: my attention is fixated on my friend, but it is also generally scanning the environment for information, and so it collected the phenomena from the conversation taking place behind me. Thus, there are two modes of the locus of attention: general attention and particular attention. When a human being is writing a sentence, they must be particularly attentive only to the process of writing; when a human being is playing soccer, they must be generally paying attention to the game itself, in order to play decently. So much for the witnessant and its locus of attention.

14. Of the Systematic Limit of Phenomenology; or, Of the Liberated Consciousness: Chalmers

What could be the systematic limit of phenomenology, or consciousness? Consider this example: Antigone is a shy and reserved girl, but during her first semester at Rutgers College, she meets a radical Hegelian-Marxian professor who encourages her to come out of her shell. How many layers of her phenomenological consciousness are there, until we reach the most uninhibited, raw version of Antigone's consciousness? Thus, the example illuminates us to the fact that there are systematic limits that ground consciousness and limit its modes. The integrated set of emotionally charged and neutral information in Antigone's programmatology of Mind is such that, before she met her radical professor, she had a very inhibited consciousness — indeed, a very inhibited Core Script. What is going on here? It must be the case that there are certain informational inhibitors against certain possible trajectories she might take in her life: these inhibitors are clusters of information that fundamentally limit the expression of Antigone's Core Script, or her Personal Identity. They are located in the systematic part of her Mind, and limit her productive consciousness — the way that she thinks, acts, and speaks. Before she meets her professor, she is shy and reserved — many branches of her possible modality are inhibited, and certainly the products of her Mind are inhibited. Until she meets her professor, she does not come out of her shell.

Thus, it is an imperative that human beings release themselves from our own mental inhibitions. Thus, human beings must *defocalize* their own conscious phenomenologies, by *defocalizing* their systematic set of integrated emotive information as held within the *mental depository*. To defocalize our sets of information is to remove the limits placed upon them. This is not to argue that we should defocalize our values and moralities — certain inhibitors are benefic, while others are malefic. How might we distinguish between the two? Certain inhibitions ground society: ethical inhibitions, for example. Certain malefic inhibitions, on the other hand, prevent human flourishing — the natural, raw expansion of a given phenomenology into an erudite, well rounded consciousness. Here, it is also reasonable to argue, for a *General Theory of Projected Consciousness*, or, the idea that consciousness is projected up from out of the brain into the sphere of the locus of attention, and from there doubly projected out into the real world; the *General Theory of Projected Consciousness* is an expansion upon famous philosopher David Chalmers's *extended consciousness hypothesis*.[127] Underneath consciousness, as it were, exists the systematic set of information that is integrated into one's Core Script. The Core Script consists of all mentally integrated information pertinent to the concept of the self, and all information that shapes and limits consciousness. Thus, the *liberated consciousness* is an aspiration that involves the complicated process of negating certain psycho-informational inhibitors in order to better liberate the Mind, so that it may flourish in a more organic and healthy way. So much for the systematic limits of phenomenological consciousness and their cure, the *liberated consciousness*.

15. Of the Freudian-Lacanian Cyclology of the Dependent Consciousness

Related to the aspiration of the *liberated consciousness*, the *dependent consciousness* is a direct result of the effects of rapportionality upon the Core Script of an individual, which in turn, limits the phenomenological consciousness of said individual. A dependent consciousness is merely one that is not independent in some way or set of ways. Modally, its operation is contingent upon and limited by factors external to itself, but nevertheless, these factors become internalized in the systematic set of information held in the mental depository. In a very real sense, these apparently Mind-external dependencies exist internally to Mind. When an individual becomes consumed by their desires — indeed, driven by them — when their General Will is polluted and intoxicated by craving — there is a dependency afoot in their psyche. Like mental inhibitors of the variety just discussed, mental dependencies may be more organic and benefic, e.g., dependency on one's friends and family. However, because mental maturity is a goal first and foremost, these dependencies must either be eradicated or limited, to whatsoever extent they are in fact malefic dependencies. One can easily imagine a person who has an overdependency on their mother, or the idea of a mother — as was demonstrated by famous psychoanalyst Sigmund Freud's reconstruction of the so-called *Oedipus Complex* — or, instead, of a person who has a cyclological dependency on abusive partners, who are emotionally unavailable and physically

---

[127] Chalmers, David John, and Tim Peacock. 2022. *Reality+: virtual worlds and the problems of philosophy.*

threatening, for example; likewise, Lacan's writings on transference, too, allow one to imagine scenarios wherein individuals are dependent upon those figures whose impressions of they transfer onto others: hence, a Freudian-Lacanian *cyclology of the dependent consciousness*.[128] Akin to the *inhibited consciousness*, the dependent consciousness is in general considered to be a malefic vibration, and indeed it is a vibration inasmuch as it is manifested in the products of Mind. Because metanoia is possible, both intentionally and organically, malefic dependency cycles may be eradicated through careful self-reflection or through psychoanalytical means. But what of rapportionality, and of the community in general? Is not community grounded upon dependency itself? While this may be the case, we have already discoursed around the idea that there are both malefic and benefic dependencies. What is the limit that distinguishes between the two? Here, we will derive a *General Theory of the Ethicality of Dependency*, by drawing upon the logic of the *liberated consciousness* itself. Any dependency that inhibits Mind from its innermost flourishing and organicity, must be considered to be malefic: e.g., the tyrannical rule of a parent who forces their child to live under a rock, socially, and never experience healthy dependencies, e.g., friendships and partnerships.

To a certain extent, even dependencies based upon ethicality are malefic: a person should not be ethical because they merely *are dependent upon ethicality, or because they take pleasure in ethicality*, but instead, because ethicality is the abstract and righteous mode of being. Ethicality is deontological duty more than anything else, it rewards the Core Script with a feeling of righteousness, but that must be tempered and limited by reason, and not be vain or frivolous in its nature. Returning to malefic dependencies, it is not always simple to ascertain whether or not a dependency is toxic or malefic, but in general, *any reason for persisting in a certain modality of being is a dependency*, thus, that is a way to begin to sniff out these dependencies. As famous philosopher Friedrich Nietzsche teases, a philosopher or analyst must have a good nose... or, must have a keen sense of intuition in order to piece everything together in the appropriate way. Thus, once we have verified that there is a reason for persisting in a given cyclological mode of production, the question must be asked: does this dependency either liberate or inhibit consciousness? Uninhibited consciousness is one of the grounding factors of the *benefic consciousness*, a concept that supersedes the benefic life because, life is grounded not in abstractions such as the concept of a trajectorial life, but instead, is grounded across temporal moments, of which phenomenological consciousness is the mediator. Thus — in general — any cyclological dependencies must be interrogated as to their true worth in an individual's programmatology.

Akin to liberated consciousness, *independent consciousness*, too, as a phenomenological mode, ought to be aspired after, as though it were a prize — because it is one of the most liberating and freeing modalities of Mind one

---

[128]   Freud, Sigmund, and Abraham A. Brill. 1938. *The basic writings*; Lacan, Jacques, Jacques-Alain Miller, and Alan Sheridan. 2019. *The four fundamental concepts of psycho-analysis*.

may possess. In fact, it is the entire Buddhist aspiration for the Core Script: liberation from attachment and cyclology; and, Buddhist conceptions of non-attachment do not negate the existence of rapportionality, but merely limit and mediate rapportionality in a benefic way. Furthermore, while there may be dependent rapportionality, there may also be independent rapportionality — without a descent into full blown political libertarianism. The key is to mitigate dependencies and independencies in such a way as is best for a flourishing human programmatology — a benefic consciousness. Thus, a *General Theory of Benefic and Independent Rapportionality*. So much for the benefic and malefic vibrations of certain cyclological productions of Mind.

16. Of Animalistic and Linguistic Phenomenology: Beyond Marx, Althusser, and Derrida

Here, before proceeding onto further phenomenological matters, it will be just to discourse around the problematic of animal consciousness, and how human beings elevated themselves up out of nature — a process that happened automatically, in alignment with the automatic faculties of Mind. As shall shortly be discussed in the subchapter on *Metalinguistics*, there is such an entity as the *Linguistic Superstructure*, that is responsible for the elevation of humankind up out of nature and into society. Some — most notably famous critic Sylvia Wynter — argue that Christianity denaturalized humankind, but nothing could be further from the truth: instead, it was the evolution and development of complex language and its concomitant Linguistic Superstructures, that allowed for a more complex *semiotics of self-reflexivity*, which was the birth of society, and, over time, civilization itself.[129] There is no distinguishing feature more prominent that separates humankind from animals than our complex, self-reflexive linguistic system. Collectively, the idiosyncratic and metafactual Linguistic Superstructures form a grand Sitrnerian spook, which, nevertheless has a subtle, albeit noumenal existence, because of human rapportionality — that is to say, that human rapports, together with projectional essentialism, account for the existence of the *collective Linguistic Superstructure*, or the total set of all Linguistic Superstructures.[130] Important to note, is that the Linguistic Superstructure has as its base, nothing other than consciousness itself. To refute the Marxian and Althusserian modalities of superstructure: how could economics be the base of the superstructure, when, first and foremost, economics is a pseudoscience dependent upon consciousness, and secondly, when the concept of property, is also dependent upon consciousness, because property is

---

[129] Wynter, Sylvia. 2003. "Unsettling the Coloniality of Being/Power/Truth/Freedom: Towards the Human, After Man, Its Overrepresentation—An Argument". CR: *The New Centennial Review*. 3 (3): 257-337.

[130] Stirner, Max. 1974. *Max Stirner, the ego and his own*. New York: Harper & Row.

a Kantian-Cognitivist Projectional Category, rooted nowhere in the world but in Mind?[131]

Thus, how could the superstructure be based upon anything but consciousness itself? Any visualization of the superstructure that ignores phenomenological consciousness and its powers, is hardly worth visualizing at all. This is to say, that the Linguistic Superstructure, is the turning back rightside up of Hegel, whom Marx turned upon his head, by arguing that the economic system was the base of the superstructure, when in fact, the Linguistic Superstructure in its actuality is far more Hegelian than it is Marxian, because, it is dependent upon phenomenological consciousness.[132] Perhaps if Marx had been a more faithful student of Hegel and his corpus, Marx might have seen that phenomenological consciousness was the root of all civilization, insofar as it is the domain of the Linguistic Superstructure. As we shall see in the next subchapter, animal consciousness rears its beastly head in the modality of fascism, which is nothing other than the natural, animalistic state of humankind, responsible for sexism, tribalism, xenophobia, hysteria, racism, and fascism. For, are not the animals in nature fascist — clinging to one another in tribes, alienating the sick and weak, parading around as brutes and the like? Humanity's hope lies in its capacity for linguistic phenomenology: its ability to apply self-reflexive concepts upon itself, which in turn, diversifies the Linguistic Superstructure, and allows for a more developed and mature society and civilization at large. How may human beings escape the human, all-too-human animalistic tendency toward fascism, if this reconstruction is truly the case? Human beings must encourage a *virtue cyclology*, and a *perpetual development of Mind*. Those are the only ways to expand our Minds, and eradicate as best as possible the animal nature within us, which is ultimately allied with fascisms and other social evils.

Against famous philosopher Jacques Derrida, *logocentrism*, or the centrality of a grand narrative, or the centrality of logic itself, of logos, is not a bad thing at all, but instead, is allied with the Linguistic Superstructure: without logocentrism, there could be no distinguishment of human from animal: therefore logocentrism deserves only the highest of praises from its critics, instead of the cool disinterested approach of Derrida himself.[133] Furthermore, to accept the arguments for rapportionality, and Kantian-Cognitivist Projectional Categories, is to reinstate a Platonism of sorts, albeit one more so allied with cognitive science than anything else — a Platonism wherein the forms exist within the Mind, akin to Kant's cognitivism.[134] Thus, tied hand and hand with the Linguistic Superstructure,

[131]   Kant, Immanuel, and Paul Guyer. 2009. Critique of pure reason. Cambridge: Cambridge Univ. Press.

[132]   Hegel, Georg Wilhelm Friedrich, and Terry P. Pinkard. 2018. *The phenomenology of spirit*; Hegel, Georg Wilhelm Friedrich. 2004. *Hegel's Science of logic*. Amherst, N.Y.: Humanity Books; Marx, Karl, and N. I. Stone. 2014. *A contribution to the critique of political economy*.

[133]   Derrida, Jacques. 1998. *Of grammatology*. Baltimore: Johns Hopkins University Press.

[134]   Kant, Immanuel, and Paul Guyer. 2009. *Critique of pure reason*. Cambridge: Cambridge Univ. Press; Plato, and John M. Cooper. 2009. Complete works. Indianapolis: Hackett.

is a *General Theory of Social Platonism*, wherein, forms exist within the minds of humans, and are projected onto the world from their consciousnesses, and are grounded by the rapportionality of individuals, indeed, even by one's self-reflexive rapport with oneself. Thus, *Social Platonism* cannot but be the case, all of these issues considered. Furthermore, it should be said, that the Hegelian-Lacanian Linguistic Superstructure, has less in common with the Marxian-Althusserian superstructure, than it does with the Lacanian symbolic register of famous psychoanalyst Jacques Lacan — which is its natural kindmate — and, indeed, could also be referred to as a *process semiotic* superstructure; more on the Hegelian-Lacanian Linguistic Superstructure in the subchapters to come.[135] So much then, for animal and linguistic phenomenology.

17. Of the Mature and Immature Consciousnesses: Kant and Honneth

Following our appraisal of the independent and uninhibited consciousness as a decent programmatology of Mind, it is now time to augment those two arguments with another metaphysical argument on the maturity of consciousness. Imagine a consciousness that is both dependent and inhibited in multiple ways: how might that affect the phenomenological development of said individual? It must be the case that, said individual, possesses an immature consciousness, insofar as their consciousness is dependent upon ultimately frivolous concerns, and is, furthermore, inhibited from developing into a mature consciousness. Supposing a phenomenological consciousness manifests the ideal conditions — of independency and uninhibitedness — are those conditions necessary and sufficient for development of a mature consciousness? Those conditions may be necessary for the development of a mature consciousness, but are not sufficient for the development of one. For, even if consciousness is uninhibited and independent, it still must develop in the right modalities in order for it to accomplish phenomenological maturity. Phenomenological maturity is consciousness that has developed in the appropriate and sufficient modalities such that it is now, what the Buddhists would call, *enlightened*. In Immanuel Kant's famous essay, *What is Enlightenment?*, he does agree with us that enlightenment involves independence, for, he declares: *dare to think!*[136] However, he does not discuss any methodology for releasing mental inhibitions, which, for many, are the predominant hindrances to enlightenment. Both in Hinduism and its offshoot, Buddhism, hindrances to enlightenment are discussed, and quite aptly so. Returning to the matter at hand: what is required beyond independence and uninhibitedness of Mind, in order to

---

135 Lacan, Jacques, and Bruce Fink. 2007. *Écrits: the first complete edition in English*. New York: W.W. Norton.

136 Kant, Immanuel, and Hans Siegbert Reiss. 2010. *Kant: political writings*. Cambridge [England]: Cambridge University Press.

accomplish a mature, enlightened — as it were — consciousness? Nothing other than *just development*, or a certain *virtue cyclology*: one must develop in the right ways, at the right times, and under the right conditions to accomplish that development.

Therefore, the development of the phenomenological consciousness of Mind must be a chief imperative of any philosophical theory of pedagogy. The mature consciousness is perhaps the closest of all the modalities of consciousness to the benefic consciousness, which is the ultimate aim of any theory of ethics, for, it is the ethical consciousness *par excellence* coupled with the automaticity of Mind such that inherent to it is a *virtue cyclology*. More on the inverse of the mature consciousness, the immature consciousness: it is retrogressive, where the mature consciousness is progressive. The immature consciousness, because it is dependent on family and other social constructions, and because it is retrogressive rather than progressive — dependent upon the past, that is — it most closely matches alongside a sort of organic fascist modality of Mind, insofar as dependent tribalisms, and anxious, paranoid inhibitions are natural modalities of Mind that must be cured through education and proper development of phenomenological consciousness. Furthermore, the mature consciousness most resembles the base animalistic modality of consciousness, insofar as it is dependent and inhibited; it is through society, the Linguistic Superstructure, and civilization, that human beings may outgrow their animal instincts and overcome them. Which political modality does the mature, enlightened consciousness, then, best suit? Because all of society is grounded on Kantian-Cognitivist Projectional Categories — the atoms that form the Hegelian-Lacanian Linguistic Superstructure — and rapportionality, the mature, enlightened consciousness will understand that without rapportionality and community, that there can be no civilization at all, but only, pure and unmediated barbarism — as has been the present state of humanity for many thousands of years, insofar as humanity engages in war and other vitriolic offenses to right, duty, and moral objectivity — all and all, humanity is responsible for egregious offenses to civilization and its concomitant virtue of civility.[137]

Thus, the mature consciousness affects a moral modality, not of community per se — for that is itself mental dependency and a Stirnerian spook more than anything else — but of rapportionality, of Hegelian and Honnethian recognition of others and their dignity, and also of phenomenological development — which is to say, the expansion of one's idiosyncratic Linguistic Superstructure.[138] Hence, the phenomenological development of consciousness is an imperative that we must all follow as though our very lives depended upon it — because, in a very real sense, they do. For, are we not called to be the best possible versions of ourselves that we can be? If we fail to accomplish the best for ourselves — and worse yet, if

[137]   Kant, Immanuel, and Paul Guyer. 2009. *Critique of pure reason*. Cambridge: Cambridge Univ. Press.

[138]   Stirner, Max. 1974. *Max Stirner, the ego and his own*. New York: Harper & Row; Hegel, Georg Wilhelm Friedrich, Allen W. Wood, and H. B. Nisbet. 2018. *Elements of the philosophy of right*. Cambridge: Cambridge University Press; Honneth, Axel. 2014. *The I in we: studies in the theory of recognition*. Cambridge: Polity Press.

we fail even to apply ourselves to the task of development — how can we claim to have lived a flourishing and fulfilled life? So much for the mature and immature consciousnesses.

18. Of Ricoeurian Narrativity and the Emotivics of Heart

Let Heart be understood to be the General Will as it were of the emotions. Because human beings have emotive and subliminal sets of information stored in their mental depositories, they are frequently limited by these sets of information. Indeed, it is precisely this information — this *subliminal prioritization* — that accounts for the specific modal trajectorics of a given person in the world across the temporal timeline — which is to say, it explains why and how they are the way they are. However, while even emotionally neutral information may impact a person's Core Script — or their personal identity — it is the emotionally positive or negative information that affects a person's Heart, or the epicenter as it were of their emotional nervous system. While the mechanisms of the emotions are both subliminal and noumenal — even though we can point to chemicals and so on, the mechanisms in the brain are far too complex for us to comprehend — the phenomenology of emotions is on the other hand far from being subliminal or noumenal. In fact, we experience emotions in a very intense, direct, and phenomenological way. Because of the reflexivity equation, all information that becomes integrated into our mental depositories is screened as either pertinent or impertinent to said individual's Core Script, or their personal identity. However, the modality of this screening is such that, as information is being integrated into the mental depository, additional sets of information — known as narratives — become attached to the original sets of information, and augment them.

Thus, we may define an emotion as a positively or negatively charged set of information that becomes augmented after its screening by the reflexivity equation. The mere charge of an emotion will not help us ascertain whether or not a given set of emotions is either malefic or benefic — that would require an extended, trajectorial reconstruction of the individual's modality. What then, may be considered the Heart of a person? It is nothing other than the complete set of their most vital emotions — the *oligarchy of the cycles* — that plays a defining role in characterizing the exact nature of their *subliminal prioritization*. Here, we may ask: how do values figure in the logic of the emotions? Returning to the reflexivity equation, we may assess that there are at least two psychosomatic modalities of values: prescriptive and descriptive. This means that there are values in human programmatology about how the world is, and about how the world should be. Yet, as we will explore at greater length in the division of this work devoted to the ethical domain, there is a third alternative here that is phenomenological rather than psychosomatic — it is nothing other than *Speculative Optimalism*, or a new *General Theory of Ethics*, that asks us to challenge our pre-existing values making use of speculative reason — the phenomenological imagination — and also to imagine the best possible values and application of those values that we can, in order to exact a more just and perfect world, along the lines of what Plato had in Mind across his various dialogues on ethics. A person's Heart may be identified — it is noumenal but may be imagined and intuited — by a trajectorial reconstruction of said individual's modality of Mind — a careful reconstruction of their production — their thoughts, actions, and speech — and of their systematology of Mind — their composite set of integrated information that is emotionally charged and augmented by other information, according to the logical results of the reflexivity equation. It should be addressed that the manner in which the author speaks of narrative is heavily influenced by the writings of Paul Ricoeur on narrative; any incoming atom of content or, likewise, set of information — emotional or otherwise — undergoing the cycle of procession, must be weaved into an informational tapestry within Mind: thus, information becomes narrativized automatically by the *automatic faculty of Mind*.[139] Because this process may be observed by human beings, it may also be referred to as a sort of so-called soft science — hence, *emotivics*; certainly Affect theorists have laudably championed endeavors of this variety.[140] So much for the emotivics of Heart.

19. Of the Operation of Austinian Performativity; or, Of the Core Script: Beyond Parfit and Calculus

Finally, we arrive at the division of this work that is dedicated to an analysis of the Core Script of human beings, or, that set of information that shapes and limits a person's modality of personal identity, and is exactly responsible for the modality of their productivity of Mind, which is to say, of their thoughts, speech, and actions. Yet, as we have seen with Antigone, is there not a performativity of consciousness? Famous philosopher and law professor Kenji Yoshino argues that human beings *cover* or conceal and inhibit their identities, so there is an element of performativity afoot in this reconstruction.[141] Thus, there must be an *Operation of Austinian Performativity*: that is to say, there must be a general modality that is presented to the world, composite both of an individual's automaticity of Mind, and their phenomenology of Mind; rooted, to be sure, in J.L. Austin's theory of *performativity*.[142] Together, the two make up the modality of Mind of an individual.

---

[139] Ricoeur, Paul. 1997. *Time and narrative*. Chicago, Ill: University of Chicago Press.

[140] Gregg, Melissa, and Gregory J. Seigworth. 2011. *The affect theory reader*. North Carolina: Duke University Press.

[141] Yoshino, Kenji. 2007. *Covering: the hidden assault on our civil rights*. New York: Random House.

[142] Austin, J. L., J. O. Urmson, and Marina Sbisà. 2009. *How to do things with words: the William James lectures delivered at Harvard University in 1955*. Oxford: Oxford University Press.

The phenomenology of Mind, however, is shaped and limited by *subliminal prioritization*, or their modal values; moreover, the phenomenology of Mind is limited by an individual's Core Script, which is responsible for their productivity in the world, in an exact and precise manner. For, it is an internal, subliminal logic of how to produce in the world. Thus, freedom is nothing other than the intentional editing of this Core Script. Perhaps a group of ten psychoanalysts from different backgrounds — in order to come as close to objectivity as possible — could analyze a patient and help them achieve intentional metanoia, or the alteration of their Core Script. It should be clear that intentional metanoia is possible, because there is a natural process of metanoia that occurs across the temporal timeline. Now, some famous philosophers get hung up about the idea of a Core Script that persists across time, and the Oxfordian Derek Parfit was one of these.[143] He endeavored to show, in his seminal *Reasons and Persons*, through many a clever and science-fiction oriented thought experiment, that the Core Script did not exist. So much for a careful explanation of modality, then, without the Core Script and its *subliminal prioritization*.

Parfit sought to show how personal identity could not exist, due to his thought experiment that involved the duplication of an individual, who, after the fact, is no longer the same individual as before — but is in fact now two individuals. Here is why that thought experiment does not hold up to the whetstone: for one, the Core Script is an internal *projected essence*, and, immediately during the process of duplication, there would exist a differentiation between the first individual and the second, duplicated individual. Secondly, Parfit was infamous for not being a shrewd mathematician. He multiplies his individual by two; suppose we multiplied the individual by forty? Or divided the individual and the duplicated individual by two, would they revert to having the same Core Script? Suppose we asked for the square root of an individual: what then? Here it should be clear: that mathematical, extensional, and quantitative reasoning should not be applied to matters so delicate as phenomenological consciousness and projected essence. In fact, Parfit's main flaw is his employment of quantitative reasoning to address an issue that is fundamentally qualitative — to return to Bergson's Theory of Qualitative Consciousness.[144] Moreover, because the Core Script also involves the phenomenology of Mind, it is at least partially a qualitative and noumenal issue; but, on the other hand, the other component of the Core Script — the systematic, integrated set of information held in the mental depository — involves deeply complicated, subliminal processes that to us human beings are at this time noumenal, perhaps forever to be so. Furthermore, a final nail in the coffin of the Parfitian criticisms of personal identity: if he and his followers are so committed to the mathematical reconstruction of phenomenological consciousness, could they please provide the human race with a calculus of the Mind? Such a calculus

---

143   Parfit, Derek. 2007. *Reasons and persons*. Oxford: Clarendon Press.

144   Bergson, Henri. 2002. *Time and free will: an essay on the immediate data of consciousness.* https://search. ebscohost.com/login.aspx?direct=true&scope=site&db=nlebk&db=nlabk&AN=790187.

is a priori impossible, because consciousness is qualitative. There may, however, be phenomenological causation — as my perceiving an impression triggers me to recall, my late nights clubbing in Berghain, for example. So much for the Core Script.

20. Of Triggernometry and the Kierkegaardian Phenomenology of Heart: Beyond Neo-Kantian Discursive Political Liberalisms; or, Of the Noumenality of Communicative Intimacy

We have already discoursed around the area of the phenomenology of the emotions, but there remain several issues to discuss, in particular, within the domain of the *Kierkegaardian phenomenology of Heart.*[145] Firstly, we must draw our attention to the *Noumenality of intimacy*, for, while we may experience phenomena around another individual or set of individuals, we may never experience the world as they experience it. While the productions of Mind do bear a general imprint of the entire set of information integrated into a person's mental depository, products — and language in general — remain paltry, flawed means of communication between individuals. Thus, intimacy, the most prized relation between two individuals, is itself alienated from our knowledge, and hence exists in a noumenal relationship to us — let this be understood to be a direct critique of Habermasian discourse ethics: for, if intimacy is noumenal, then how is discourse possible?[146] Discourse may be accomplished merely through instinctive action and instinctive intuition — not rationality — which is another critique of Habermasian discourse ethics. Indeed, even though we may be aware of our own phenomenologies, we are ourselves estranged from the innermost mechanisms of our Hearts and our Minds — thus, a complete knowledge of the self is another noumenal issue for human human beings — insofar as it remains out of reach for us. A knowledge of the Core Script, however, may be intuited by the phenomenological imagination: that is the closest we may get to a knowledge of the self. The Core Script may best be identified by ascertaining the specific triggers pertinent to a given individual's phenomenology, using of course the phenomenological imagination.

Thus, there must be room for a *phenomenology of the trigger*, in order to ascertain the deepest, most fundamental drives of the Core Script. Certainly, the *phenomenology of cyclology* too must play a role in the identification of the more serious, fundamental drives inherent to the Core Script. Famous existentialist philosophers Martin Heidegger and Jean-Paul Sartre, too, were invested in the

---

[145]   Kierkegaard, Søren, Howard V. Hong, Edna H. Hong, and George Pattison. 2009. *Works of love*; Kierkegaard, Søren, Howard V. Hong, and Edna H. Hong. 2000. *The essential Kierkegaard*. Princeton, N.J.: Princeton University Press; Carlisle, Clare. 2020. *Philosopher of the heart: the restless life of Søren Kierkegaard.*

[146]   Habermas, Jürgen, and William Rehg. 2015. *Between facts and norms contributions to a discourse theory of law and democracy*. Cambridge: Polity Press.

phenomenology of the trigger, Heidegger in *Being and Time* and Sartre in *Being and Nothingness*; however, the flaw in their reconstruction was that they believed the fundamental trigger to be the *nothing*.[147] As we saw very early on in this work, whether or not there is such an entity known as the nothing is indeed a profound question, however, it is a noumenal inquiry insofar as its answer remains out of our reach as human beings. Thus, the true trigger *par excellence* of the modality of Mind and Heart is nothing other than Noumenality itself. It is the noumenal that vexes us, causes wonder in us, and triggers us more than anything else. How does my partner feel about me? Am I destined to succeed in this life? Who really am I? All of these are questions with noumenal non-answers. However, because we may use our phenomenological imaginations to intuit certain areas of the Core Script, we may at least make progress in these noumenal domains. Thus, there may be, to a limited extent, a certain triggernometry, or a measurement of the triggers that impact our Modalities of Mind and Heart; so much for triggernometry.

21. Of the Freudian-Lacanian Cyclology of Heideggerian Phenomenological Mood

While we have discoursed on the phenomenology of Heart, we have yet to discuss how the phenomenology of Heart colors the phenomenology of Mind in general. At every given moment, the Phenomenology of Heart manifests itself in a certain *Mood,* or an emotional coloring of consciousness. Mood is a manifestation of the relevant set of information that is the Core Script, and is the reaction of the individual to his or her encountered phenomena. Here, however, the noumenal can trigger the Mind and Heart whenever the individual encounters a noumenal entity, whether in the world or as a product of their Mind. Of course, thought, as a product of the Mind occurring within the domain of the locus of attention, can never be noumenal itself, but it may however represent certain noumenal concepts and entities: take for example whenever a person ponders the meaning of life, or the phenomenology of a bat, or the existence or nonexistence of the nothing — all questions are, for us, noumenal. Because Moods repeat, it is the case that there is a general cyclology of mood that occurs within the psychosomatic modality of an individual. The psychosomatic modality of an individual is the unified entity composed of the human Heart and anthropomodal Mind, which in sum total is the way humans operate in the world, at any rate.

Because moods repeat, there is such a metaphysical entity as the *Mood Cycle,* that involves qualitative phenomenological causation; phenomena, whether self-produced (thought) or impressionistically perceived from the world, can affect the Mind and Heart just as long as the locus of attention is attuned to it, and in

---

[147]   Heidegger, Martin, John Macquarrie, and Edward S. Robinson. 2019. *Being and time*; Sartre, Jean-Paul, and Sarah Richmond. 2021. *Being and nothingness: an essay on phenomenological ontology.*

fact, these phenomena, in addition to the systematic faculty of Mind, are exactly responsible for modality of mood; here, the *Mood Cycle* may also be described as the *Affect Cycle*; cycology, as discoursed around earlier in the text, is rooted in the Freudian-Lacanian concept of *repetition*; whereas Mood, to be sure, is rooted in Heidegger's phenomenological discussion of Mood in *Being and Time*.[148] Again, the reflexivity equation resurfaces during our reconstruction: for, Mood is effectively determined by the reflexivity equation, which is constantly and automatically screening phenomena both self-produced (thought) and impressionistically world-induced. As is shortly to be discussed, a Mood may be perceived either by the individual experiencing said mood, or instead may be intuited by others by experiencing the *vibes* emanated from the productive individual's productions, e.g., their thoughts, speech, and actions. So much for the Freudian-Lacanian Cyclology of Heideggerian phenomenological mood.

22. Toward a General Theory of Productive Vibes: Of Freudian Subliminal Prioritization

While the absolute mood of an individual may be noumenal to themselves and to others, phenomena related to a mood may be witnessed either by the individual themselves or by others around them. How so? Because a *General Theory of Productive Imprint* is already on the table, we already can know that the products of some individual's Mind are reflective of their entire modality of Mind insofar as a product is modal, or particular, specific, and logical. Thus, every product of Mind has a logic to it, and hence, Mind may be considered to be a function, while products of Mind may be considered outputs of that very same function. Thus, as in mathematics, the output of the function always bears the logic of the function — its very modality is such that it is constructed along the lines of the limits of the function itself. Thus, by extension, it is not only an individual's modality of Mind that may be represented in the products of that Mind, but also, it is the case that an individual's mood may be represented in their products of Mind — again, in the thoughts, actions, and speech of that individual. Which specific particulars of the product of Mind in question, allow us to ascertain the general mood of an individual? It must be the case that, just as there is a General Will, there is also a subliminal General Will — the *subliminal prioritization* — that consists of emotively charged information, and so on; to be sure, inherent in the entire corpus of Freud, is the notion that one's productions of Mind, e.g., one's thoughts, actions, and speech, almost always have a subterranean component involved in their production by said Mind; hence, the *Theory of Subliminal Prioritization* is grounded by Freudian

---

[148]   Freud, Sigmund, and Abraham A. Brill. 1938. *The basic writings*; Lacan, Jacques, Jacques-Alain Miller, and Alan Sheridan. 2019. *The four fundamental concepts of psycho-analysis*; Heidegger, Martin, John Macquarrie, and Edward S. Robinson. 2019. *Being and time*.

psychoanalysis, but also by the Freudian-Lacanian concept of drive.[149] Thus, the question of how a product relates to its producer's psychosomatic composition involves an analysis both of the phenomenological General Will and the subliminal General Will — which when unified together, form the *Composite Will*, which will be the archstone to ascertaining what particular mood an individual may be in at a given time. It is the Composite Will that explains drives and how they function in human programmatology. Thus, any product of the Mind, reflective of the Mind of its producer will have, modally accentuated *vibes* inherent to the product itself based on the modality of said product. This is not to say that the product has any meaning in itself, separated from projected, idealistic consciousness — recalling our reconstruction of *projectional essentialism* — but rather, it is to say, that the modality of the product is such that, based on its form, we may infer and intuit that certain vibes affected the modality of the product.

What, then, happens, when we have a concealed and unliberated consciousness, that attempts to disclose as little information as possible in his or her products of Mind? Perhaps it is even the case that, being a limited consciousness, his or her own *thoughts* disclose very little information, even to his or herself in his or her own Mind. Then, in that case, the vibes of a product would be discreet rather than flagrant, but nevertheless still inferable from the modality of the product. Thus, toward a *General Theory of Vibes*, there are both malefic and benefic vibes, inferable from the products of Mind. Thus, there are malefic and benefic thoughts, actions, and speech. However, this subchapter is not the place to discuss such matters, as they will be discussed in the portion of the work dedicated to ethics. To clarify: a malefic vibe might be inferred from, for example, the inane ramblings of an unmedicated man encountered on the metro. A benefic vibe might be inferred from the mental productivity of Mother Theresa, for example. Human beings infer vibes from every single phenomena they come into contact with, so long as it occurs from an organism capable of sophisticated production. Even a caterpillar's products give off vibes, a wiggle here, a wiggle there, *"please do not touch me..."* go the vibes of the poor creature. Because vibes are metafactual components of products of Mind, it follows that there is a cyclology of vibes, insofar as there is a cyclology of products in general. So much for a *General Theory of Productive Vibes*.

23. Of Metalinguistics and the Chalmersian Enmeshed Consciousness

Let *Metalinguistics* be understood to be the domain wherein certain metaphysical aspects of language are discussed and interrogated. In this following division of

---

[149]   Freud, Sigmund, and Abraham A. Brill. 1938. *The basic writings*; Lacan, Jacques, Jacques-Alain Miller, and Alan Sheridan. 2019. *The four fundamental concepts of psycho-analysis*.

the work, numerous issues around the issue of metalinguistics will be discussed, including: linguistic pragmatism, the Linguistic Superstructure, metaphysical indebtion, linguistic projectional essentialism, and objective essentiality. Most important of all of these issues, of course, is the concept of Temporal Projective Categoricism, or the projecting of phenomenological consciousness into the world; built up off of, to be sure, Kant's categories put into conversation with Hegel and Whitehead's process, temporalized philosophies.[150] Thus, the world is a basin for consciousness, and consciousness becomes enmeshed in the modality of the world; this is especially the case when human beings encounter *artistic products* of Mind, or works of art. As shall be discussed in the division of this work dedicated to aesthetics, projective consciousness actually *inhabits* the modality of the work of art, becoming enmeshed with it, akin to famous philosopher David Chalmers's theory of *extended consciousness.*[151] Behind the locus of attention, the witnessant projects its phenomenological consciousness into the world, and consciousness is projected onto objects in the world that may serve as *abilitators*, insofar as they enable human beings to imagine different modalities of being. However, Temporal Projective Categoricism — which is fundamentally *projective consciousness* — is not just vital to aesthetics, but also to linguistics, for, it is the ground of the Hegelian-Lacanian *Linguistic Superstructure*, or, the metafactual, self-reflexive, Lacanian-symbolic system of language dependent upon consciousness itself, that, because of its self-reflexivity, diversifies itself and the consciousness of individuals.[152]

There are also *idiosyncratic Linguistic Superstructures* that are epiphenomenal to an individual's consciousness — which is to say, they metafactual. Responsible for the development first of society, and later of civilization itself, the Linguistic Superstructure is the key distinguishing feature that human beings have that separates them from the rest of the animal kingdom. To be sure, animals employ semiotic systems too, but these are mostly of a primitive modality compared to the complex linguistic structure that human beings possess. Again to be discussed, is the concept of *indebtion*, which is a Kantian-Cognitivist Projectional Category that manifests in either guilt or physical debt — it is egregious, to be sure.[153] However, there are both malefic and benefic varieties of indebtion: for example, when a baby is born, society has certain expectations for it — for example, that the baby will learn how to speak, and will be encouraged to speak from a young age — moreover, *social indebtion* occurs when an individual emerges into the community at birth, and then participates, albeit without consent

[150]   Kant, Immanuel, and Paul Guyer. 2009. *Critique of pure reason.* Cambridge: Cambridge Univ. Press; Hegel, Georg Wilhelm Friedrich. 2004. *Hegel's Science of logic.* Amherst, N.Y.: Humanity Books; Whitehead, Alfred North. 1990. *Process and reality: an essay in cosmology ; Gifford Lectures delivered in the University of Edinburgh during the session 1927-28.* New York: Free Press u.a.

[151]   Chalmers, David John, and Tim Peacock. 2022. *Reality+: virtual worlds and the problems of philosophy.*

[152]   Hegel, Georg Wilhelm Friedrich. 2004. *Hegel's Science of logic.* Amherst, N.Y.: Humanity Books; Lacan, Jacques, and Bruce Fink. 2007. *Écrits: the first complete edition in English.* New York: W.W. Norton.

[153]   Kant, Immanuel, and Paul Guyer. 2009. *Critique of pure reason.* Cambridge: Cambridge Univ. Press.

— because they are so young — in a sort of *autocontractualism*, or an indebtion into society, duties, social contracts, rights, etc. This variety of indebtion has a benefic vibration, because it is the ground — with projective consciousness — of society and civilization itself at large. Without social indebtion, there could be no *science of ethics*, and no *genealogy of right*, and hence, no society at all. Further along in this division of the work, will emerge, a discussion of the nature of objectivity, and an argument will be borrowed from Saint Anselm in order to argue for a *General Theory of Objectivity*.[154] So much, then, for prefatory remarks on the subdivision of this work called *Metalinguistics*.

24. Of Austinian Linguistic Pragmatism and the Leibnizian General Theory of Projectional Optimalism

Philosopher J.L. Austin made famous the idea that language can be used to affect real change in the world, i.e., that there is such an entity known as a speech act.[155] As should be clear from our *General Theory of Production*, there are not just speech acts, but also somatic acts and mental acts. But all of that is a terribly banal observation, from the vantage point of a more developed *Freudian-Lacanian General Theory of Production*, and it is not immediately clear why J.L. Austin's *How to Do Things With Words* was treated to be such a breakthrough in the literature on language. Perhaps because, that was a time before a serious theory of linguistics was afoot. At any rate, language may be used in a broad number of ways, indeed, because it is a form of production. Because all meaning stems from the Mind, as explained by the *Theory of Projectional Essentialism*, language is hollow, or *empty*, as Max Stirner or the Buddhists might say — it has no inherent meaning outside of Mind.[156] That is one of the many reasons why a science of hermeneutics is even possible at all, because human beings project *the best they can* onto words, signs, and everything else. Thus, a General Theory is in order: the *Leibnizian General Theory of Projectional Optimalism*, or the idea that, human beings really do try — their phenomenologies and their automaticities — really do try — to understand the products of another individual's Mind, albeit according to and limited by their own modality of production and worldview; the *General Theory of Projectional Optimalism* is named after Leibniz on account of his infamous optimism,

[154]   Anselm, Brian Davies, and G. R. Evans. 1998. *The major works Anselm of Canterbury*. Oxford; New York: Oxford University Press.

[155]   Austin, J. L., J. O. Urmson, and Marina Sbisà. 2009. *How to do things with words: the William James lectures delivered at Harvard University in 1955*. Oxford: Oxford University Press.

[156]   Stirner, Max. 1974. *Max Stirner, the ego and his own*. New York: Harper & Row; Nagarjuna. 2022. *Root Stanzas Of The Middle Way: the Mulamadhyamakakarika*. [S.l.]: Shambhala.

specifically his *Best Possible World* optimism; therefore, the argument is Leibnizian in *spirit*, if not *letter*.[157]

A phenomenology of language is required for language to enter into the processional phase, insofar as the locus of attention and witnessant must both be alert to the language, but language is mostly processed on a subliminal level — we have already discussed a *General Theory of Processionality* in the very beginning of the work. Furthermore, language, being a form of production, necessarily has a *focalization* — a set of limits — that both explains its modality, and explains how others experience its modality. Thus, language may be used in any number of ways — there is no imperative here to delineate all the modalities of use of language — such a project would be appropriate for an unotherwisely busied, precocious graduate student. Furthermore, we are currently seeing a return to the hieroglyphic modality of language through the world popularity of emojis — or the popularization of specific emotive modes of communication; which is not to say that many other languages, too, do not resemble hieroglyphics, however. Whether all communication will eventually be communicated through atomistic emojis is a speculative inquiry not suited for this work, but, nevertheless, is a worthwhile speculative inquiry, to be sure. So much for linguistic pragmatism.

25. Of the Genealogy of the Hegelian-Lacanian Linguistic Superstructure

As discoursed over early on in the work, especially evinced during the exposition of the metaphysics of corporations, there exist certain entities that are born of the dual unification of *projectional essentialism* and *rapportionality*. Projectional essentialism, at its root, is dependent upon consciousness for its existence. Here, it would be elegant to bring in the metaphysics of famous philosopher René Descartes, who argued for a hierarchy of metaphysical structures, based upon their dependency on one another; for Descartes, and also for famous Heideggerian theologian Paul Tillich, God functions as the Ground-of-Being, or the Aristotelian prime mover, upon whom all other layers of the metaphysical hierarchy are dependent on.[158] How does this relate to language? Simple. Before human beings evolved the capacity for speech and its later accessory, writing, they could still communicate through productions of their Mind — just as regular organic animals do to this very day. Here, then, one could bring in famous philosopher

---

[157]   Leibniz, Gottfried Wilhelm. 2008. *Discourse on metaphysics, and the monadology.* New York: Cosimo Classics.

[158]   Descartes, Rene, and F. Sutcliffe. 2005. *Discourse on Method and the Meditations.* https://www.vlebooks.com/vleweb/product/openreader?id=none&isbn=9780141944203; Tillich, Paul, and F. Forrester Church. 1999. *The essential Tillich.* Chicago, Ill: University of Chicago Press; Aristotle. 1990. *Aristotle: Metaphysics.*

Jürgen Habermas's *Theory of Communicative Action*, but also, J.L. Austin's *How to Do Things with Words*, in order to ground the idea that human beings, prior to language and writing, communicated through the products of their Mind — through their behavior and vocality.[159] Thus, for a long period of human history, human beings could only communicate, as it were, through Walt Whitman's *barbaric yawps*, which, despite their limitations, sufficed to effect communication.[160] However, as soon as more complex modalities of communication evolved, projectional essentialism took a stronger hold on humanity, and changed our primitive ancestors in innumerable ways. Perhaps the most gargantuan of all these shifts, was the emergence of a *Linguistic Superstructure*, or, before the existence of writing, a certain metafactual, new hierarchization dependent upon consciousness itself.

Thus, phenomenological consciousness itself is the base, where complex language is the superstructure. To this day, humankind is both benefited and plagued by the Hegelian-Lacanian Linguistic Superstructure.[161] More than any other reason for the emergence of civilization, complex language stands out because it allowed for differentiation whereas more primitive modes of communication — *barbaric yawps* — were not able to do so. Thus, as soon as Mind evolved the linguistic structures requisite for complex language, this complex Linguistic Superstructure started to form. Complex language allowed for the emergence of an expanded, projectional reflexivity equation, that, because it could turn upon itself and label itself, soon expanded into the self-referential concept of a *society*, which, in turn, as it grew more and more exponentially complex, grew into the behemic concept of *civilization* itself. The family, corporations, political economy, theories of ethics and value, theories of love and partnership, etc., all fall into the domain of the self-reflexive, Hegelian-Lacanian *Linguistic Superstructure*. Departing from Marxian and Althusserian views of the superstructure, this work claims that the Linguistic Superstructure is fundamentally based upon, and dependent upon, *consciousness* as its base — which is more of a Hegelian and Lacanian view, grounded in the Lacanian symbolic register.[162] For, how could the base of the superstructure be mere matter, or physicality, when, without Kantian-Cognitivist Projectional Categories, there could never have existed the differentiation of matter, let alone the projectional category of property so inherent

---

[159]   Habermas, Jürgen. 2007. *The theory of communicative action*. 1, 1. Boston, Mass: Beacon Press; Austin, J. L., J. O. Urmson, and Marina Sbisà. 2009. *How to do things with words: the William James lectures delivered at Harvard University in 1955*. Oxford: Oxford University Press.

[160]   Whitman, Walt, and Justin Kaplan. 1984. *Complete poetry and collected prose: Leaves of grass (1855), Leaves of grass (1891-92), Complete prose works (1892), Supplementary prose*. New York, N.Y.: Library of America.

[161]   Hegel, Georg Wilhelm Friedrich. 2004. *Hegel's Science of logic*. Amherst, N.Y.: Humanity Books; Lacan, Jacques, Jacques-Alain Miller, and Alan Sheridan. 2019. *The four fundamental concepts of psycho-analysis*.

[162]   Hegel, Georg Wilhelm Friedrich, and Terry P. Pinkard. 2018. *The phenomenology of spirit*; Hegel, Georg Wilhelm Friedrich. 2004. *Hegel's Science of logic*. Amherst, N.Y.: Humanity Books; Marx, Karl, and N. I. Stone. 2014. *A contribution to the critique of political economy*; Lacan, Jacques, and Bruce Fink. 2007. *Écrits: the first complete edition in English*. New York: W.W. Norton.

to the grand pseudoscience that is economics?[163] Perhaps famous philosopher Karl Marx's greatest flaw was to critique capitalism on its own terms — to resort to blaise economic modes of argumentation — when all he had to do was apply an *a priori* ethical critique of capitalism, as shall be done further along in the trajectory of this work?[164] Without a doubt, Marx was insecure about his roots in philosophy, and especially insecure about the Hegelian roots of his thought. This author has no such insecurities about the Hegelian or Platonic influences upon his thought, and in fact wields such influences, and is proud of them, especially of the Platonic influences upon his thought! Returning to the Linguistic Superstructure, because of the constantly reprojected reflexivity equation — which itself is an automatic cycle of the Mind — the Linguistic Superstructure continues to diversify itself, and reflexively, diversify us. Thus, the Hegelian-Lacanian Linguistic Superstructure influences the base of consciousness — which was originally the base, but now, because of the reflexivity equation, there has evolved a certain dualism — hence, the superstructure is now indistinguishable from its base; the ladder has been climbed, and afterward, toppled over, to borrow a Wittgensteinian motif.[165]

However, it is clear that, in at least one respect, consciousness remains the base of the superstructure, to that extent that, as soon as a human consciousness expires, the idiosyncratic Linguistic Superstructure of an individual perishes along with said individual, leaving behind, what famous philosopher Jacques Derrida referred to as the semiotic *trace*.[166] Indeed, Derrida thought that all language and writing involved the *trace*, or mere semiotic representation of some product of Mind. With Derrida, the products of mind do indeed leave a *trace*, or an *imprint-of-Mind* in the world. Returning to rapportionality, the Linguistic Superstructure is grounded upon it, in addition to projectional essentialism, which both in turn, are grounded upon phenomenological consciousness. As mentioned above, there exists both the *Hegelian-Lacanian Linguistic Superstructure* and the *Idiosyncratic Linguistic Superstructure*, the first of which, is the set of all idiosyncratic Linguistic Superstructures that, because of holism, takes on a new metafactual, metaphysical existence: however, the collective Linguistic Superstructure is metafactual, and must be considered to be what famous philosopher Max Stirner called a spook: it does not exist in itself, but is dependent upon consciousness, or the ego: that is to say, there is no such entity as a *body politic*, or a *nation-state*: both are hideous spooks, and are very destructive toward the goal of a universal peace manifested across the world: a so-called nation-state is merely imaginary lines drawn upon an imaginary map, and so on and so forth.[167]

---

[163]   Kant, Immanuel, and Paul Guyer. 2009. *Critique of pure reason*. Cambridge: Cambridge Univ. Press.

[164]   Marx, Karl, Ben Fowkes, and David Fernbach. 1990. *Capital: a critique of political economy*; v.1. London: Penguin Books in association with New Left Review.

[165]   Wittgenstein, Ludwig. 2022. *Tractatus Logico-Philosophicus*. [S.l.]: Penguin Books.

[166]   Derrida, Jacques. 1998. *Of grammatology*. Baltimore: Johns Hopkins University Press.

[167]   Stirner, Max. 1974. *Max Stirner, the ego and his own*. New York: Harper & Row.

The idiosyncratic Linguistic Superstructure, which also has a metafactual, metaphysical existence, definitely involves Freudian-Lacanian repetitive cycles, at least in abstract Platonic form, because the Linguistic Superstructure involves products of mind. Just as the superstructure affects consciousness, so too, does the idiosyncratic superstructure — or personalized superstructure — affect the consciousness of its own individual. It involves the cyclologies, modalities, and trajectorics of how an individual employs language, and hence, with the Wittgensteinians and Heideggerians, it directly shapes how a person experiences the world, for, the "limits of my language are the limits of my world," and, "language is the house of Being".[168] It follows that, because Linguistic Superstructures are metafactual, they are noumenal, and so must be inferred and intuited by the phenomenological imagination. So much, then, for the *Linguistic Superstructures*.

26. Of the Nietzschean Metaphysics of Indebtion: Speech Act Par Excellence II

The Epistles of Saint Paul are righteously quick to lambaste debt of *any* kind, and indeed, as we have previously explored, earlier on in the work, inherent to the inquiry of questionologistics, is the concept of indebtion — or the deliberate or indeliberate casting of a debt of information and time onto another individual, or, perhaps, onto a machine, for, how often have we plugged inputs into our computers?[169] Is not the relationship between human and machine similar to the relationship between human and human? Indebtion may either be benefic or malefic, grounded upon whether the indebtion is of a more high caliber, and more serious in its nature. For, once one is indebted, one is essentially a slave to the debt — as Saint Paul is so quick to realize. For, how could one serve two masters at once? Both God and the debtor? Here, there is a general argument against debt of any kind in general, but our main focus is to be on the specific modality of debt either incurred or distributed by means of language. To be sure, metaphysical indebtion is a mechanism of the Linguistic Superstructure, because indebtion is a quality *affected* by language, and hence is of a more metafactual, metaphysical variety. Here we might consider: what of the indebtion imposed upon us by our values and moral structures? Is that not a modality of debt that we constantly have to "pay our dues" for? Precisely for that reason, as mentioned above, we must distinguish between benefic and malefic indebtion, because some debts — for example, duties

---

[168]   Freud, Sigmund, and Abraham A. Brill. 1938. *The basic writings*; Lacan, Jacques, Jacques-Alain Miller, and Alan Sheridan. 2019. *The four fundamental concepts of psycho-analysis*; Plato, and John M. Cooper. 2009. *Complete works*. Indianapolis: Hackett; Wittgenstein, Ludwig. 2022. *Tractatus Logico-Philosophicus*. [S.l.]: Penguin Books; Heidegger, Martin. 2009. *On The Way To Language*. San Francisco: Harperone.

[169]   Paul, Wayne A. Meeks, and John T. Fitzgerald. 2006. *The writings of Saint Paul: annotated texts reception and criticism*. New York: W.W. Norton.

in general, or duties to society — must be paid on a regular and immediate basis, but, are not of a malefic kind: whoever, except perhaps for that lonestar, Nietzsche, called morality a malefic modality of indebtion?[170]

Focused on guilt, especially in his *On the Genealogy of Morals*, Nietzsche claims that ascetic priests encouraged ascetic so-called virtues to the masses, through all modalities of indebtion, and so on: even Immanuel Kant critiqued so-called *priestcraft* in his *Religion Within the Limits of Reason Alone*.[171] The difference, of course, between Kant and Nietzsche, is that, for Kant, the Platonic, Western tradition of morality was valid, whereas Nietzsche thought it ought to be overturned across a *transvaluation of all values*.[172] What does need to be transvaluated, however, are all modalities of malefic indebtion: "don't you owe me some respect, aren't I your father?" It may well be the case that so-and-so Joe is your father, however, that whole nonsense about respecting your parents merely because they are your parents, is an egregious form of indebtion, and out to be castrated out of the economy of values. One is best able to ascertain a malefic modality of indebtion when one especially feels the weight or gravity of the moral scenario: when the Heart is heavy, indebtion is at work. Thus, in accordance with the postulates of the liberated consciousness and the independent consciousness, we must condemn unequivocally any modalities of malefic indebtion, for, indebtion, truly, is the science of enslavement. Later in this work, we shall discuss economic indebtion, an arrangement of society so degenerate and animalistic — tribalistic truly to its core — that it perhaps sets up indebtion to be the *social evil par excellence.* So much — for now — on linguistic indebtion and its discontents.

27. Of Projectional Essentialism and Objective Essentiality: Nietzsche, Fish, and Dworkin

Long ago, we discoursed around the concepts of focalization, and defocalization. And, imperative to consider in this discussion, is the *General Theory of Productive Imprintation*, or, the idea that, each product of Mind — whether a thought, speech, or action — bears a modal imprint of the programmatology that birthed it into emergence. Again, for a product of Mind to have a focalization, means for it to have a set of limits: what distinguishes it from every other possible entity across all possible worlds? Nothing other than its focalization. Now, because of *projectional essentialism*, all units of language must necessarily have focalizations, too: that is

---

[170]   Nietzsche, Friedrich, and Walter Arnold Kaufmann. 2011. *On the genealogy of morals*. New York: Vintage Books.

[171]   Kant, Immanuel, Theodore M. (Theodore Meyer) Greene, and Hoyt H. Hudson. 1960. *Religion within limits or reason alone.*

[172]   Kaufmann, Walter Arnold, and Friedrich Nietzsche. 2011. *Beyond good and evil: prelude to a philosophy of the future.* New York: Vintage Books.

to say, modal and conceptual limits of production. A word that is produced from a programmatology of Mind is produced *according to the logic of that Mind, and only that Mind.* It may well be that an individual has dependencies upon certain modalities of language, forced upon them, for example, by a teacher or a parent, perhaps, however, even though this person is dependent upon the logic of another Mind, those inhibitors and limits are themselves internal to the individual's Mind, and hence all dependencies are sourced internally, even if their referent is external, e.g., Jerry Fodor's famous *Granny.* Here, philosopher Jacques Derrida might agree, that projective, mental focalization is all we can infer about language: there is a limit, involved, however, this limit is itself noumenal — because, essences involve the complete set of information across all possible worlds about a certain entity, and hence, absolute essences are noumenal to us; however, partial essences are the modes of essence involved in focalizations, and the limits of Mind.[173] Here, we encounter a peculiar issue: what are the limits of human programmatology? Certainly, our programmatologies do not involve *absolute* and *objective essences*, but instead, involve *partial* and *limited* essences.

Here, we come across the issue of *essential objectivity*: is it possible? Certainly so. For, if we have one perspective, we may imagine, it exists plotted on the Imaginary Graph of Being; hence, we may use our phenomenological imaginations to intuit the concept of a *perfect viewpoint*, or an *absolute* and *objective* viewpoint. Here, the reader may be reminded of Saint Anselm's argument for a *perfect being*, namely, God; if a perfect being can exist, then it does exist, etc. If a perfect viewpoint could exist — which is to say, a perfect essence — then without a doubt, and without all of the baggage of Saint Anselm's argument, one can argue that, yes, indeed, an *objective viewpoint* may exist, and that an *absolute essence* may exist.[174] Here, it would be elegant to ground the legitimacy of this argument by hybridizing it with three prominent figures: Friedrich Nietzsche, Stanley Fish, and Ronald Dworkin.[175] Nietzsche argues for a sort of *perspectivism*, and, he argues, that *Truth*, is a Platonic idea, akin to the idea of God; hence, if we are *social Platonists* — which we are — then, it follows that we ought to both agree and disagree with Nietzsche. First, we agree with his *perspectival relativism*, while, at the same time, we disagree with him over whether or not *objective Truth* or *objective essence* exists: in fact, we believe that objective Truth does exist. Fish argues for a *reader response criticism*, which is the idea, akin to projectional essentialism, that the reader of a text interprets the text according to their own modality of Mind: hence, there are *partial viewpoints*, akin to Nietzsche's *perspectival relativism*, or the idea that

---

[173]   Derrida, Jacques. 1998. *Of grammatology*. Baltimore: Johns Hopkins University Press.

[174]   Anselm, Brian Davies, and G. R. Evans. 1998. *The major works Anselm of Canterbury*. Oxford; New York: Oxford University Press.

[175]   Kaufmann, Walter Arnold, and Friedrich Nietzsche. 2011. *Beyond good and evil: prelude to a philosophy of the future*. New York: Vintage Books; Dworkin, Ronald. 1986. *Law's empire*. Cambridge, Mass. u.a: Belknap Pr. of Harvard Univ. Pr; Fish, Stanley Eugene. 2003. *Is there a text in this class?: the authority of interpretive communities*. Cambridge, Mass: Harvard Univ. Press.

everyone has their own perspective and worldview. Compare Nietzsche and Fish's views, with the views of legal philosopher Ronald Dworkin, who, in his magnum opus, *Law's Empire*, argued that judges — are we not all judges of the text that is the world? — have rose-tinted lenses, which is to say, that each judge brings their own worldview to their practice of jurisprudence.

The three of these prominent figures, all agree, that *perspectival relativism* is the case — not moral relativism — and, once we have that view successfully on the table, it is simpler to apply Saint Anselm's reasoning to the logic of our inquiry: *if worldviews exist, then a perfect worldview can exist, which is none other than the absolute set of all possible Kantian-Cognitivist Projectional Categories which may be applied to the information present in the world — or in the text, for example.*[176] Thus, to consider the *objective worldview* is to consider a defocalized worldview without limits: a worldview without distinctions between views and information: instead, it simply captures all of the informational facts and metafacts — the perspectives grounded in phenomenological consciousness, and so on — inherent in a given world locale. Wittgenstein, too, argued for the existence of worldviews; if he were not so academically illiterate, perhaps he would have come across Saint Anselm?[177] So much for Projectional Essentialism and the *Anselmian General Theory of Objectivity.*

28. Of the Subliminal and Semiotic Language of Thought: Beyond Fodor

One of famous philosopher Jerry Fodor's most important contributions to philosophy, is none other than his view that there is a *language of thought*, or, an internal means of subliminal, systematic communication that grounds phenomenal thoughts and all other products of Mind.[178] The language of thought can be read as a noumenal systematicity that exists underground consciousness, and, hence, may be understood to scaffold consciousness. The language of thought is not the best terminology for what it is supposed to represent, however. For, no doubt, the language of thought is employed by the following automatic programs of Mind: the subliminal prioritization of entities as cognitized in, the simultaneous construction of products of Mind, the integration and narrativization of information, the logic of which information is effectively emotional or not — based upon the reflexivity equation. Where Fodor appears to be original in discussing the language of thought, really, the language of thought has its roots in Freudian discussions on

176 Kant, Immanuel, and Paul Guyer. 2009. *Critique of pure reason.* Cambridge: Cambridge Univ. Press.

177 Wittgenstein, Ludwig. 2022. *Tractatus Logico-Philosophicus.* [S.l.]: Penguin Books.

178 Fodor, Jerry A. 2010. *The language of thought.*

the subconscious.[179] Obviously, there would have to be such a subliminal semiotic system of the subconscious in order for the Mind to function that way that it does — in the ways we have only just listed immediately above — so, all in all, the language of thought is neither a revolutionary idea nor a particularly original one. If the terminology of the language of thought is malefic in some way, how might we go about reconstructing and redefining the term? First, it is malefic insofar as Fodor calls it both a *language* and also a language of *thought*. Let us start with why the language of thought is not in fact a *language*: it is moreso a *subliminal semiotic system* than it is a language per se, because, firstly, there is no phenomenology behind it, and the term language implies that there is a witnessant behind the production of words, speech, signs, etc., which, obviously the language of thought cannot have, because it is a subliminal semiotic system.

Secondly, the language of thought is not a language of *thought* because thought is fundamentally *phenomenal*, or may be perceived by the witnessant — it is phenomenal in the Mind's eye, as it were, and as Fodor understands the language of thought, it is more so a system *underground* or *subliminal* to our phenomenologies: therefore, because thought is phenomenal, Fodor's language of thought cannot be phenomenal, because it is a subliminal system that exists underneath consciousness, as it were, outside the scope of the witnessant: the true language of thought cannot be witnessed, and all thoughts are phenomenal, therefore, the language of thought is a terrible set of terms to describe what it is attempting to describe. Therefore, we must rename the language of thought, perhaps to the *Subliminal Systematic Functionality of Mind*. Subliminal, because it is outside of the scope of consciousness; systematic, because it involves an intricately intertwined system of modules and so on; functional, because these modules all function and even undergird products of Mind, etc.; and of Mind, of course, because the *Subliminal Systematic Functionality of Mind* is part of the *automatic programmatology of Mind*, as discussed earlier on in this chapter. So much for a critique of Fodor's Language of Thought, and its replacement: the *Subliminal Systematic Functionality of Mind*.

---

[179]   Freud, Sigmund, and Abraham A. Brill. 1938. *The basic writings.*

Chapter III

OF METAPOLITICALITY

THIS division of the work shall tackle issues inherent to any aesthetics, ethics, or politics. All three involve the imagination, but in three different respects. Aesthetics involves the *intuitive imagination*, or the faculty of the imagination to intuit; clearly, there is an obvious relation between epistemology and aesthetics, for precisely the reason that both domains of philosophy involve intuition. Out of aesthetics, grows ethics — a view shared by Kant in his *Critique of the Power of Judgment* — except that, for your author, ethics involves the *speculative imagination*, or the faculty of the imagination that ponders what one ought to do.[180] Out of ethics, grows politics — except that politics involves the *concrete imagination*, or that imagination that seeks to morph its intuitions and speculations into concrete and physical realities. In the division of this work labeled *Aesthetics*, several issues involving intuition will be interrogated, and from these philosophical interrogations will follow several conclusions about metaphysics and epistemological assessment in general. First, however, the issue of zeitgeistology shall be discussed; after that, shall follow a discussion of so-called *species aestheticism*, or the notion that aesthetics must be limited strictly to the modality of the species involved in the aesthetic assessment taking place at a certain time. After that, will follow a discussion of the *work of art* and its *axic alignment* to the Platonic Imaginary Graph of Being, which will be shown to be the true whetstone according to which beauty must be not only tested but refined. Following that discussion, will be another one, except this time one on the issue of *bipartite aesthetic informativity* and its relation to the *aesthetic intuitive thought*. Then, will follow, a discussion of the assessment of the *mature consciousness*, which will be argued to be the modality of consciousness best suited to processing aesthetic assessments; other consciousnesses will develop after the accomplishment of the *mature consciousness*, but all of these consciousnesses will not make any further progress in the domain of *aesthetic assessment* past the degree to which the *mature consciousness* accomplishes *just assessments*.

After that, Lord Byron's modality of consciousness shall be extrapolated from him and formulated into the so-called *fashionable consciousness*, or that consciousness capable of conforming to the needs of its time period, and,

---

[180] Kant, Immanuel, and Paul Guyer. 2009. *Critique of the power of judgment.* Cambridge, UK.: Cambridge University Press.

indeed, the needs of any time period: the *fashionable consciousness* is necessarily cosmopolitan, in that regard.[181] Following the discussion of Lord Byron, *die Unterfrau* shall be introduced as a foil to Nietzsche's Übermensch; furthermore, *die Unterfrau* embodies none other than the *revolutionary consciousness*, or that consciousness that most resembles the Socratic questioning of the status-quo — said discussion shall conclude the division of this work labeled as *Aesthetics*.[182] As aforementioned, the *Ethics* will grow up out of the *Aesthetics*, and begins with an exposition of the *Benefic Speculative Formulation*, or that thought experiment responsible for the establishment of the eighteen ideal principles of morality. Then, the contentions of the *mature consciousness* shall be delved into, these being, imperialism contra indigeneity: akin, of course, to Habermas's distinction between the system and the lifeworld.[183] Thus, imperialism functions as the systematic component of society, whereas indigeneity represents the Habermasian lifeworld. After that, will follow a discussion of the Rawlsian game theoretics of civilization, and how game theory is relevant to the *Benefic Speculative Formulation* that is responsible for the phenomenological derivation of the eighteen ideal principles of morality.[184] Then, the *Benefic Speculative Formulation* will be carried out to its endpoint: *harmony*. Before *harmony* may be derived, first consciousness must undertake the odyssey that is the *Benefic Speculative Formulation*, and subliminally or consciously comprehend the meanings of the various eighteen ideal principles of morality. Let, therefore, the *Benefic Speculative Formulation* function as a so-called *genealogy of morals*, but not in the Nietzschean fashion. Instead, this trajectory is much more so related to a Hegelian framework than to a Nietzschean framework: and in fact, Nietzsche's *On the Genealogy of Morals* is hardly worth reading at all, on account of its being more about *priestcraft* than it is about morality itself.[185] Here, it may be worth arguing that the *Benefic Speculative Formulation* functions as a superior model for the development of morality in individuals than Lawrence Kohlberg's *Theory of Moral Development*.[186] After the eighteen ideal principles of morality have been comprehended by the *benefic consciousness*, said consciousness contemplates what justice might be, and concludes that justice is nothing other than a *harmony* of the eighteen ideal principles of morality. After that, the infamous Wittgensteinian duckrabbit returns to the forefront of our philosophical interrogations: Whitehead's *process philosophy* and Derrida's *deconstruction* are

[181] O'Brien, Edna. 2019. *Byron in love.*

[182] Nietzsche, Friedrich Wilhelm, Adrian Del Caro, and Robert B. Pippin. 2006. *Nietzsche: thus spoke Zarathustra.* Cambridge: Cambridge University Press.; Plato, and John M. Cooper. 2009. *Complete works.* Indianapolis: Hackett.

[183] Habermas, Jürgen. 2012. *The theory of communicative action.* 2, 2. Boston, Mass: Beacon Press.

[184] Rawls, John. 1999. *A theory of justice.* Cambridge, Mass: Belknap.

[185] Nietzsche, Friedrich, and Walter Arnold Kaufmann. 2011. *On the genealogy of morals.* New York: Vintage Books.

[186] Kohlberg, Lawrence. 1986. *The philosophy of moral development: moral stages and the idea of justice.* Cambridge [u.a]: Harper & Row.

combined, according to the wisdom of the ontologically versatile duckrabbit, in order to form a sober *process ethics*, or an ethics dominated by the notion that the ethical *absolute* is noumenal to us, rather than knowable, and, furthermore, subdominated by the notion that, due to zeitgeistal *autodiversification*, ethics must never make proclamations, but merely *perpetual speculations*.[187] After that, Kant and Rand are put into conversation with one another, and the *altruistic consciousness* synthesizes with the *selfish consciousness*, in order to form the *polyintentional consciousness* capable of performing actions both for itself and for others, in a polyintentional manner as described earlier in this work.[188]

Then, a *genealogy of right* is performed, and the genealogical origins of right are shown to be the dues owed to an individual from society grounded in said individual's *autocontributionality* to society. Following that dialectic, will be perhaps the most important issue in the entire book: *Theogenesis*, or *Birth of God Theology*, which is the theology of the Pauline *unknown god* who has yet to emerge in the total set of all possible worlds, but whose eventual coming into being is inevitable, given that such a being has an eternity to come into being, and therefore will emerge someday either as a *Boltzmann god* or as a *synthetic god* of some civilization's own creation.[189] The discussion of *theogenetics* concludes the division of the work labeled as *Ethics*. Just as the *Ethics* grew up out of the *Aesthetics*, so too does the *Politics* grow up out of the notions established in the *Ethics* in a developmental fashion. Elements from the *Ethics*, too, will furnish the developmentally mature political theories presented in the *Politics*. First, the *Politics* will establish a theory of personal identity to counter the so-called Parfitian nihilistic view of personal identity: let this theory be known as the *Holistic Theory of Personal Identity*, which is rooted in nothing other than *phenomenological constructivism*, or the view that consciousness is responsible for everything in the Habermasian lifeworld.[190] After that, will follow an exposition of a *Tripartite Nietzschean Theory of Political Anthropomodalisms*, these three anthropomodalisms being, asceticism, decadence, and apollonianism; Nietzsche's analysis of slave morality will figure largely in that analysis.[191] Following that exposition, a discussion of *political innate ideas* will

---

[187] Wittgenstein, Ludwig, G. E. M. Anscombe, Peter M. S. Hacker, and Joachim Schulte. 2010. *Philosophische Untersuchungen = Philosophical investigations*. Chichester, West Sussex, U.K: Wiley-Blackwell; Whitehead, Alfred North. 1990. *Process and reality: an essay in cosmology; Gifford Lectures delivered in the University of Edinburgh during the session 1927-28*. New York: Free Press u.a.; Derrida, Jacques. 1998. *Of grammatology*. Baltimore: Johns Hopkins University Press.

[188] Kant, Immanuel, Jens Timmermann, Mary J. Gregor, Immanuel Kant, and Immanuel Kant. 2014. *Groundwork of the metaphysics of morals: a German-English edition*; Rand, Ayn, and Leonard Peikoff. 2014. *Philosophy: who needs it*. New York: Signet. http://rbdigital.oneclickdigital.com.

[189] Paul, Wayne A. Meeks, and John T. Fitzgerald. 2006. *The writings of Saint Paul: annotated texts reception and criticism*. New York: W.W. Norton.

[190] Parfit, Derek. 2007. *Reasons and persons*. Oxford: Clarendon Press; Habermas, Jürgen. 2012. *The theory of communicative action*. 2, 2. Boston, Mass: Beacon Press.

[191] Nietzsche, Friedrich, and Walter Arnold Kaufmann. 2011. *On the genealogy of morals*. New York: Vintage Books

ensue, followed by a presentation of the *Theory of Instinctive Production*, itself a foil for the Habermasian *Theory of Communicative Action*, in that it argues that instinct is responsible for the social order, rather than rationality.[192] After that, will follow a discussion of so-called *polynomial dialectics*, the *masterscript*, and the *social narrative*: three theoretical tools that will aid us in comprehending the hypercomplexity of the political situation at any given point in time. Following that discussion, will be another one on the so-called *Karmic Social Idealistic Matrix Theory*, which analyzes the Foucauldian concept of the panopticon, except that it expands it to be a *social panopticon* responsible for human reputations.[193] Furthermore, Spivak's *subalternity* becomes complemented by the conceptual class of *celestials*, who together make up the class of citizens whose social status is responsible for their possessing the social quality of *celestiality*.[194] Once that discussion is concluded, one of the most important series of subchapters in the entire book follows: a series of philosophical interrogations *toward political justice*, of which there are nine. First, the so-called *Kantian consciousness*, named due to its interest in three questions — *what can I know, what should I do, and what can I hope* — begins to question and synthesize all of the elements of the former consciousnesses it has gone through in its earlier developmental history: ultimately, the teleological destination of the inquisitive *Kantian consciousness* is none other than the *democratic consciousness*, which functions as the teleological endpoint in the development of consciousness; this claim is akin to Fukuyama's assessment of liberal democracy as the teleological endpoint of political development, except that it involves phenomenological consciousness instead of modalities of government.[195]

Next in the *toward political justice* subchapter series is an exposition of the *right to personhood*, which integrates the components of the *Holistic Theory of Personal Identity* into a concrete political framework. Next in the series of *toward political justice* chapters is a discussion of both the right to political justice and the right to political scaffolding. The right to political justice involves the concrete manifestation of the eighteen ideal principles of morality as derived through the *Benefic Speculative Formulation* into a system of rights. The right to political scaffolding, on the other hand, comprehends the Nussbaumian *fragility of goodness*, and consequently entails both a concrete political mediation of human instinctivism due to repressive political structures, and a set of political structures designed to nourish and complement human consciousness such that it might functionally optimally.[196] After the discussion of the three chief rights, these being, the right to personhood, the right to political justice, and the right to political

[192] Habermas, Jürgen. 2007. *The theory of communicative action*. 1, 1. Boston, Mass: Beacon Press.

[193] Foucault, Michel, and Alan Sheridan. 2020. *Discipline and punish: the birth of the prison*.

[194] Spivak, Gayatri Chakravorty, Donna Landry, and Gerald MacLean. 1996. *The Spivak reader: selected works of Gayatri Chakravorty Spivak*. New York, NY: Routledge.

[195] Kant, Immanuel, and Paul Guyer. 2009. *Critique of pure reason*. Cambridge: Cambridge Univ. Press; Fukuyama, Francis. 2020. *The end of history and the last man*.

[196] Nussbaum, Martha Craven. 2011. *The fragility of goodness: luck and ethics in Greek tragedy and philosophy*.

scaffolding, there follows a presentation of the novel *Aristotelian Metaphysical Theory of the Individual and of the Nation-State*, which basically applies Aristotle's metaphysical theory of four causes to both the individual and to the nation-state at large, and argues that instead of having four causes, both the individual and the nation-state have four *motivators* that best explain their functionality in the world.[197] The elaboration of this theory will ground the next four subchapters in the *toward political justice* series: *Just Mind Theory, Just Rule Theory, Just Environment Theory, and Just Economy Theory. Just Mind Theory* argues that the teleological endpoint of the development of human consciousness is none other than the *democratic consciousness*; this subchapter traces the development of consciousness from the primitive *dependent consciousness* all the way up to the *democratic consciousness*. Next, comes *Just Rule Theory*, which argues that the teleological development of rules culminates in a *democratic constitution*, hence, *democratic constitutionalism*.

Just Environment Theory culminates in the *democratic universal safe space*, borrows heavily from Habermas's theory of social pathologies, and returns to the dialectic the conflict between indigeneity and imperialism, with the result being the need for a universal safe space to protect indigeneity from the myriad forms of imperialisms.[198] Last in the Aristotelian subchapter subseries, comes *Just Economy Theory*, which culminates in the *democratic universal economy*, which argues not for an impotent political federation of nation-states, but for an *economic syncretism* that will truly deincentivize war and other wastes of human capital permanently. Lastly, comes one of the most important subchapters in the entire work: the discussion of *Just World Theory*, which traces the genealogical development of international *harmony* all the way up from the most primitive of the anthropomodal concepts: need and instinct. Thus, the *just world* involves the *democratic consciousness, democratic constitutionalism*, the *democratic universal safe space*, and the *democratic economy*: truly, the *just world* is nothing other than the *democratic world*. With the conclusion of that subchapter, so concludes the division of this work labeled *Metapolitics*.

OF AESTHETICS

In this division of the work labeled *Aesthetics* we shall interrogate several issues surrounding aesthetics. First, we will delve into an analysis of *zeitgeistology*, or the study of zeitgeists. Then, we will discuss aesthetic emotivisms — or general theories of aesthetics based upon the emotions — and will consider whether or not these modalities of aesthetics are repugnant or not, and, whether or not emotivisms really reduce down to *species aestheticisms*, or theories of aesthetics that are relative to the given species of an organism, for example, the aesthetics

---

[197] Aristotle. 1990. *Aristotle: Metaphysics*.

[198] Habermas, Jürgen. 2012. *The theory of communicative action*. 2, 2. Boston, Mass: Beacon Press.

of a shark. Then, we shall consider the *work of art* as distinguished from all other worldly entities, as an entity whose telos is to captivate consciousness in particular. Then, we will consider how to come as close as possible to an *absolute assessment* about a work of art, contrasted with a *subjective assessment*. We will then bring into the discussion a useful theoretical and hypothetical tool, the *Imaginary Graph of Being*, or the imaginary set of Plato's forms and their relations to each other.[199] Ultimately, human beings may imagine and intuit this *Imaginary Graph of Being*, so whether or not the forms actually exist, is a noumenal question; however, no matter what the answer is to that question, these forms exist in our faculties of cognition and hence have a very real, phenomenological and systematic existence. Then, we will consider what it is like to have an *aesthetic phenomenology*, or a phenomenology that is interacting with a work of art. After that, we will discuss a theory of *Bipartite Informativity* and the *aesthetic intuitive assessment*, according to which, our information about a work of art has two sources: the information that protrudes up out of the work of art itself, and the information stored in our mental depositories. Then, we will discuss how an intuitive assessment is a product of Mind, and hence, follows the process of production outlined earlier in this work.

After that, we consider how we may shift our assessments from mere *species assessments* to *absolute assessments*, with help from the *Imaginary Graph of Being*, or the total set of Plato's forms and their relations to each other. Then, we will discuss the aesthetic assessments of the *mature consciousness*, which are more competent when it comes to making *just assessments* than are other modalities of consciousness. Then, we will produce a *Universal Theory of Fashionable Consciousness*, or a theory about that consciousness that transcends its own time and becomes universally fashionable across all time periods. That argument will involve an aufhebung the phenomenologies of John Keats and the Marquis de Sade, two opposites, whose golden mean is none other than the phenomenological consciousness of George Gordon, Lord Byron: hence, the *Byronic consciousness*.[200] Then, at the very end of this chapter, will be discussed a *General Theory of Aesthetic Unorthodoxy*, which culminates in the postulance of the *phenomenology of die Unterfrau*, or the unorthodox consciousness that is fundamentally responsible for superseding the zeitgeist and producing novel, fashionable products of Mind. As usual, the noumenal aspects of our inquiries shall be highlighted, and, especially in the case of *die Unterfrau*, will be discussed in terms of how they can be interrogated and best understood. So much for the prefatory remarks on the division of this work labeled *Aesthetics*.

---

[199]   Plato, and John M. Cooper. 2009. *Complete works*. Indianapolis: Hackett.

[200]   Roe, Nicholas. 2013. *John Keats: a new life*. https://archive.org/details/johnkeatsnewlifeooooroen; Schaeffer, Neil, and Donatien Alphonse Francois de Sade. 2001. *The Marquis de Sade: a life*. London: Picador; O'Brien, Edna. 2019. *Byron in love*.

1. Toward a General Theory of Platonic-Hegelian Zeitgeistology; or, Of the Metaphysics of Fashion

That the zeitgeist is an epiphenomenal entity dependent upon the Hegelian-Lacanian *Linguistic Superstructure*, is a claim few would reject: for, how could the given culture of a populace not be dependent upon the phenomenological consciousnesses that make up said populace?[201] Furthermore, the zeitgeist may be described as the emotional coloring of the Linguistic Superstructure. In *The Republic*, Plato argues for a body politic that is a holistic superstructure of the polis, constituted by atomistic individuals: here it would be strategic to borrow his reasoning for another mode of argument, namely, toward the formulation of a *General Theory of Platonic-Hegelian Zeitgeistology.*[202] Let us now consider Plato's theory of souls, for which there is Mind, Emotive Spirit, and Generative Body. To borrow his holism of the polis, where the sum of the individuals of a polis is not the same as the entire group of them conceived of together as a whole, suppose we applied his political holism to the Hegelian zeitgeist, what then? It is not too controversial to agree with Plato that there are three chief modalities of the human superstructure: again, Mind, Emotive Spirit, and Generative Body. What happens when we add temporality into the mix with political holism? We arrive precisely at the zeitgeist: or, at the concept of a holistic cultural alterity: an ever changing modality of culture. This ever changing modality of culture is, as we have already argued, dependent upon the Linguistic Superstructure and its natural capacity to diversify cultural matters, which first occurs by altering the modalities of production inherent to the mind. The Linguistic Superstructure is responsible for altering the functions that produce our products of Mind, to be sure. Agreeing with Plato, have we not already argued for a *Kierkegaardian phenomenology of the Heart*, in the division of this work labeled *Anthropocognitivity?*[203] Thus, to reduce political holism to its component — the individual — we arrive at three chief components of the zeitgeist, across every moment of time hitherto, notwithstanding some radical evolution of humankind that would render this theory obsolete. On the one hand, there is the part of the zeitgeist pertinent to Mind: *intellectual fashion*.

On the other hand, there is the part of the zeitgeist pertinent to Emotivics: *emotional fashion*. On the third hand, there is the part of the zeitgeist pertinent to the Generative Body: *appetitive fashion*. While it may be that political holism is a Stirnerian spook — insofar as the zeitgeist is noumenal, of course — for how could it be quantified in a scientific manner? — the zeitgeist nevertheless, like its

---

[201]   Hegel, Georg Wilhelm Friedrich. 2004. *Hegel's Science of logic*. Amherst, N.Y.: Humanity Books; Lacan, Jacques, Jacques-Alain Miller, and Alan Sheridan. 2019. *The four fundamental concepts of psycho-analysis*.

[202]   Plato, G. R. F. Ferrari, and Tom Griffith. 2013. *The republic*. Cambridge: Cambridge University Press; Hegel, Georg Wilhelm Friedrich, Robert F. Brown, Peter Crafts Hodgson, and William Geuss. 2019. *Lectures on the Philosophy of World History, Volume I: Manuscripts of the Introduction and the Lectures of 1822-1823*.

[203]   Kierkegaard, Søren, Howard V. Hong, Edna H. Hong, and George Pattison. 2009. *Works of love*.

parent the Linguistic Superstructure, has a certain metaphysical, qualitative, and metafactual existence: it exists without existing, as it were, because, fundamentally, it is a geometry of consciousness, and is exactly dependent upon consciousness for its metafactual, inferrable, and hypothetical existence. Because of its explanatory power, the concept of the zeitgeist is useful to us, and so on. Here, it would be prudent to recall that in our analyses of Anthropocognitivity, we discoursed around the issues of the emotional charge of information stored in the mental depository. Thus, there is an inherent link between the phenomenological matters and the *automatic* and *systematic* matters involving emotivics. They are intertwined in such a way that there may be emotionally charged information, but they are not totally intertwined, because there is such a thing as emotionally neutral information: that the towel that is hanging up on the towel rack, over there, for example. To magnify our reconstruction once more — returning to the zeitgeist — intellectual and emotional fashions are also intertwined, because fundamentally political holism is dependent upon its parts, and, the nature of the parts is reflected in the *general nature* that is the zeitgeist. A zeitgeist is merely the metafactual total set of individual modalities at a certain point and time. Thus, the science of zeitgeistology is the science of *fashion*, and all culture is merely some modality of *fashion*. What then, is the ground of fashion? Nothing other than the Linguistic Superstructure, that naturally diversifies itself through the process of *autodiversification*, which is the root of all social change. Here, Marx might complain: "is not the economic base the root of all change, fundamentally?"[204]

There, we must reply: certainly not, for, economics, again is an egregious metafactual pseudoscience dependent upon phenomenological consciousness — nothing more and nothing less. Therefore, while it may seem that the economic base is responsible for all social changes, it is really the case, that economics is merely a *social category* privileged by the *subliminal prioritizations* of every single individual with power and influence in society. Thus, the question of how to affect cultural change, and fashion itself, must reflexively turn back upon the *subliminal prioritizations* of the collective set of individuals: those sets and those sets alone must be interrogated to affect real and substantive change. Furthermore, because there is zeitgeistal diversification through the Linguistic Superstructure, and because there is progress, due to the process of zeitgeistal *autodiversification*, it follows that it may be prudent to argue that the *project* of aesthetics may one day become complete, as was Hegel's view.[205] However, because the Linguistic Superstructure may diversify itself an infinite amount of times, there is no such concept of a *complete aesthetics*. Therefore, the project of aesthetics — and ethics — is in a state of *perpetual incompletion*, which is to say, that these two projects that are aesthetics and ethics, are nothing other than *perpetual endeavors*. Hence,

---

[204] Marx, Karl, Eugene Kamenka, and Karl Marx. 1983. *The portable Karl Marx.*

[205] Hegel, Georg Wilhelm Friedrich, Robert F. Brown, Annemarie Gethmann-Siefert, Heinrich Gustav Hotho, and Georg Wilhelm Friedrich Hegel. 2014. *Lectures on the philosophy of art: the Hotho transcript of the 1823 Berlin lectures.* Oxford: Oxford University Press.

the theoretical emergence of a Whiteheadian-Derridean *process aesthetics*.[206] So much — for now — on the *General Theory of Platonic-Hegelian Zeitgeistology.*

2. Beyond Species Aestheticism: Beyond Hume

Many philosophers proclaim: the science of aesthetics, to whatever extent there may be one, is really only a science of the emotions — this view has been called emotivism, and so on. Famous philosopher David Hume's view on aesthetics may be reduced to the fundamental implication of his theory: it leaves judgment in the hands of the subject; however, any theory of subjective aesthetics is necessarily a theory of *species aestheticism*, for it does not rely upon the universal and absolute Platonic Imaginary Graph of Being.[207] One can see how this view becomes immediately repugnant to us interrogators of reason, when one turns it on its head: suppose then we had an aesthetics from the viewpoint of the shark? An ethics from the viewpoint of the shark? One is reminded here of Nietzsche's perspectivism, perhaps even a certain relativity of morals.[208] *How repugnant!* While on the one hand, the *anthropomodal power of assessment* — as has been rigorously analyzed by Immanuel Kant in his *Critique of the Power of Judgment* — is a fruitful and indeed useful reconstruction, it could never be the case, that such a subjective theory of aesthetics, could lay claim to a justified and rigorous status, for even if subjective aesthetics may hold a hegemonic influentiality over the minds and hearts of human beings: what is the use of a subjective theory of aesthetics, if the beautiful is relative, which, by extension, means that the ethical is relative?[209] For, aesthetics and ethics are necessarily intertwined, and even Kant acknowledges that moral ideals are associated with aesthetic ideals: for this author, they are necessarily linked. For, the aesthetic imagination is the ground of all ethics, and likewise, ethics informs aesthetics: who ever would argue in support of unethical art? Returning to Immanuel Kant, it is very eccentric of him to argue for a certain mode of subjective aesthetics, because, for him, there could never be any such thing as a subjective ethics; on the other hand, Habermas shrewdly argues that Kant's ethical theory is too monological in that it focuses on the self-discursive narratives an individual presents to themselves, contra Habermas's discourse

---

[206] Whitehead, Alfred North. 1990. *Process and reality: an essay in cosmology; Gifford Lectures delivered in the University of Edinburgh during the session 1927-28*. New York: Free Press u.a.; Derrida, Jacques. 1998. *Of grammatology*. Baltimore: Johns Hopkins University Press.

[207] Hume, David. 2013. *Of the standard of taste: post-modern times aesthetic classics*. [Place of publication not identified]: Birmingham Free Press.

[208] Kaufmann, Walter Arnold, and Friedrich Nietzsche. 2011. *Beyond good and evil: prelude to a philosophy of the future*. New York: Vintage Books; Nietzsche, Friedrich, and Walter Arnold Kaufmann. 2011. *On the genealogy of morals*. New York: Vintage Books.

[209] Kant, Immanuel, and Paul Guyer. 2009. *Critique of the power of judgment*. Cambridge, UK.: Cambridge University Press.

method of morality.[210] At any rate, Kant's moral works are in direct conflict with his aesthetic works, as was realized, all-too-realized, by his Romantic critics, especially Hegel, who kick-started his career with the unification of subjective and objective phenomenologies.[211]

Here, it would be prudent, to follow along the path of Hegel, and accept that, while there is such a thing as the anthropomodal power of assessment, there is also such a thing as *absolute assessment*, or *objective assessment*.[212] Just as we argued for a *Anselmian Theory of Objectivity*, we may too argue for an *Anselmian Theory of Absolute assessment*, for, if we can imagine one viewpoint, we may imagine a perfect viewpoint, that sees both from its over perspective, and also from the total set of all perspectives, and indeed, also comprehends the so-called non-perspective.[213] Thus, for aesthetics as well as for ethics, *perfection* is the ultimate aspiration of any possible enterprise involving the two. Again, we must distinguish between the *perfect* or *unlimited view* and the *imperfect*, or *limited view*. Any embodied, physical view must necessarily be a limited and imperfect view, for, everyone will agree that human beings — or sharks — have certain cognitive limits, and so on. Thus, for each embodiment, there must necessarily be such a thing as *an optimalistic cognization of beauty*, which is itself a *golden mean* between the perfect view and the imperfect view. The pure, imperfect view is one that is purely limited, and does not transcend its limitations, whereas the perfect view is transcendental and has no limits. Thus, through transcendence, we may arrive at a so-called *mixed viewpoint* — or an Aristotelian *golden mean* — made up partially of perfect and unlimited assessments and imperfect and limited assessments.[214] How may we inform our imperfect viewpoints at least partially with the form of perfect viewpoints?

We must return to the mentalist *Idiosyncratic Cognitive Graph of Being*, and its sibling, the *Imaginary Graph of Being*, which, represents entities both real and unreal — perfect forms, whether or not they exist — which is ultimately a noumenal question — a question that we can only rely upon Saint Anselm to dig us out of, which is to say, to rescue us from the trench of Noumenality — these imaginary forms may be imagined on the *Imaginary Graph of Being*. Whether one is a realist or a hypotheticalist about the *Imaginary Graph of Being*, once it is on the table, it informs our understanding and better explains reality: let it therefore be understood to have, very probably, a real existence — conservatively — at least in the human imagination, which, again, is the cognitivist view of Kant.[215] Thus,

---

[210] Habermas, Jurgen. 1996. *Moral consciousness and communicative action*. Cambridge, MA: MIT.

[211] Hegel, Georg Wilhelm Friedrich, and Terry P. Pinkard. 2018. *The phenomenology of spirit*.

[212] Ibid

[213] Anselm, Brian Davies, and G. R. Evans. 1998. *The major works Anselm of Canterbury*. Oxford; New York: Oxford University Press.

[214] Aristotle, and Charles David Chanel Reeve. 2014. *Nicomachean ethics*. Indianapolis: Hackett Publishing Co.

[215] Kant, Immanuel, and Paul Guyer. 2009. *Critique of pure reason*. Cambridge: Cambridge Univ. Press.

across the Imaginary Graph of Being, we may intuit points on the graph and compare them to points as perceived in the Ontological Graph of Being — or the Graph of the World. Even though the Ontological Graph of Being is noumenal to us, it nevertheless, may be intuited — and differentiated — through projectional consciousness and its concomitant phenomena, projectional essentialism. Thus, we must augment our modalities of critique — of which there are two modes — automatic and phenomenological — by informing them — literally in-forming them — with forms intuited from the *Platonic Imaginary Graph of Being*.[216] More on *axic alignment* in the next subchapter.

3. Of the Work of Art and its Axic Alignment on the Platonic Imaginary Graph of Being

Every work of art necessarily has some formal alignment with points on the Imaginary Graph of Being. Thus, the beautiful work of art is the work of art that, formally, exists *parallel* to some set of elegantly positioned forms on the Imaginary Graph of Being. Likewise, the ugly work of art exists in a parallel relation to some malefic coordinate series on the Imaginary Graph of Being. Now, how may we critique the work of art — let alone anything else? — as mentioned in the previous subchapter, there are two modalities of critique: *automatic* and *phenomenological*. These two modalities of critique conform to our earlier analyses of the dual programmatologies of Mind: the automatic and phenomenological programs of Mind. Phenomenological critique is when our consciousness *inhabits* or *immerses* itself in the work of art, because the work of art is limited, and thus, when consciousness projects itself upon that set of limits, it is itself limited: thus the work of art, and indeed, the whole world, limits an individual's phenomenology in this manner. The automatic programmatology of Mind plays a role, here, too; thus, we must propose a *Bipartite Theory of Critique*, or perhaps, of hermeneutics and interpretation at large. As we perceive the work of art phenomenologically, the Hegelian-Lacanian *Linguistic Superstructure*, which is epiphenomenal to consciousness, and yet, also informed by the systematic set of information in the mental depository, plays a role, too: the role that the Linguistic Superstructure plays, is none other than this: it allows us to differentiate the work, to whatsoever extent the limits of the work allow this to be done — for, the work of art fundamentally protrudes a set of information into the world: the rest is interpretive: hence, Derrida's arguments about polysemia — or multiple meanings — and so on. But what of the collective Linguistic Superstructure, or, the zeitgeist

---

[216]   Plato, and John M. Cooper. 2009. *Complete works*. Indianapolis: Hackett.

itself? How can we explain why fashion changes?[217] Certainly, there is such a thing as *autodiversification*, so, with Hegel, as humanity continues to span further and further across the temporal timeline, there is such a thing as *a progress* — or *diversification* — of the Linguistic Superstructure.

Why — among the ages — are there different styles of art? Simple, because, as the human race continues along the temporal timeline, as a civilization, we are inching closer and closer to the capacity for *absolute assessment*, which is to say, that our viewpoints are continually diversifying and becoming better and better. Still, even apart from the diversity of fashions, what explains why certain modalities of art — products of Mind — are fashionable at certain times? It must be that the *subliminal prioritization*, of society at large, is none other than, from within us, *inarticulably mesmerized* by certain works of art — or products of Mind. Furthermore, this *mesmerization* involves the specific trajectorics of zeitgeist — individuals bear all of the culture they have experienced in their systematic sets of information, and thus, are limited by this informational exposure: for example, Samuel Johnson, born into his own times, developed tastes and *subliminal prioritizations*, according to the modality of the zeitgeists of his times.[218] And, even as autodiversification — or *social metanoia* — occurs, there are nevertheless phenomenological limits — as Hegel so justly argued for in the *Phenomenology of Mind*.[219]

Thus, until we reach the point of *absolute assessment*, the human race remains trapped in an epoch of *partial assessment*, and must rely faithfully upon the *Imaginary Graph of Being* to direct it in the right ways, when it comes to the ever-expanding *process* that is itself the science of aesthetics and the science of ethics. As mentioned earlier in this work, the fundamental unit of historical diversification is nothing other than the *trigger*, and among the total set of triggers, is the *aesthetic trigger*: or the trigger related to fashions. Thus, there are three modalities of the aesthetic trigger: intellectual, emotive, and appetitive — following along with, again, Plato's theory of souls. And, triggers hit idiosyncratically close to home, because of the reflexivity equation: and, if there is such a thing as the *collective Linguistic Superstructure*, or, the *zeitgeist*, then, there is such thing as the *collective trigger*, or, the notion that the form of an entity especially triggers to the total set of one collective of peoples — fixed, of course, to a certain moment on the temporal timeline — fixed to a certain zeitgeist, as it were. So much for axic alignment.

---

[217]   Hegel, Georg Wilhelm Friedrich. 2004. *Hegel's Science of logic*. Amherst, N.Y.: Humanity Books; Lacan, Jacques, and Bruce Fink. 2007. *Écrits: the first complete edition in English*. New York: W.W. Norton; Derrida, Jacques, and Barbara Johnson. 2017. *Dissemination*.

[218]   Boswell, James, and Marshall Waingrow. 2019. *Boswell's Life of Johnson: an edition of the original manuscript*. Edinburgh: Edinburgh University Press.

[219]   Hegel, Georg Wilhelm Friedrich, and Terry P. Pinkard. 2018. *The phenomenology of spirit*.

4. Toward a General Theory of Aesthetic Phenomenology Alongside the Aesthetic-Theory-of-Being-in-the-World: Fish and Chalmers

Let the world be understood to be a basin for phenomenological consciousness; a basin, because, the world is fundamentally noumenal to us, but, through phenomena, we may interact with it; because our phenomenological consciousnesses are projected into the world, our *witnessants* inhabit the world: call this the *General Theory of the Inhabitancy of the Witnessant*. For phenomenological consciousness to inhabit the world is for it to fit into and be sculpted, molded even, by the modal structure of some given information in the world: our consciousnesses are *limited* by the world and its concomitant information, which is to say, that our consciousnesses project into the world, and, are in turn, conditioned by the world, and framed in such and such a way. Certain entities in the world have a telos such that they are designed to exploit the fact of our projectional consciousnesses, and thus, they are designed in order to quite literally capture and captivate consciousness: call these telic entities, the *works of art*. Now, the works of art are an especially captivating modality of the world, for they are designed to capture our attention, to lull us into self-reflexivity, to compare ourselves to the work of art itself. Because of projectional consciousness, the qualitative mental causation that occurs in Mind by gazing at the spectacle of the work of art, is such that, whatever occurs in the Mind of the perceiver, comes from within their own internalized, systematic set of emotionally charged information held in the mental depository. However, the modality of the work of art is such that it does limit the possible reactions an individual may have to the work, for, like any other physical entity in the world, it protrudes information out into the world, and hence, there is a limit — but by no means a necessity — placed upon the conscious Mind that gazes at the work of art. Which figures have argued for something similar?

Famous philosopher David Chalmers, for example, argues for extended consciousness, or the idea that the Mind extends into the world.[220] Famous professor Stanley Fish argues for, as we have seen earlier on, a certain *reader response criticism*, wherein individuals project their own consciousnesses and systematic sets of emotionally charged information onto the text, or, the world in general — or, *the work of art*.[221] Because the fundamentals of the world are noumenal to human beings, they are left to sift through a series of mere *impressions of the world*. Returning to *extended consciousness*, there is such a thing as *enmeshed consciousness*, or consciousness enmeshed with phenomena perceived and informed by the world. Thus, when human beings gaze at the work of art, they become enmeshed with it; however, this is also the case with all entities in the

---

[220] Chalmers, David John, and Tim Peacock. 2022. *Reality+: virtual worlds and the problems of philosophy.*

[221] Fish, Stanley Eugene. 2003. *Is there a text in this class?: the authority of interpretive communities.* Cambridge, Mass: Harvard Univ. Press.

world: what we perceive through our witnessant and its locus of attention, impacts our Minds either on a conscious or subliminal level. Furthermore, when the work of art becomes enmeshed with a Mind, the work of art serves as an *abilitator*, or an entity that enables the Mind to climb up the ladder, as it were, into a certain domain of phenomenological consciousness. Returning to the Noumenality of the work of art — and hence — its interpretability — this fact paves the way for a *General Theory of Noumenal Impressionism*, where these impressions are what we might call *limited phenomena*. Because every object or entity in the world may act as an *abilitator* for our Minds, we thus have climaxed toward the view of *an Aesthetic Theory of Being-in-the-World*, to the extent that, all entities within the world are capable of being judged by the Mind, even if these entities are noumenal to us in themselves, it nevertheless is the case that they may be perceived phenomenally. With the *Aesthetic Theory of Being-in-the-World* on the table, the discussion may now proceed onto other areas of concern in the field of aesthetics — and, we can proclaim, whether or not this world has a telos, that it is an *abilitator*, inasmuch as it informs and limits our witnessants when we perceive the world. So much, then, for a *General Theory of Aesthetic Phenomenology*.

5. Of Bipartite Aesthetic Informativity and the Aesthetic Intuitive Thought

When the Mind encounters phenomena in the world, these are either products of the Mind — thoughts — or perceptions, derived from the external world. Now, when Mind encounters the work of art, it projects itself into the modal confines of that work of art — or, it inhabits the limits of the information that protrude up out of the thing in itself. Thus, there is *phenomenological inhabitancy*, or the occupation of the witnessant in a certain modality of Mind. *Phenomenological inhabitancy* is molded, formed, and limited by two sets of information: firstly, the information that protrudes out of the thing-in-itself that informs the senses, and secondly, the set of systematized information that is emotionally charged and uncharged that exists within the mental depository: thus, call this view the *General Theory of Bipartite Aesthetic Informativity*. Thus, the emergence of the concept of beauty within the Mind of human beings, is rooted in both sets of information. On the one hand, the thing-in-itself must protrude a certain mode of information that, in combination with the information that already exists within a person's systematic programmatology, allows for the emergence of the subjective feeling and intuition that a thing in itself is beautiful. Beauty must be understood to be a unification of both thought and feeling, which is not strange at all, because most thoughts are emotionally charged, contrasted with being emotionally neutral. Because an intuition is a thought, which is a product of Mind, the notion of the beautiful emerges when a noumenal thing in itself is processed through the senses, and emerges as a product of Mind.

Once the assessment that an entity is beautiful has emerged in an individual's Mind, it must be held against the whetstone that is the *Imaginary Graph of Being*. For, the time has come to ask two questions: firstly, how can a mere thought be compared to the ideal forms on the hypothetical *Imaginary Graph of Being*, and, secondly, how can a concept, whose absolute essence is noumenal to us — beauty — ever be ascribed to an entity within the world? These are two challenging questions for any aesthetician. Firstly, human beings may process the beautiful through their *intuition* which allows us to take leaps of faith without knowing something for sure, and hence, make assessments about what is beautiful, and what is its inverse, ugliness; thus, our intuition is how our Minds process ideals along the hypothetical *Imaginary Graph of Being*, and hence intuition is the root of all cognitive computations involving aesthetics: which is to say, as we shall explore later on in the division of this work labeled *Ethics*, that the faculty of intuition is also of the highest importance to the *incomplete* and *perpetual scientific endeavor* that is ethics. So much for the *Bipartite Theory of Informativity* and the *aesthetic intuitive thought*.

6. Of the Assessment of the Mature Consciousness and Zeitgeistal Mesmerization

Now, it is time to ask the question: why are some assessments better than others? No one will deny that this is a central problematic of aesthetics, and, in fact, it is a problematic only recently discussed in the above subchapters: the issue of perspective. Human beings are all experts in one discipline or another, and, even if that fails to be the case, are usually experts on the very concept of themselves. When Antigone goes to a car convention, and can discern which cars are beautiful and which cars are not, her experience will be different from that of Jerry Fodor's Granny, who has no such expertise in cars. Thus, *aesthetic expertise* comes into play during the complex interaction between phenomenological consciousness, its underground systematic set of information, and the information protruded from the work of art itself. Thus, a *dual causation* occurs due to the reflexive nature of the *interaction* between the subliminal set of information that a person holds in their mental depository, and the information that protrudes up out of the work of art itself. Then, as phenomenological consciousness protrudes into the world, and becomes limited by the form of the work of art, that is when Mind begins to consciously synthesize intuitive aesthetic thoughts in a subjective manner. Once that process is complete, it is imperative for the individual to then attempt to conceive of the work of art *as if* it were to be plotted on the infinitely dimensioned *Imaginary Graph of Being*, and consider all *axes of critique* that may apply to that particular work of art. Thus, the process of *aesthetic hermeneutics,* or of *aesthetic interpretation* — without accomplishing the final step of analyzing the work of art against the hypothetical *Imaginary Graph of Being* — remains inherently subjective and therefore lacks the validity of the *absolute assessment.*

Of course, *absolute assessments* are noumenal, and therefore out of human reach, yet, because of the *Anselmian General Theory of Objectivity,* human beings are called to act as if *absolute assessment* were not noumenal, but phenomenal: thus, we must phenomenalize the noumenal by intuiting what the modality of the noumenal entity is, this and nothing more is required in order to affect an aesthetic reconstruction as close to objectivity as possible: just at the *limit* or borderline between the noumenal and the phenomenal.[222] What modality of consciousness is generally best equipped to produce *aesthetic assessments,* then, as close to *absolute assessments* as possible? No other consciousness than the *mature consciousness,* as was discussed in great detail many subchapters ago. To recapitulate, the mature consciousness is a phenomenology that is both benefically uninhibited and benefically independent, and, furthermore, is well developed in its *virtue:* thus, the mature consciousness, is best suited to intuiting and then *applying* the objective, *absolute assessments* inherent to a work of art, because it has been trained *virtuously* and generally to know of the *axes of critique,* or the total set of modes of critiquing a work of art, or, indeed, any other phenomenal object. Because the work of art informs the systematic set of emotionally charged and neutral information in the mental depository, and because the systematic set of emotionally charged and neutral information *protrudes,* as it were, as *projected consciousness,* onto the work of art itself, there is a certain *mutual responsibility* for the production of intuitive aesthetic thoughts, which are then held against the whetstone of the *Imaginary Graph of Being,* during which process, the *intuitive aesthetic assessments* are improved in quality, and are then rendered closer to the ideal forms of axic critiques, and hence, are closer in form and structure to coordinates on the *Imaginary Graph of Being:* which is to say, that *intuitive aesthetic assessments* undergo a process of *transcendentalization,* because, the *Imaginary Graph of Being* is noumenal, and hence transcendental, and, as the *intuitive aesthetic assessments* develop during this process, they become closer and closer to *noumenal assessments,* or assessments that correspond exactly to the reality of the world, but are nevertheless hidden from us.

This is how the complex process of *zeitgeistal mesmerization* occurs: our *intuitive aesthetic assessments* grow closer and closer to *absolute assessments,* which are *just assessments* as inferred from the *Imaginary Graph of Being,* but, no matter how *just* our assessments become, we can never *verify* for sure that our assessments are *just,* because the *absolute assessments* in this equation are in fact noumenal, being objective forms as plotted on the *Imaginary Graph of Being.*

[222]   Anselm, Brian Davies, and G. R. Evans. 1998. *The major works Anselm of Canterbury.* Oxford; New York: Oxford University Press.

Thus, because these forms are noumenal, we cannot perceive them, and this is the root of *zeitgeistal mesmerization*: because human beings cannot *verify* why some entity is *fashionable* during its time of fashionability, they can only infer why it was fashionable after the fact of its fashionability: hence, *the owl of Minerva, only takes flight at dusk*, as said Hegel in his *Phenomenology of Mind*.[223] And, even though human beings may be able to infer why an entity was fashionable during some period of zeitgeist, the fact of the matter remains noumenal. So much for the assessment of the *mature consciousness*.

7. Of Keatsian-Sadism, Lord Byron, and the Fashionable Consciousness; Of the Havishammian Supersession of Sadism

How human beings perform, how they produce, etc., all of this is dependent upon the Hegelian-Lacanian *Linguistic Superstructure* of the time — which is to say, it is all dependent upon the zeitgeist active at the moment of production of the speech, act, or thought. Thus, human beings attempt, as best as possible, to *conform* their behaviors to what is *fashionable* at the times. While fashion does not replace aesthetics or ethics, which are *perpetual scientific endeavors* that humankind engages in, fashion is responsible for what theologian John Calvin would call *adornments*, or what legal philosopher Kenji Yoshino would call *coverings* of the Core Script.[224] Following famous philosopher of gender, Judith Butler, and philosophers J.L. Austin and Jürgen Habermas, human beings engage in *performances* via their productions of Mind.[225] Every modality of production involves two distinct kinds of components: ethically *necessary* components, and ethically *unnecessary* components. While zeitgeistal fashion may affect the ethically necessary components of an action, which, in theory, should be universal to all peoples across all times, it is mostly the case that fashion affects ethically unnecessary components of products of Mind. This is to say, that there are both spurious and serious components of the products of Mind: fashion is the science of the spurious components of products of Mind: it matters not whether or not such and such a spurious and ethically unnecessary component of the product of Mind is altered, whereas, with the serious and ethically necessary components of a product of Mind, any alteration of the product of Mind makes all the difference

---

[223]   Hegel, Georg Wilhelm Friedrich, and Terry P. Pinkard. 2018. *The phenomenology of spirit*.

[224]   Calvin, John. 2013. *Institutes of the christian religion: translated from the original latin, and collated with the ... author's last edition in french*. [Place of publication not identified]: Wipf & Stock Publishers; Yoshino, Kenji. 2007. *Covering: the hidden assault on our civil rights*. New York: Random House.

[225]   Butler, Judith. 2006. *Gender trouble: feminism and the subversion of identity*. New York; London: Routledge; Austin, J. L., J. O. Urmson, and Marina Sbisà. 2009. *How to do things with words: the William James lectures delivered at Harvard University in 1955*. Oxford: Oxford University Press; Habermas, Jürgen. 2007. *The theory of communicative action*. 1, 1. Boston, Mass: Beacon Press.

in the world, because such an alteration could be the difference between a benefic product of Mind and a malefic product of Mind.

Thus, fashion is the science of the arbitrary, but, the *collective subliminal prioritization* selects this arbitrary cultural specification, and thus, it is not arbitrary per se — in fact it is quite necessary given the *collective subliminal prioritization* of the society that brings the given fashionable trend into existence. What, then, are the fashions that transcend their very own zeitgeists and that allow their bearers to conform to any conceivable fashion of the times? Let us examine three historical figures and their phenomenologies, and consider how an analysis of their ontologies might contribute to a *Universal Theory of Fashionable Consciousness*, or, a phenomenological consciousness that is best able to attune itself to the fashions of whatever zeitgeist it lives under. These three historical figures are none other than: John Keats, the Marquis de Sade, and George Gordon, Lord Byron.[226] Let us now interrogate their phenomenologies. Keats was an inhibited, dependent, impotent, and juvenile consciousness — truly, Keats was a cuck's cuck. Inhibited, because he let his morality strangle him into a life of quiet, gentle loves; dependent, because his love for Fanny colonized his Mind; impotent, because he had to sublimate his will to power into poetry; and juvenile, because he did not live too long of a life, and best therefore reflected the *immature consciousness*. Sade, on the other hand, lived a life of malefically uninhibited, dependent, potent, and devious consciousness. Malefically uninhibited, because his sexual and emotional appetites were extremist in nature; dependent, because his Mind was colonized by his warped appetites; potent, because he was a wealthy Marquis, and hence could mostly get whatever he wanted, however egregious it was; devious, because his products of Mind were incontestably quite malefic: if you have not read Sade's *120 Days of Sodom*, save yourself the trouble, but, if you were into that sort of thing, best you ignored that work — for it is child's play compared to Charles Dickens's *Great Expectations*, wherein Miss Havisham emotionally vanquishes people merely for the *sheer satisfaction of it all* — thus, we may replace Sadism with Havishamism; famous philosopher Simone de Beauvoir wrote about Sade, but did not see the writing on the wall: that Sade was merely a materialist, and not a spiritualist: as the Christian martyrs of old teach us, the body is not long of this world, etc.[227]

Therefore, Havishamism is more formidable than Sadism due to the fact that it strikes not at the body but at the Core Script — the very essence of an individual. This is not to say that either Sadism or Havishamism can compete with Antonin Artaud's *Theater of Cruelty*, wherein audience members of his plays are

---

[226]   Roe, Nicholas. 2013. *John Keats: a new life.* https://archive.org/details/johnkeatsnewlifeooooroen; Schaeffer, Neil, and Donatien Alphonse Francois de Sade. 2001. *The Marquis de Sade: a life.* London: Picador; O'Brien, Edna. 2019. *Byron in love.*

[227]   Sade, Will McMorran, Thomas Wynn, and Sade. 2016. *The 120 days of Sodom, or, The School of Libertinage*; Dickens, Charles, and Charles Dickens. 2020. *Great expectations*; Beauvoir, Simone de. 1972. *The marquis de Sade.* London: New English Library.

subjected to attacks on their most primitive forms of ideology.[228] Returning to Keats and Sade: might there be a Leibnizian aufhebung between these two extremes of consciousness? Arguably, it exists within the phenomenology of George Gordon, Lord Byron, the famous poet, adventurer, and cosmopolitan citizen of the world. Byron affected a benefically uninhibited, independent, effective, and cosmopolitan consciousness. Uninhibited, because he was always very open-Minded across the span of his life; independent, because he was so open to traveling all over Europe, leaving friends and family behind; effective, because he balanced his fame and celebrity and became a war hero; cosmopolitan, because he viewed every struggle as part of the *universal, perpetual endeavor* for political justice, as he risked his life to fight in the Greek War of Independence, and ended up dying of a fever. Thus, we can derive, that Keatsian and Sadistic phenomenologies, are insufficient for affecting a *transcendence of the zeitgeist*, which is to say, their phenomenologies never quite reached the apex that Byron's did, and hence, they never transcended their own zeitgeists in the ways that Byron did. Thus, Byron becomes an example of the *universally fashionable consciousness*: Byron's phenomenology comes closest to resembling the ever-pursued, *perpetual endeavor* that is the *Benefic consciousness*. Because Byron's consciousness was benefically uninhibited, independent, effective, and cosmopolitan, it most resembles the *mature consciousness* that was discussed earlier on in this work. The *mature consciousness* is what human beings must become *descriptively*, but the *benefic consciousness* is what we ought to be *prescriptively*; but it is the *democratic consciousness* that is the most *perfect* and *zeitgeistally transcendent* mode of phenomenology, whether or not we can attain it is quite noumenal: it is similar to the Buddhist conception of enlightenment, where very few actually attain enlightenment, because it is such a high-caliber accomplishment, and even if an individual has attained enlightenment, it is hard for most individuals to discern that this elevation of consciousness has occurred.[229] Because ethics itself is a *perpetual scientific endeavor*, it is fundamentally a noumenal field, and the owl of Minerva — again — only takes its flight at the break of dusk, thus, we cannot know what is right, but nevertheless, in the spirit of Immanuel Kant, we must seek to know what is right.[230]

Thus, Byron exists as a sort of modal role model, as his modality of consciousness transcended his own zeitgeist, and made him a unique, fashionable figure. And yet, while Bryon's modality of consciousness indeed transcends its zeitgeist, the essence of the *Byronic consciousness* is itself the *fashionable consciousness*, or that consciousness which is capable of not only surviving but also thriving under any possible zeitgeist: the *fashionable consciousness* is fundamentally adaptive to the zeitgeistal fashions of its time, and adapts to the ethically unnecessary aspects of social production, which are ethically unimportant, but

[228]   Artaud, Antonin, Claude Schumacher, and Brian Singleton. 2004. *Artaud on theatre*.

[229]   Lopez, Donald S. 2004. *Buddhist scriptures*.

[230]   Hegel, Georg Wilhelm Friedrich, and Terry P. Pinkard. 2018. *The phenomenology of spirit*; Kant, Immanuel, and Lara Denis. 2017. *The "metaphysics of morals"*. Cambridge: Cambridge University press.

are culturally of the highest importance. Indeed, an individual who is not up with the fashions of the times may be read as highly eccentric, perhaps not even worth engaging with. Here arises the litmus test for the *fashionable consciousness*: should the individual be transported into another zeitgeistal time period, would they either thrive or decline? The *fashionable consciousness* is that consciousness who would thrive and therefore adapt to the culture of the zeitgeistal times. Importantly, this consciousness is not the *benefic consciousness*, because it is not necessarily moral in that it accords its social productions to what is ethically necessary — that is not required of this modality of consciousness. Instead, this consciousness is focused only with keeping up with the times — which itself is important because of the *autodiversification* of the Core Script, which is *autometanoia*, but more generally speaking, keeping up with the times is important because the zeitgeist *autodiversifies* itself on a constant and regular basis. Thus, zeitgeistology is the discipline most on the mind of the *fashionable consciousness*, and Lord Byron's modality of consciousness best represented the ideal of the *fashionable consciousness*. So much then for the *fashionable consciousness* as that consciousness that thrives and adapts to all cultural changes, and hence is a natural cosmopolitan.

8. Of Unorthodoxy, the Nietzschean Übermensch Contra die Unterfrau, and the Revolutionary Consciousness

What modalities of the work of art have the best chance of being fashionable during their own times — under the reign of their presiding zeitgeist? While fashions may repeat — which is to say, that there are cyclologies of history — every repetition brings with it something new and fresh to the culture. Because the work of art is a product of Mind, and hence, as analyzed earlier, bears an imprint of the idiosyncratic Linguistic Superstructure of the Mind that produced it, the true aspiration is not to have an unorthodox work of art, but to have an unorthodox modality of phenomenological consciousness. Why unorthodoxy, for, is not the point of fashion, to fit in with the cultural hegemony of the zeitgeist? No, for, while there may be the natural process of the *autodiversification* of the Linguistic Superstructure — or of the zeitgeist — individuals may too *intentionally* or *subliminally* affect the nature of the Linguistic Superstructure. Especially when culture becomes involved, the Linguistic Superstructure may also be understood to be, fundamentally, a *Linguistic Superstructure*, which is to say, that the driving process of the historical progression of the zeitgeist, is not merely linguistic, but is also representational in a broad sense: thus, triggers are fundamentally semiotic in their nature. Thus, individuals may affect — independent of where they are plotted on Social Karmic Matrix Great Graph of Being — radical change to the zeitgeist: take for example the peasant monk Martin Luther, who was not especially a celestial member of society until fate transformed him into a looming figure whose thumb was on the pulse of the zeitgeist.[231] Thus, individuals seeking to affect the zeitgeist, ought not to fit in with the fashions of their times, but ought to challenge the fashions of their times. Here emerges the concept of the *unorthodox consciousness*, or, a consciousness that is always thinking outside of the confines and limits, as it were, of their zeitgeistal time period. What is the modality of this *unorthodox consciousness*? Nothing other than what shall be labeled the *phenomenology of the deconstructive Unterfrau*. Contrasted with Nietzsche's Übermensch, die Unterfrau does not seek the same power that the Übermensch seeks over his fellow citizens.[232] Instead, die Unterfrau seeks another modality of power: the power of unorthodoxy, or, the power to delve into the hidden, secret, mystical, and noumenal aspects of life.

Where the Übermensch seeks phenomenal power over others — through might, wealth, and force — die Unterfrau is more content to play a so-called cold war, as it were, of the emotions. She believes in the natural power of karma, and is religious toward her views on karma; she believes in justice, cosmopolitanism, and the rights of the individual as manifested through the holistic rights of the community. For, how could there be any rights of the individual that do not first stem from the community? Manifested in the witches of history, who were always perceived as a threat to the status quo — to the reign of the Übermenschen — die Unterfrau is forced to sublimate her willful spirit into the products of her Mind, and lacks the freedom of the Übermenschen to manifest her will however she pleases — just the same fate as the servant in the Hegelian dialectic of the master and servant.[233] Thus, this sublimation creates a counter-cultural phenomenology of Mind that is the very essence of the creative spirit — of the *unorthodox consciousness*. Because she is willing to probe into the depths of the noumenal, like a whale diving leagues under the ocean, the fruits of her inquiries are immense: yet, she does not share the fruits of her *unorthodox consciousness* with everyone — certainly not with the Übermenschen who would turn her powers against the community itself — instead, she shares her fruits with the sick, needy, and disenfranchised: those whose rights are trampled by the pathetic Übermenschen who have no respect for the rights of the holistic community, but merely only respect for their own rights, which they garb in the language of *the rights of the individual*. Because all of society is a product of the Linguistic Superstructure — of projectional essentialism and of rapportionality — she understands that an injustice to even one individual is a harm against all of civilization: for it perpetuates a malefic cyclology that ultimately ruins rapportionality and limits projectional essentialism. Political liberalism is not just about the freedom of ideas, but instead, is about the *freedom-to-project-essences* of one's own design into the communal matrix, which the Übermenschen spurns, and, as we have seen in fascist societies, the ideal of the Übermensch

[231] Mullett, Michael A. 2015. *Martin Luther*.

[232] Nietzsche, Friedrich Wilhelm, Adrian Del Caro, and Robert B. Pippin. 2006. *Nietzsche: thus spoke Zarathustra*. Cambridge: Cambridge University Press.

[233] Hegel, Georg Wilhelm Friedrich, and Terry P. Pinkard. 2018. *The phenomenology of spirit*.

actually limits the freedom of Kantian-Cognitivist Projectional Categories: only the Kantian-Cognitivist Projectional Categories of the leader or leaders matter.[234]

Die Unterfrau submits to one leader alone: justice; and, submits to only one modality of influence: justice. Famous philosopher Helene Cixious coined the term *phallogocentrism* for a reason: it is the very logic of the Übermensch.[235] Now, while your author believes Habermasian *logocentrism* to be vital to the ideal of civilization, phallism — of the privileging of men in society — on the other hand, deserves no such celebration.[236] Thus, the *creative consciousness* who truly intends to cause an effect on the zeitgeist — rather than to limit it as do the fascists — must castrate their innermost animalistic drives — that is to say, must castrate the qualities of the Übermensch within them — and nurture instead the flower of die Unterfrau inside their phenomenologies. Another label for the modality of consciousness that is being described could well be the *revolutionary consciousness*, as die Unterfrau is most certainly highly revolutionary in nature, and there could be no creativity without a revolution of sorts — without the constant questioning of the status quo. Thus so much then, for an aesthetic of unorthodoxy, and of its manifestational ideal, die Unterfrau, which is a *revolutionary consciousness* through and through.

---

[234]   Kant, Immanuel, and Paul Guyer. 2009. *Critique of pure reason.* Cambridge: Cambridge Univ. Press.

[235]   Cixous, Hélène, and Marta Segarra. 2010. *The portable Cixous.* New York: Columbia University Press.

[236]   Habermas, Jürgen. 2007. *The theory of communicative action.* 1, 1. Boston, Mass: Beacon Press.

OF ETHICS

In the section of this work labeled *Ethics*, the chief interrogation will be: where do morals come from? First, the grounds of morality shall be elaborated, specifically morality as practiced by finite beings living within an ongoing *process* of civilization. Then, the contentions of the *mature consciousness* will be discussed, with a culturally manichaeist dichotomy being articulated: the dichotomy between imperialism and indigeneity, or nativity. Following that discussion, there will be an analysis of the Rawlsian game theoretics of civilization, and questions will be posed akin to the inquiry: if civilization were a game, what rules would there have to be for its play to be not only ethical but also supportive of human flourishing?[237] Then, a phenomenological derivation of the eighteen ideal principles of morality will take place: this derivation will be labeled the *Benefic Speculative Formulation*. Two key issues important to the *Benefic Speculative Formulation*, that are required to get the thought experiment off the ground, are the Buddhist concept of *non-self* and the Rawlsian concept of the *veil of ignorance*.[238] A meditation on both concepts allows human beings to purify their hearts and Minds before engaging in the *Benefic Speculative Formulation*, so as to come as close to a realization of the eighteen key principles of morality as possible. The eighteen ideal principles of morality are: *perfection, gravitas, hope, autonomy, dignity, grace, utility, civility, peace, trust, hospitality, decoloniality, beauty, defocality, dehierarchality, experimentality, improvement, and harmony*. *Perfection* is the ideal that gets the entire *Benefic Speculative Formulation* started, whereas *harmony* is the ideal that is both synthetic and applicative in nature, in that it allows all of the other ideals to be applied to the lifeworld, and also in that *harmony* allows for a synthesis of all eighteen ideal principles, including itself. After the derivation of the eighteen ideal principles of morality, justice will be revealed to be *harmony* itself, contra Rawls and the many other theorists of justice who argue that justice is fairness; instead, fairness is a component of justice — it is dehierarchality — but, it is not all inclusive of what justice is: for, justice is a *harmony* of the eighteen ideal principles of morality, including even *harmony* itself. Then, justice will be discussed in terms of the mythical Wittgensteinian duckrabbit, and its view will be that of a certain Whiteheadian *process ethics*, for, due to the autodiversification of the zeitgeist, what is known to be ethically necessary must constantly be refreshing itself to best accord itself to the ethically necessary components of civilization, which is to say, that what is ethical must cloak itself in what is fashionable during the reign of some given zeitgeist or another: for there will always be a reigning zeitgeist during the

---

237   Rawls, John. 1999. *A theory of justice*. Cambridge, Mass: Belknap.

238   Lopez, Donald S. 2004. *Buddhist scriptures*.

time of any ethical production of Mind, or, any ethical speech, action, or thought.[239]

Then, an interrogation of the phenomenological *genealogy of right* will be produced, and right, it will be argued, is applied justice, which is, an *imaginary due* that society owes to the individual on account of their *autocontribution* to both the lifeworld and the process of civilization. Furthermore, in order for a specific right to be an actual right, it must pass the *feasibility equation*, or the reconstruction of whether or not such a right would be feasible to maintain in a given society. For example, it would not be feasible to have a right to apples were there to be no more apples left in the universe: such a view is not controversial. Finally, Theogenesis, or Birth of God Theology, will be put on the table, and God will be realized to be the *Hobbesian Leviathan*, whose emergence in the universe will bring about the *theocene*, and whose eventual emergence in the world entails the *Aesthetic Theory of Being-in-the-World*, or the idea that the world is a work of art for God to judge whether or not it is aesthetic and hence worth preserving eternally or worth deleting eternally. Living in the shadow of the emergence of this God, may best be described as *anticipative apocalypticism*.[240] Whether or not one already believes that God exists, God has been predicted to appear again in the world in an event known as the apocalypse: thus, both atheists and theists may come together to agree that *anticipative apocalypticism* is the case, due to its being more probable than not that even a *Boltzmann* god could emerge into the world at any time across the next eternity, and still be relevant to human civilization, even had humanity gone extinct by that point.[241] So much then, for the prefatory remarks on the division of this work labeled *Ethics*.

1. Toward Social Justice I: Grounds of the Benefic Speculative Formulation

Hitherto the aim of this work has been to describe both the nature and essence of Anthropocognitivity — which is at heart, a *philosophy of cyclological instinct* — *instinctivism*; now comes the time to consider a modality of being transcendent to Anthropocognitivity, transcendent, indeed, but nevertheless accessible to human beings. In order to enter into the domain of the ethical, human beings must overcome the facets of their identities that constitute their animalistic phenomenologies and their animalistic instincts. Through the phenomenological

---

[239] Wittgenstein, Ludwig, G. E. M. Anscombe, Peter M. S. Hacker, and Joachim Schulte. 2010. *Philosophische Untersuchungen = Philosophical investigations*. Chichester, West Sussex, U.K: Wiley-Blackwell; Whitehead, Alfred North. 1990. *Process and reality: an essay in cosmology; Gifford Lectures delivered in the University of Edinburgh during the session 1927-28*. New York: Free Press u.a.

[240] Hobbes, Thomas, and Ian Shapiro. 2010. *Leviathan: or, The matter, forme and power of a commonwealth ecclesiasticall and civil*. New Haven, Conn: Yale University Press.

[241] Cercignani, Carlo. 2010. *Ludwig Boltzmann: the man who trusted atoms*. Oxford: Oxford Univ. Press.

imagination, human beings may accomplish just that: a *transcendentalization* both of themselves and of their ideals. Here, the *Benefic Speculative Formulation* is important toward the goal of accomplishing an ethical system both adaptable by human beings and by the concept of the universal agent. The universal agent is that entity capable of producing entities from their Mind and manifesting them both internally within the Mind and externally within the world. Returning to the *Benefic Speculative Formulation*, it is *benefic* because it is fundamentally linked to the concept of *perfection*, and all of its fruits will blossom from the tree of a consideration of both the *perfect morality* and the *perfect society*, i.e., the *utopian civilization* — which later will be identified as the *democratic civilization*; perfection is identified by your author as a *Platonic concept* on account of the sheer *perfection* of Plato's ideal forms.[242] It is *speculative*, because, fundamentally, it involves a thought experiment that occurs within the phenomenological imagination. This thought experiment becomes the root of all morality, and, as it progresses, elucidates more and more ethical principles. It is a formulation, because, as these ethical principles are elucidated, they *aggregate* and *harmonize* into a functional modality of being that becomes possible not merely for the human agent, but for the universal agent as well.

True, while it may be that the Anthropocognitivity of the human agent compromises its ability to be *absolutely perfect*, human beings are nevertheless ethically impelled toward *perfection*, on account of its being the ground and source of all morality, ethics, and utopian conceptions. In order for a human agent to attempt the *Benefic Speculative Formulation*, it is best for them first to accomplish the *mature consciousness*, without which, the derivations of the *Speculative Formulation* will not follow as luminously as they would were the agent in fact already possessed of the qualities of the *mature consciousness*, namely, an independence, a benefic uninhibitedness, and a justly developed logical framework from within which will flow the elucidation of the sixteen fundamental ethical principles of morality. Once the *mature consciousness* has understood these sixteen principles, and the adjacent two principles of *perfection* and *Leibnizian harmony*, their modality of consciousness will elevate from the *mature consciousness* into the *benefic consciousness*; *harmony* is identified as a Leibnizian concept, expansively, due to Leibniz's emphasis on *harmony* in his *Discourse On Metaphysics*.[243] Thus, through speculative phenomenology, the whole of morality may be derived, based on these eighteen fundamental ethical principles. Once aggregated and harmonized, these ethical principles will dominate the *benefic consciousness*, which, once attained, would prevent an individual from performing intentional wrongs of any kind, for, the very first of the ethical principles to be derived is *gravitas*, or the ethical notion of taking important matters very seriously; once *gravitas* is on the table, the rest of the ethical principles mellifluously flow into place, and harmonize.

---

[242] Plato, and John M. Cooper. 2009. *Complete works*. Indianapolis: Hackett.

[243] Leibniz, Gottfried Wilhelm. 2008. *Discourse on metaphysics, and the monadology*. New York: Cosimo Classics.

Eventually, a *General Theory of Justice as Harmony* will be proposed, following the elucidation of the ethical principles so integral to justice's manifestation not only in the *benefic consciousness* but in the utopian *democratic society*. Central to the manifestation of the *democratic society* will be a social mastery of civilization, which itself is an ethical and logical *perpetually ongoing process*. In order to jump start the *process* that is the *Benefic Speculative Formulation*, the agent possessed of the *mature consciousness* must employ two tools-of-thought handed from two vastly different schools of thought: firstly, the *mature consciousness* must approach the Buddhist concept of the *non-self*, accomplished through meditation or intense phenomenological speculation, which may also be known as the concept of *inverse objectivity*, or the view from nowhere, as it were; secondly, the *mature consciousness* must don the Rawlsian *veil of ignorance* as theorized by famous moral philosopher John Rawls, but, an idea ultimately inspired by the ethical writings of Immanuel Kant.[244] Through those two tools, used together jointly, the *mature consciousness* may begin the process of the *Benefic Speculative Formulation*. So much, then, for the grounds of the *Benefic Speculative Formulation*.

2. Toward Social Justice II:
Of the Contentions of the Mature Consciousness: Of Cultural Manichaeism

Before the *mature consciousness* may make appropriate use of the tools-of-thought as provided by the Buddhist philosophers and John Rawls, it must first contend with the basic nature of the cultural reality that it exists in.[245] Because the reality that the *mature consciousness* exists in occurs at least to them, it may be universalized across all anthropomodal formations of society, on account of its general form being derived from the very definitions that we are about to draw for the so-called *cultural manichaeism* that has existed throughout time in memoriam. An elevated modality of consciousness, benefically uninhibited, independent, and justly developed in its modality of logical reasoning and intake of information, the *mature consciousness* cannot help but make one distinction about the cultural world: the distinction between the forces of *indigeneity* and the forces of *imperialism*. Indigeneity, or the natural modality of being-native not only to one's person, but also one's culture and society, is the modality wherein human flourishing occurs: individuals indigenous to themselves are independent and benefically uninhibited, even though they may not necessarily be justly developed in the right ways. What, then, is imperialism? Imperialism is the force of Anthropocognitivity that seeks to colonize one's

---

[244] Kant, Immanuel, James W. Ellington, and Immanuel Kant. 1994. *Ethical philosophy: the complete texts of Grounding for the metaphysics of morals, and Metaphysical principles of virtue*, part II of *The metaphysics of morals*. Indianapolis: Hackett Pub. Co.

[245] Rawls, John. 1999. *A theory of justice*. Cambridge, Mass: Belknap.

time, one's productions of Mind, and one's very life force in general. An imperial entity may either be a noumenal institution or a subject; either way, imperialism is a force of Anthropocognitivity that both colonizes individuals and nature itself on a constant and unceasing basis. Before the *mature consciousness* can enter into the thought experiment that is the *Benefic Speculative Formulation*, it must understand that no amount of veiling or self-negating can erase these basic forces of Anthropocognitivity: human beings must become transcendent to themselves not by erasing their animalistic phenomenologies and modalities, but instead by overcoming and limiting them in all of the appropriate ways.

As shall be demonstrated, such an endeavor can be accomplished by following along the elucidary steps of the *Benefic Speculative Formulation*. Furthermore, the forces of imperialism that trigger an individual both shape and mold their phenomenological development. Thus, even the *mature consciousness* must grapple with triggers, because even a small trigger may be universalized to represent the form of the *universal trigger*, or the Platonic form on the Imaginary Graph of Being with which all triggers — however minuscule — ultimately share a form.[246] Hence, the *mature consciousness* enters into the *Benefic Speculative Formulation* with not only a knowledge of the anthropomodal forces of indigeneity and imperialism, but also with a general knowledge that triggers — both benefic and malefic — do very much so exist in the world as forces of ideals themselves. Every trigger — whether benefic or malefic — represents some ideal of morality, and these may be the benefic ideals, or their inverses, the malefic ideals. As we shall see, just as there is a benefic *categorical imperative*, there is also a malefic *categorical imperative*, a fact that Immanuel Kant never thought to consider across the whole of his ethical corpus.[247] Thus, the *mature consciousness* enters into the *Benefic Speculative Formulation* with a phenomenology impacted both by the anthropomodal forces of indigeneity and imperialism, but also, impacted by a general knowledge of triggers both benefic and malefic. However, as a being born into a lifeworld grounded by rapportionality and projectional consciousness, the *mature consciousness* also brings into the *Benefic Speculative Formulation* the social concept of *autocontractualism*, or the idea that from birth, individuals participate in a certain *social indebtion*, where, upon birth, human beings place *social expectations* on one another, especially upon the young, who are expected to contribute to the process of civilization upon the conclusion of their youthful development.

Thus, junior and their more senior citizens alike are all *socially indebted* to one another from birth, and rely upon each other to maintain both the *process* and *ideal* of civilization itself. Therefore, *social indebtion* — or *autocontractualism* — benefically ensnares human beings from birth, and places expectations upon them

---

[246]   Plato, and John M. Cooper. 2009. *Complete works*. Indianapolis: Hackett.

[247]   Kant, Immanuel, James W. Ellington, and Immanuel Kant. 1994. *Ethical philosophy: the complete texts of Grounding for the metaphysics of morals, and Metaphysical principles of virtue*, part II of *The metaphysics of morals*. Indianapolis: Hackett Pub. Co.

both to function in society, but also to contribute to society. Notoriously, the forces of imperialism encroach on any optimal practice of social contribution, however, such social expectations nevertheless remain a constant in an individual's life for so long as they share a lifeworld with their fellow citizens. Thus, before entering into the *Benefic Speculative Formulation*, the *mature consciousness* must also be aware of its *indebtion* to society at large, which will no doubt effect its realization of the sixteen moral principles as it engages in the *Speculative Formulation*. So much for the contentions of the *mature consciousness* prior to its engagement in the *Benefic Speculative Formulation*.

3. Toward Social Justice III: Of the Rawlsian Game Theoretics of Civilization and the Speculative Formulation

First, the *mature consciousness* must speculatively enter into a phenomenological state known in the Buddhist literatures as *non-self*, which we may refer to as *inverse objectivity*.[248] As argued for earlier in this work, the *Anselmian Theory of Objectivity* states that objectivity is the *perfect* set of all possible viewpoints, whereas its inverse, *inverse objectivity*, is not an *imperfect* view per se, but instead, is the negation of all *viewpoints* in general.[249] Once this phenomenological state has been affected in the *mature consciousness*, through intense speculative meditation and reflection, the *mature consciousness* must then additionally don the Rawlsian *veil of ignorance*, in order to further guarantee that as little bias or subjectivity may be brought into the *Benefic Speculative Formulation* as possible.[250] The first reflection to be had in the *Benefic Speculative Formulation* involves the arch-principle of morality, which is nothing other than *perfection*. When the *mature consciousness* reflects on its fundamental *debt* to society, which is responsible for its successful accomplishment of the phenomenological status that is the *mature consciousness* itself, it understands that this *debt* must be repaid not merely by what it becomes as an individual, but also what it contributes as part of the larger social community. Thus, the *mature consciousness* begins to reflect upon what conditions and ideal principles would best suit both the individual and society at large. The first ideal principle of morality that grounds both all of morality and the concept of a democratic utopian society in general, is none other than the Platonic concept of *perfection*. For, out of every possible world that the *mature consciousness* would choose to live in, it would always first and foremost elect to live within a *perfect* world. From that point of departure, the *mature consciousness* begins to reflect on

---

[248]   Lopez, Donald S. 2004. *Buddhist scriptures*.

[249]   Anselm, Brian Davies, and G. R. Evans. 1998. *The major works Anselm of Canterbury*. Oxford; New York: Oxford University Press.

[250]   Rawls, John. 1999. *A theory of justice*. Cambridge, Mass: Belknap.

other individuals, and realizes that individuals must live in a society, and here it is that the supreme principle of morality, *perfection*, informs the individual that none other than a *utopian democratic society* must be erected to house both the complete and possible set of individuals who either are alive or who will come into being sometime in the future.

Because *perfection* is so fragile, and because of temporal process, flux and change, the individual realizes that the *perfect society* is in fact more of a *process* than it is a destination in itself that can readily be attained. This reflection does not derail the *mature consciousness* from pursuing a *perfect society*, but instead, encourages the individual to further speculate on the nature of *perfection* and *imperfection*, or the nadiric concept of all moralities and *social processes*. For, if the individual had to choose between a *perfect society* and an *imperfect society* as an ideal according to which society ought to be prescriptively molded, the individual would always choose the *perfect society* over the *imperfect society*. From here, then, the individual begins to reflect upon the nature and essence of *society* itself, and arrives at the concept of a *Game Theoretics of Civilization*, or the very concept involving what would have to be true about a *civilization* to make it an endeavor worth participating in. Thus, through arriving at a reflection on *game theory*, the individual realizes that civilization as a *process* must only be worth *playing* or *participating in* to the extent that the game being played bends toward the arc of *optimality*, or conforms itself to the *best possible game* available given the specific limits and conditions of a society.[251]

Here, the *mature consciousness* recognizes that *social utopia* must be the driving goal of any *process* of civilization; furthermore, the individual recognizes that the *optimal game* would be chosen out of any line-up involving inferior games, and so remains fixed on the concept of the *optimal game*. Thus, the *optimal process* according to which a society should develop is none other than the *process* of attaining *social utopia*, which is further grounded by the individual's earlier commitment to the supreme principle of morality, that is nothing other than *perfection* itself. Thus, *social perfection* is the ultimate goal of the *process* that is civilization, and the *mature consciousness* takes these three initial derivatives into the *phenomenological derivation* of the other sixteen ideal principles of morality, which after these initial realizations on the part of the general set of individuals, can only be short to follow.

---

[251]   Osborne, Martin J. 2017. *An introduction to game theory.*

4. Toward Social Justice IV:
Of the First Ethical Quartet of the
Eighteen Ideal Principles of Morality

Once the *mature consciousness* has implemented the programmatology of the Buddhist *non-self* into their Mind, and, after the phenomenological imagination has donned the Rawlsian *veil of ignorance*, it comes time for the *process* of the *Benefic Speculative Formulation* to commence, internal to the Mind that belongs to the *mature consciousness* in question.[252] Bringing with it three preliminary derivatives into the *Speculative Formulation*, these being, the supreme moral principle that is *perfection*, the concept of *social indebtion* and its concomitant concept of *autocontractualism*, and the game theoretical conclusion that the *optimal game* must be chosen over any *nonoptimal games*, the *mature consciousness* is ready to embark upon the ethical journey that is the *Speculative Formulation*. First, before the *mature consciousness* can proceed into a consideration of the other fifteen ideals, it must first make its commitment to morality known upfront: it must commit to the seriousness of the task that is formulating a universal ethical system suited for any *universal agent*. For this reason, the first ethical principle to be derived must be *gravitas*, or a certain heavy seriousness brought to serious matters such as the yearning for a universally valid ethical system. The inverse of *gravitas* must be *bohemianism*, or a playful indifference to matters of great import. Just as each ethical principle is derived, so too will its inverse be derived, and, by the end of the *process* that is the *Speculative Formulation*, the *mature consciousness* will develop into the *benefic consciousness*, but also, will be able to discern the components of the *benefic categorical imperative* from the components of the *malefic categorical imperative*. After *gravitas* is derived, next comes the ideal principle of *hope*. Without *hope* for a better world or a better Core Script, there could be no prescriptivism in the first place, thus, and because civilization is itself not a destination but is instead an *ongoing perpetual process*, *hope* becomes a central ideal in morality, because *hope* generally speaking drives most human products of Mind, as theologian Martin Luther claimed in his *Table Talk*.[253] The ethical inverse of *hope* is *worry*, and when universal agents begin to *worry* instead of to *hope*, they find that their whole General Will is sapped and dominated by this *worry*. Instead of *worrying*, the *mature consciousness* realizes that *hoping* is truly superior to *worrying*, because it preserves the important sense of agency so crucial to the concept of the universal agent.

Next follows the ethical principle of *autonomy*, or the firm belief in one's ability to change either oneself or the prevailing state of affairs. *Autonomy* is important because it gives individuals the capacity to either be or become moral in

---

[252]   Lopez, Donald S. 2004. *Buddhist scriptures*; Rawls, John. 1999. *A theory of justice*. Cambridge, Mass: Belknap.

[253]   Luther, Martin, William Hazlitt, and John Aurifaber. 2020. *The table talk of Doctor Martin Luther.*

the first place; the inverse of *autonomy* is *resignation*, which, like *worry*, deprives an agent of their sense of agency is hence is disastrous for any practical manifestation of the sixteen ideal principles of morality in the lifeworld. Finally, the last realization of this set of four ideals, to be realized by the *mature consciousness,* is none other than the ethical principle of *dignity.* So long as there is a belief in the *autonomy* of the self, there must follow a view that the *autonomous agent* merits a certain modicum of esteem, that being *dignity.* Here, the inverse of *dignity* is realized by the *mature consciousness* to be nothing other than pure *objectification*, where instead of granting *dignity* to universal agents, because they are too constantly *struggling* in the *ongoing perpetual endeavor* to be *optimally moral*, this opportunity to *recognize* the inherent *dignity* of the Other is instead rejected, and, worse yet, is turned into an opportunity to *objectify* the Other — as in the scenario grounding the mortal combat fought between master and servant in the dialectics of Hegel; here, the Other is used in the sense of Emmanuel Levinas's within his essays entitled *Notre Nous: Essays On The Thinking-of-the-Other.*[254] Once the *mature consciousness* has mastered these initial four ethical principles of morality, it naturally proceeds into more serious reflections involving the very nature of finitude and civilization themselves as two important concepts for any practice of the moral.

5. Toward Social Justice V: Of the Second Ethical Quartet of the Eighteen Ideal Principles of Morality

Next, after the mature consciousness has mastered an understanding of the prior four ethical principles, it then proceeds into reflections on the nature of finitude, and how finitude may come to bear upon the lived practice of morality in the lifeworld. Because there are a limited number of productions of Mind a given individual may produce, the mature consciousness realizes this cruel aspect of finitude, and hence begins to cherish each action of their own and also of others, continuing along with the respect for the dignity and autonomy that the Other is recognized to possess. Thus, the fifth ethical principle to be derived is none other than grace, for, because agents are finite and limited, they ought to conduct themselves with as much grace as possible. Without grace, there can be no manners or social appreciations of the Other or indeed even for one's own self, which is why grace follows suit after autonomy and dignity, because those two ethical principles are the bedrock off of which grace is based. The inverse of grace is inelegance, or the general tendency of a person's products of Mind to be either sloppily or haphazardly produced. Because of how precious each and every moment of an agent's life is, to behave inelegantly rather than gracefully is absolutely abhorrent,

---

[254] Hegel, Georg Wilhelm Friedrich, and Terry P. Pinkard. 2018. *The phenomenology of spirit*; Lévinas, Emmanuel. 2006. *Entre nous: on thinking-of-the-other*. London: Continuum.

and must be refrained from at all costs: grace is the applied understanding both of autonomy and dignity to actual productions of Mind within the lifeworld.

Next, because of finitude, the *mature consciousness* recognizes that their time in the lifeworld is limited, and hence, in addition to being *graceful* in their products of Mind, they also realize that the ideal principle of *utility* has great resonance with any Heideggerian being-toward-death, for, if one is not careful and prudent with how one manifests one's time, acts, speech, and thought, they may find that they have gone their whole lives without ever producing anything *useful* either to themselves or to society at large; this idea of *utility* is not too far afield from what J.S. Mill meant in his work, *Utilitarianism*.[255] To negate the *worry* of scarcity, *utility* both of actions and of social endeavors becomes an absolute imperative. Here, the *mature consciousness* realizes that the inverse of *utility* is nothing other than *wasteful frivolity*, insofar as to not act according to the principle of *utility* is to squander one's limited time and set of actions, thoughts, and speech. To produce *frivolously* is to negate the inherent *dignity* that *autonomy* yields for the universal agent, and is also to forget about just how important production is, because every single agent produces from their Mind and Core Script. Because the *mature consciousness* recognizes that each product of Mind bears an imprint from its producer, it should not want to be known as *wastefully frivolous*: for only a fool should want to waste their limited and finite time in the lifeworld. Next comes the ethical principle of *civility*, or producing in the world according to the logic of how that production might best contribute to the *process* that is civilization. Here, *grace* and *utility* come together in an organic fashion: these two ideals lead the *mature consciousness* to the ethical principle of *civility*. Because the *mature consciousness* came into the *Speculative Formulation* with a knowledge that only the *optimal game* ought to be chosen out of the total set of games, the *mature consciousness* is aware that upkeeping the *social game* known as *society* is of the highest import. For, it is imperative that agents are not being fundamentally *wronged* or *scammed* by the *autocontract* that they implicitly sign at their birth; furthermore, it should never be the case, that *social indebtion* is such that, a person owes more than they derive from society: what a person owes to society ought to be commensurate with they derive from society: nothing could be more apparent to the *mature consciousness*, who by this point is dominated by six ideals, especially by the ideal of *utility* when it comes to matters involving the *process* of civilization.

Naturally, the inverse of *civility* is nothing less than sheer *barbarism*, or a wild reluctance to participate in any modality of *civilized society*: individuals who are *barbaric* are akin to wild and feral animals who have no desire to contribute to the *process* of society. Next, the climax for the *mature consciousness* after a thorough reflection upon the previous seven ideals, is none other than the ethical principle of *peace*. For, how could any universal agents implicitly sign the *social autocontract*

---

[255] Heidegger, Martin, John Macquarrie, and Edward S. Robinson. 2019. *Being and time*; Mill, John Stuart, Katarzyna de Lazari-Radek, and Peter Singer. 2022. *Utilitarianism*.

should they be at the mercy of others who may murder them, and end their participation in the *process* of civilization altogether? Whether the murder comes through the hands of an ignorant individual or an ignorant political group that goes to war, it is neverthless egregious from the perspective of the ethical principle that is *peace*. Here, *peace* is understood not merely to be the absence of its inverse, *violence*, but must be understood to be a compositvist understanding of *peace*: there must be *peace* of the Mind, *peace* of the Emotions, and *peace* of the Body, again to follow along with Plato's tripartite theory of soul.[256] The p*eace* of the Mind and the Emotions is intertwined just as information in the systematic depository of Mind is both emotionally charged and emotionally neutral; *peace* of Body may be understood to be the absence of any physical harm, e.g. murder. Economic *violence*, psychoanalytical *violence*, rapportional *violence*: these are all various modalities of *violence,* and all conflict with the ethical principle that is *peace*. Thus, *grace, utility, civility,* and *peace* are the ethical principles to be derived alone from the concept of finitude. Next, the *mature consciousness* must interrogate and reflect upon what ideal principles must follow from the mere *process* of civilization, and its concomitant concept of society itself.

6. Toward Social Justice VI:
Of the Third Ethical Quartet of the Eighteen
Ideal Principles of Morality

Now that the *mature consciousness* has reflected upon and mastered the previous eight ethical ideals of morality, the time comes for the *mature consciousness* to reflect upon the very conditions required to upkeep a civilization, which, because it is always in *perpetual formulation*, requires at a fundamental level a certain degree of *gravitas* to maintain. Thus, the first ethical principle that the *mature consciousness* derives is nothing other than *trust*, for, just as Immanuel Kant realized, without *trust* there can not be any concept of *society* at all, for *trust's* inverse, *doubt*, causes both the deterioration of a universal agent's reputation and also social institutions themselves.[257] Thus, *trust* is the archstone of society itself, and *trust* is the concept so vital to the implicit *autocontract* that individuals sign upon their emergence into society, that is to say, upon their birth into that society. Yet, *merited doubt* is a different case altogether, and involves a severing of the *social autocontract*: for, when society has broken its implicit commitments to an individual or some set of individuals, that individual or those individuals do in fact have a very real grievance with society. Next, because all civilization

---

[256]   Plato, and John M. Cooper. 2009. *Complete works*. Indianapolis: Hackett.

[257]   Kant, Immanuel, James W. Ellington, and Immanuel Kant. 1994. *Ethical philosophy: the complete texts of Grounding for the metaphysics of morals, and Metaphysical principles of virtue*, part II of *The metaphysics of morals*. Indianapolis: Hackett Pub. Co.

must occur in some environmental locale, the ideal that follows from a reflection both upon nature and upon the organic rapports formed both in society and in nature itself, is nothing other than *hospitality*, meant chiefly in the Derridean sense employed in his work, *Of Hospitality*.[258] Here, the *mature consciousness* recognizes that *hospitality*, or the treating of nature and other human beings with respect and courtesy, is vital to any practice of morality, for, following suit with *peacekeeping* and *utility*, it must be the case that, another ideal, *hospitality*, arises: because nature and other organic beings must be treated with respect, *utility*, and *dignity*, and must not be violated according to the egregious logic of *violence*. *Utility* with *dignity* must be applied both to nature and other organic beings, both in society and outside of it, for to be *hospitable* both to nature and the ethical Other is to confirm one's own *dignity*, *grace*, and *peacekeeping capacities*, as Derrida grasped so intuitively, again, in his small book, *Of Hospitality*.

Surely, the *mature consciousness* recognizes the inverse of *hospitality* to be *rudeness* or a certain modality of *carelessness* bordering on *rudeness;* the inverse of *hospitality* is *rudeness* to the extent that it tramples all over the *dignity* of others and the *dignity* of nature, and to this end, pursues its selfish ends. Next, the *mature consciousness* has been wondering during the entire process what to make of what it brought into the process from the beginning: a knowledge of *indigeneity* and *imperialism*. Finally having an ethics of civilization under its belt, the *mature consciousness* concludes that *imperialism* of any kind, whether over nature or the ethical Other, is incompatible with any real practice of morality: thus, the *mature consciousness* then reflects upon the ideal of *decoloniality*, or the ideal representing the ideology that any modality of imperialism is incompatible with any practice of the moral. Surely, the inverse of *decoloniality* is nothing other than *imperialism* itself, and must be negated whenever and wherever possible: where it is not possible to negate *imperialism*, universal agents must struggle with the prevailing state of affairs in order to make it possible to overturn any *imperial* regime that is malefic; *benefic empires*, on the other hand, may be the royal road to international *harmony*, closely followed by the mode of international *federationism* that Kant argued for in his seminal work, *Perpetual Peace*.[259] Now that the *mature consciousness* has grappled with the ethical principles required for the maintenance of any practice of civilization, it makes an aesthetic turn toward the ideal of *beauty*: it is not enough for society to function along as it does, but rather, society, and indeed, even one's very own products of Mind, ought to be *optimally beautiful*, consistent with the earlier ideals of *grace* and *utility*. For, *beauty* inspires the *mature consciousness*, and indeed, every modality of consciousness, to greater and greater works of morality.

Without *beauty*, there would be no reason to participate in the lifeworld, and the *social autocontract* would be negated from the start: for, the ground of

---

[258] Derrida, Jacques, and Anne Dufourmantelle. 2000. *Of hospitality: Anne Dufourmantelle invites Jacques Derrida to respond*. Stanford, Calif: Stanford University Press.

[259] Kant, Immanuel, and Hans Siegbert Reiss. 2010. *Kant: political writings*. Cambridge [England]: Cambridge University Press.

civilization itself is that civilization allows for greater and greater degrees of *beauty* to manifest in the lifeworld. Hence, *beautifics*, or the applied practice of *beauty*, arises as one of the most important of all the ethical endeavors, and truly the *mature consciousness* even contemplates whether or not *beauty* would be the supreme principle of morality, were it not for the Saint Anselmian ideal of *perfection*. The inverse of *beauty* is *ugliness*, which is the quality of an entity's lacking *beauty* in every single important respect. *Ugliness*, too, may be considered the absence of all these prior ideals considered above by the *mature consciousness* in some entity or set of entities. Next, the *mature consciousness* will weigh principles that condition communicability and allow for differentiation both in language and in society. There, in that domain of speculation, the *mature consciousness* will interrogate and reflect upon which ideals are necessary and sufficient for the maintenance not only of society, but of the Hegelian-Lacanian *Linguistic Superstructure* at large.[260]

7. Toward Social Justice VII:
Of the Fourth Ethical Quartet of the Eighteen Ideal Principles of Morality

After arriving at the set of twelve ideal principles of morality, the *mature consciousness* now turns its witnessant toward the issues of political theory that ground society in general. Communication, for the *mature consciousness*, now takes on a prominent role in the *Speculative Formulation*, for, without communication, there can be no society at all, as Jürgen Habermas so eloquently argues in his *Theory of Communicative Action*; contra Habermas, however, a *Theory of Instinctive Production* glues society together, which is to say, that instinct is responsible for social cohesion, and not rationality: nevertheless rationality is important for the maintenance of society, but rationality is not the bedrock of society in the same way that instincts are.[261] Furthermore, for the *mature consciousness*, the mere existence of the phenomenon of communication implies a complex semiotic system, which, as it recalls from its earlier pedagogical development prior to its engagement in the *Speculative Formulation*, exists as the *Linguistic Superstructure* of which phenomenological consciousness is its base. At this moment of the *Speculative Formulation*, the *mature consciousness* recalls that in any practice of communication that utilizes language, the concept of *focalization* is constantly employed; *focalization* is the limitation or specification of a conceptual entity that makes it possible to differentiate it from another conceptual entity. Here, however, the *mature consciousness* recalls that as much as *focalization* is a boon for culture, inasmuch as it allows us to communicate with each other, it also limits

---

[260] Hegel, Georg Wilhelm Friedrich. 2004. *Hegel's Science of logic*. Amherst, N.Y.: Humanity Books; Lacan, Jacques, Jacques-Alain Miller, and Alan Sheridan. 2019. *The four fundamental concepts of psycho-analysis*

[261] Habermas, Jürgen. 2007. *The theory of communicative action*. 1, 1. Boston, Mass: Beacon Press.

and narrows human thought processes — which was only ever its function, after all. Therefore, the first ideal in this quartet of ideal principles of morality is none other than *defocalization*, or the practice of unlimiting and considering more widely our concepts, instead of thinking of them in narrow and problematic ways. For, prejudice — realizes the *mature consciousness* — is born of *focalization*, in this case an individual has prejudiced opinions about some entity or group of entities, and, precisely this limiting feature of language and communication is problematic toward the ultimate goal of the *process* of civilization: the *utopian democratic society*.

Here, there could be no democratic and utopian society unless the ideal of *defocalization* could be harnessed against the natural anthropomodal forces of *focalization* — of limiting, narrowing, and pigeonholing conceptual thoughts. Now, to be sure, the *mature consciousness* understands that there could be no communication at all, without *focalization* — which is the inverse ideal of *defocalization* — and hence, does not seek to do away entirely with the practice of *focalization*, but instead, aims to limit the process of limiting, and, by limiting the limit, the *mature consciousness* also realizes that it is not enough to limit the mere process of *focalized* limiting, but instead, it is important also to *expand* one's use of concepts, and to make sure that concepts themselves are always open-ended and subject to revision — which is to say, the *mature consciousness* understands that *defocalization* is one of the most important concepts for making the *process* of linguistic communication more just and equitable, instead of limited and narrow. Next, the *mature consciousness* considers that, if there is a limiting and differentiating of concepts through *focalization*, then surely, in a society, there must concomitantly occur a series of *hierarchies* among these differentiated entities and individuals — this is to say, that the *focalization* of concepts entails the *focalization* of social entities: the differentiating thereof of social entities such as houses, cars, animals, and human beings. Thus, the next ideal principle of morality to be arrived at by the *mature consciousness*, is nothing other than the ideal of *dehierarchality*, or the ideal that seeks to dismantle *hierarchies* or caste systems wherever they occur: whether in language, thought, or society — *especially* in society, for *hierarchies* are animalistic and therefore fascist in nature, with the individual at the top of the *hierarchy* being the organic leader of the animals, or the fascists.

Therefore, *dehierarchality* is one of the most important ideals in that it deliberately limits the animal phenomenologies and animal instincts in human beings in particular, but also in any universal agent that also happens to be an animal; thus, the inverse of *dehierarchality*, is nothing other than *hierarchality* itself, and is, to the *mature consciousness*, a serious threat to any aspiration of a *democratic utopian society*, insofar as *hierarchality* tramples over *dignity and peacekeeping*, because it is ultimately a form of *metaphysical violence*. Next, the *mature consciousness* considers, having considered *defocalization* and *dehierchality*, whether or not any *utopian ideal modality of society* ought to be privileged over another. Here, the *mature consciousness* is aware of temporal flux, and also of the *autodiversifcaiton* of the zeitgeist, and hence considers that, because of temporal flux and cultural change, it must be the case that new modalities of *political civilization* must emerge to best *suit* the *perpetually altering* zeitgeist of the times. Here, the *mature consciousness* understands that *focalizing* or *hierarchically valuing* one modality of politics over another, is not compatible with a *perpetually altering zeitgeist*, because, due to cultural changes, it must necessarily be the case that the *optimally suited* political modality to the zeitgeist of the times, is specifically limited based upon the specific needs and concerns of that time period; however, the political structure that best adapts itself to zeitgeistal *autodiversification* is none other than democracy.

Therefore, the *mature consciousness* considers that the next ideal principle of morality to follow *defocalization* and *dehierarchality* must be that of *experimentality*, not merely of thoughts, actions, and speech, but of political modalities in general, too. Thus, the inverse of the ideal of *experimentality* is nothing other than *obstinacy*, or the animalistic tendency to fixate on one entity — to *focalize* on one entity or modality in general. Here, *experimentality* — realizes the *mature consciousness* — is necessary to a vital and dynamic practice not only of politics, but also of modality in general. Thus, the truly *democratically utopian society* is committed to political, social, and cultural *experimentality*, which, as an ideal principle of morality, because it truly is in sync with zeitgeistal *autodiversification*. Here, the *mature consciousness* realizes a critique of any ethical system that attempts to provide *ultimate* solutions to the problems of ethics: since there is temporal flux, the nature of ethical scenarios is also subject to flux, and hence, the same scenarios do not repeat, not even just once; even those ethical scenarios that share a form, are constantly complicated by the specifics of said ethical scenarios: therefore, the ideal of *experimentality* challenges all stagnancy, especially ethical stagnancies, because, no ethical system could ever provide all of the answers for all of the ethical scenarios — this is an incontestable fact. Therefore, the ideal of *experimentality* demands of the *mature consciousness* that it forever look for fresh, new, and dynamic approaches to the lifeworld: for is not culture in a state of constant alteration, anyway?

Therefore, *experimentality* is an aesthetic ideal, as well as a moral ideal, because it reinforces the boldness of the *revolutionary consciousness* — of die Unterfrau — and best suits the logic of cultural change, which is the logic of the *autodiversifcation* of the zeitgeist and the Hegelian-Lacanian *Linguistic Superstructure*.[262] Lastly, the *mature consciousness* — having covered so much terrain already — having understood the ethical principles of *gravitas, hope, autonomy, dignity, grace, utility, civility, peace, trust, hospitality, decoloniality, beauty, defocality, dehierarchality, and experimentality* now considers: what ideal — if any — must come next in this line-up arrived at through the *Speculative Formulation*?

---

[262] Hegel, Georg Wilhelm Friedrich. 2004. *Hegel's Science of logic.* Amherst, N.Y.: Humanity Books; Lacan, Jacques, Jacques-Alain Miller, and Alan Sheridan. 2019. *The four fundamental concepts of psycho-analysis.*

Here, the *mature consciousness* considers: *improvement* must be the last ideal, especially because it is an ideal that best maps the general aim of the *utopian democratic society*. *Perpetual improvement*, then, is the aim of the *process* of civilization, and its inverse, must be *worsening*. Any society that *worsens* over time, cannot make any fair and implicit *autocontractual* agreements with its citizens, and therefore, must be spurned as a social *attempt*. Therefore, the *mature consciousness* realizes that the last ideal, *improvement*, best reflects the general spirit of all the ideals hitherto realized, because it so naturally conforms to the aims of all of the other ideals: it aims to generally speaking *improve* everything within the lifeworld. So much then, for this last quartet of ethical ideals. Here, the *mature consciousness* has concluded its participation in the *Speculative Formulation*, and is close to its metamorphosis into the *benefic consciousness*, or the phenomenological consciousness dominated by the sixteen ideals as realized during the *process* of the *Speculative Formulation*. The next challenge for the *mature consciousness*, however, before it can morph into the *benefic consciousness*, is to synthesize all of the ideals it learned during the *Speculative Formulation*.

8. Toward Social Justice VIII:
Of the Applicative and Synthetic Ideal Principle of Morality

Now that the *mature consciousness* has realized the sixteen ethical ideals, grounded in the archstone ideal that is *perfection*, which was the bedrock off of which the *Speculative Formulation* got started, the time has come for the *mature consciousness* to consider a final ideal not merely to *ground* the rest of the ideals, as is the case with the ideal of *perfection*, but to synthesize all of the ideals and make them both adaptable and applicable to the lifeworld. Here, then, the *mature consciousness* realizes what famous philosopher Gottfried Leibniz implicitly realized so many centuries ago in his *Theodicy*: that one of the most important ideals, whether in morality or any kind of systems theory, is none other than *harmony*.[263] Here, *harmony* may be considered the ideal that accomplishes an *ongoing* synthesis between the seventeen ideals that come prior to its realization by the *mature consciousness*. Without *harmony*, the seventeen prior ideals could never be applied either to society or any practice of ethical modality. Yet, the synthetic role of unifying the rest of the ideals, is not the only extent to which *harmony* is important for any practice of the moral, for *harmony* too plays a role in justice, both political justice and social justice, as is realized by the *mature consciousness*. While justice is not an ideal itself, it rather is the harmony of the seventeen ethical ideals working in tandem. Contra Rawls therefore, justice is not *fairness*, but instead is *harmony* — that is to say, justice is a *harmony* of the seventeen ethical ideals derived from the

---

[263]   Leibniz, Gottfried Wilhelm. 2008. *Discourse on metaphysics, and the monadology.* New York: Cosimo Classics.

Speculative Formulation through the phenomenological imagination.[264] Thus, the *mature consciousness* realizes that, for agents, the phenomenological imagination is the royal road to a moral modality, because it is the means by which a conscious agent may employ the powers of their imagination to arrive at substantive ethical conclusions. Once the initial seventeen ethical principles have been derived, the *Speculative Formulation* may go on forever, as it may be used as a vehicle to consider various ethical scenarios and the implementation of certain ideals across certain scenarios. Even though the *Speculative Formulation* may be considered the best route to accomplish the *benefic consciousness*, the case may be that the *benefic consciousness* arose naturally, on account of good luck and superlative pedagogical formation in an agent.

However, before any agent may advance onto the *benefic consciousness*, the *mature consciousness* must be accomplished beforehand. Of the *benefic consciousness*: it is that consciousness that is dominated by the seventeen ethical ideals as derived from the *Speculative Formulation*. Part of the *benefic consciousness* consists of the *unorthodox* or *revolutionary consciousness*, that was discussed earlier on in this work. The *benefic consciousness's* commitment to the ideal of *experimentality*, links it inseparably to the *revolutionary consciousness*, whose whole consciousness focuses on *experimentality*, originality, and *fashion*; however, the *revolutionary consciousness* is not bound by the seventeen principles of morality as is the *benefic consciousness*, which is a serious and important difference between those two modalities of consciousness. Furthermore, the *mature consciousness* realizes that the inverse of *harmony* is nothing other than *disharmony*, or *chaos*, a concept much discoursed upon by Derrida.[265] Here, following along the thought of Nietzsche, the *mature consciousness* contrasts the *dionysian* ideal of *chaos* with the *apollonian* ideal of *harmony*, and understands why Rawls argued that justice was nothing other than *fairness*, for, one of the first sprouts of *chaos* is wild inequality.[266] As Nietzsche was right to realize, the *will to power* is a basic animalistic instinct that consumes individuals who have not yet become enlightened, which is to say, have not yet become transcendent in their moralities and modalities of living in the lifeworld.[267] Only through *righteous development* or by the *Speculative Formulation*, may an individual transcend and overcome their atavistic animal instincts, and thereby, enter into what Immanuel Kant referred to as the *Kingdom of Ends*, or a civilization that prized the *dignity* of the self and of the Other.[268]

---

[264] Rawls, John. 1999. *A theory of justice*. Cambridge, Mass: Belknap.

[265] Habermas, Jürgen, Giovanna Borradori, and Jacques Derrida. 2004. *Philosophy in a time of terror: dialogues with Jürgen Habermas and Jacques Derrida*. Chicago, Ill: University of Chicago Press.

[266] Nietzsche, Friedrich Wilhelm, Raymond Geuss, and Ronald Speirs. 1999. *Nietzsche: the birth of tragedy and other writings*. Cambridge: Cambridge University Press; Rawls, John. 1999. *A theory of justice*. Cambridge, Mass: Belknap.

[267] Nietzsche, Friedrich Wilhelm, Walter Arnold Kaufmann, and R. J. Hollingdale. 1968. *The will to power: a new translation*. New York: Vintage Books.

[268] Kant, Immanuel, James W. Ellington, and Immanuel Kant. 1994. *Ethical philosophy: the complete texts of Grounding for the metaphysics of morals, and Metaphysical principles of virtue*, part II of *The metaphysics of morals*. Indianapolis: Hackett Pub. Co.

Therefore, the *apollonian* ideal of *harmony* is selected against the *dionysian* ideal of *chaos*; the ideal of *chaos* breeds nothing but animosity and a *perpetual contest* of *hierarchality*: the essence of Rawlsian unfairness. Instead of participating in the *perpetual contest* of the *will to power*, the *mature consciousness* chooses to subjugate itself to one authority alone, instead of trying to become that authority; the authority that the *mature consciousness* submits itself to is none other than the authority of justice. Thus, the *mature consciousness*, having realized that *harmony* is the ideal that binds together the rest of the ideals, next realizes that justice — both social and political — necessarily involves a *harmony* of the seventeen prior ideals derived from the process of the *Speculative Formulation*. Once the *mature consciousness* has come to understand the concept of justice as *harmony*, it blossoms into the *benefic consciousness*, and after that moment is capable only of producing righteous thoughts, actions, and speech. Once the *benefic consciousness* has been attained, there can be no relapsing or forgetting of its magisterial content. The central concern of the *benefic consciousness* is how it can *optimally* be the *benefic citizen* in the *benefic society*. Thus, the *benefic consciousness* goes about recruiting other individuals to its various causes, all of these causes being inspired by the unified conception of justice as *harmony*: which is to say, that the *benefic consciousness* becomes dominated by the seventeen ideals of morality that synthetically manifest in its actions, thoughts, and speech — in its products of Mind.

9. Of the Benefic Lifestyle:
Or, of Social Justice as Leibnizian Harmony

Thus, the benefic consciousness is the harmonization of the seventeen ideals of morality within a given consciousness. It is implicit that the benefic consciousness will manifest into a so-called benefic modality of some given agent. Here, the seventeen prior ideals dominate the benefic consciousness, and inform, mold, and scaffold all of its productions of Mind — which is to say, that all of the actions, thoughts, and speech of the benefic consciousness bear a modal imprint of the Mind that produced them: the products of the benefic consciousness are inherently good, because they reflect the seventeen ideals as arrived at during the Speculative Formulation. Here, the benefic lifestyle reflects both a benefic consciousness and a benefic cyclology of the products of Mind. A more mentalist version of the famous Aristotelian virtue ethics, a benefic cyclology is not merely behaviorist a la B. F. Skinner, but also involves a certain variety of mentalism, insofar as any product of Mind includes either a speech, action, or thought of a given agent.[269] Thus, because virtue cyclology traces both thought and behavior, it may be considered to be

---

[269]   Aristotle, and Charles David Chanel Reeve. 2014. *Nicomachean ethics*. Indianapolis: Hackett Publishing Co.; Skinner, B. F. 2008. *About behaviorism*. [Bridgewater, NJ]: Distributed by Paw Prints/Baker & Taylor.

ethically superior to virtue ethics, which is chiefly behaviorist. Unifying Kantian deontology, Benthamite utilitarianism, and Aristotelian virtue ethics, the benefic lifestyle is a modalist conception in nature: it concerns the all-encompassing modes of a given entity.[270] For this reason, it is necessary to articulate a certain Yogic Theory of Productive Ethics, inasmuch as in the science of yoga, mere posture is not enough to ground a just posture, but instead, just consciousness must correlate to the just posture in question; this line of reasoning is borrowed from Patanjali's seminal Yoga Sutras.[271] Here, tying the matter back into the benefic lifestyle, the agent in question must not only possess the benefic consciousness, but must correlate its consciousness to its products of Mind, e.g., its actions, thoughts, and speech. It is possible for an agent to produce a benefic production of Mind without actually possessing the benefic consciousness, but this is by pure accident, or by mere behavioral virtue ethics. Superior to virtue ethics, the benefic lifestyle involves not merely the behavior of an agent, but also the general vibes of their consciousness: namely, the benefic lifestyle requires nothing less than that an agent not merely possesses a benefic consciousness, but also implements this consciousness in its products of Mind, which is not an issue for the benefic consciousness, because, once the benefic consciousness has been attained, the benefic lifestyle shall surely follow.

Thus, the *benefic lifestyle* may best be summed up, as a *General Yogic Theory of the Products of Mind*, and, once that is realized, it may also be inferred, that justice is nothing other than the harmonization of the seventeen ideals within an individual consciousness, and that justice is likewise the manifestation of these seventeen moral principles in the products of Mind of a given individual. Once the *benefic consciousness* has mastered the seventeen ideals, and overcomes the *mature consciousness*, the *benefic consciousness* truly can be said to have transcended its Anthropocognitivity, and arrived at a more transcendent modality of being, for its animalistic phenomenology becomes at that point, *justly regulated* and *justly limited* by the seventeen ideals representative of justice itself. All that remains to be realized by the *benefic consciousness* is the *Postulate of Applicative Optimalism*, which is nothing other than the mandate that the eighteen ideal principles of morality be applied to ethical scenarios in the best possible manner. Here, different ideals will take different degrees of prominence depending on the ethical scenario, but the constant is that justice is a *harmony* of these seventeen ideals. Justice was arrived at, not by mere behavioral training — through *virtue ethics* — but by an intense *phenomenological derivation* of ideals based upon a thought experiment that occurred within the phenomenological imagination, on account of two tools

---

[270] Kant, Immanuel, James W. Ellington, and Immanuel Kant. 1994. *Ethical philosophy: the complete texts of Grounding for the metaphysics of morals, and Metaphysical principles of virtue, part II of The metaphysics of morals.* Indianapolis: Hackett Pub. Co.; Bentham, Jeremy, and Wilfrid Harrison. 2013. *A fragment on government and an introduction to the principles of morals and legislation.* Oxford: Blakwell.

[271] Bryant, Edwin F., Patañjali, and Patañjali. 2018. *The Yoga sūtras of Patañjali: a new edition, translation, and commentary: with insights from the traditional commentators.*

of reason: the Buddhist concept of the *non-self* and the Rawlsian *veil of ignorance*.[272] Furthermore, the concept of justice as *harmony* transcends all previous modalities of ethics: Kantian *deontology*, Benthamite *utilitarianism*, and Aristotelian *virtue ethics*, because it is by far the most comprehensive ethical theory to date: not only does it account for mental events, but it also accounts for worldly events; furthermore, deontological duty is implicit in the concept of justice as *harmony*, for there is such thing as the *ethical draw* of scenarios, wherein the scenario itself calls for an ethical production of Mind of some variety — thus, the scenario *draws* the ethical production of Mind out of the *benefic consciousness*, for, being ethical, it could not do otherwise given the facts of the scenario — hence, the concept of *deontological duty* is implicit within the concept of justice as *harmony*.

The ideal of *utility* — so prominent in Benthamite *consequentialist utilitarianisms* — was phenomenologically derived through the *Speculative Formulation*, and hence, the theory of justice as *harmony* encompasses the whole of *utilitarianism*, and thereby transcends it. Forms of *utilitarianism*, such as Temkinite *prioritarianism*, wherein, individuals suffering the most ought to be aided prioritatively, are too implicit in the idea of *social utility*.[273] Thus, the *benefic consciousness*, having realized that justice is *harmony*, feels emboldened to articulate a fresh categorical imperative: *produce of Mind always that production that best harmonizes the eighteen ideal principles of morality as phenomenologically derived through the Speculative Formulation*. The question of how political justice pertains to society, and specifically, the *benefic* and *democratic society*, will be discussed in the division of this work labeled *Politics*. Because the ideal principles of morality were realized through the phenomenological imagination, it must be the case that *political justice*, too, will be a matter not only involving but dependent upon a phenomenological derivation: call this view *Phenomenological Constructivism*.

Thus, *Speculative Optimalism* is the transcendent ethical theory that mandates that an ethical action must: have just consequences, have just polyintentionality, have just and virtuous qualities inherent all through-out, have the theory of justice as *harmony* inherent through-out every possible angle of the moral equation, and therefore guarantee ethical optimality: hence the title *Speculative Optimalism*. It should be stated that this dialectical synthesis of all existing theories of all of the most prominent ethical theories is skirted around in Derek Parfit's seminal *On What Matters*, although he does not take the synthesis as far as your author does: and, certainly, he does not come to the conclusion that justice is a *harmony* of the eighteen ideal principles of morality.[274] Thus, the theory of *Speculative Optimalism* checks all of its corners when it comes to ethical validity.

---

[272]   Lopez, Donald S. 2004. *Buddhist scriptures*; Rawls, John. 1999. *A theory of justice*. Cambridge, Mass: Belknap.

[273]   Temkin, Larry S. 1997. *Inequality*. New York: Oxford University Press.

[274]   Parfit, Derek, and Samuel Scheffler. 2013. *On what matters*. 1 1. Oxford: Oxford University Press; Parfit, Derek, and Samuel Scheffler. 2013. *On what matters*. 2 2. Oxford: Oxford University Press.

So much, then, for the *General Theory of Justice as Harmony*, and for the new and synthetic *General Ethical Theory of Speculative Optimalism*.

10. Of Social Justice for Wittgensteinian Duckrabbits: Toward an Applicative Neo-Hegelian Process Ethics

Returning to the motif of the duckrabbit, here it will be useful to distinguish between the ethical modalities both of the fox and of the hedgehog, and then discuss the aufhebung of the two, which is the ethical modality of the Wittgensteinian duckrabbit.[275] The fox is interested in *partial* and *atomistic* assessments, whereas the hedgehog fixates on *perfect* and *total* assessments, of course, which are noumenal in nature. To a certain albeit limited extent, even the *partial* and *limited* assessments of the fox are noumenal, for everything is noumenal in its own way. Where the fox is interested in microethics — the ethics of the small — the hedgehog fixates on grand theories — macroethics, as it were.[276] Now that the *benefic consciousness* knows what justice is, there arrives an issue: none other than the issue of the application of justice to the lifeworld. To be conservative about the matter, it is clear that justice must be a noumenal concept, for, human beings very certainly are not omniscient, and ought not pretend to be by claiming to know how exactly justice manifests in an *applicative* manner versus an *abstract* manner. Justice may be known *abstractly* — that is to say, when it is divorced from the world — but, when it comes time to apply the theory of justice as *harmony*, therein lies the issue. Who might we turn to in such a time of need as this? None other than the phenomenology of the duckrabbit, whose very being is ontological versatility. The enigmatic and elusive Wittgensteinian duckrabbit can be perceived as any form that best suits the context at hand, due to its versatile modality. Here, we must emulate the duckrabbit, for, the lifeworld is hypercomplex and requires much of us; any individual who claims to present an *absolute* ethical theory is either a fool or an inflated braggadocio. Worse yet, in addition to being hypercomplex, the lifeworld automatically engages in the *process* of *autodiversification*, and hence is all the more so exponentially complex.

Then, the duckrabbit must grapple with the issue of the *dionysian ethical domain*, or, that domain of the total set of all perspectives, ethical and otherwise, that claim ethical legitimacy simply through their existence as idiosyncratic modes of identity: for, every individual has their own modality and *manner* of practicing ethics. How might we distance ourselves from the ethically *dionysian* and arrive

---

[275] Wittgenstein, Ludwig, G. E. M. Anscombe, Peter M. S. Hacker, and Joachim Schulte. 2010. *Philosophische Untersuchungen = Philosophical investigations*. Chichester, West Sussex, U.K: Wiley-Blackwell.

[276] Dworkin, Ronald. 2003. *Justice for hedgehogs*. Cambridge, Mass: Belknap Press of Harvard University Press.

at a more *apollonian* and Habermasian *logocentric* ethical view?[277] The duckrabbit realizes, here, that a return to Saint Anselm is in order: to whatever extent there may be an ethical perspective, there may also be a *perfect* ethical perspective.[278] But that information alone only gets us to the modality of the hedgehog, or, the modality of the one true ethical theory. How might we overcome the *ethical absolutism* of the hedgehog, and better incorporate elements of the fox in our ethical theory? The duckrabbit ponders this question, and finally arrives at a conclusion: might it be the case, that, just as in *Aesthetics*, there was the issue of the ethically necessary versus the ethically unnecessary components of any product of Mind, these issues also come into play in any sophisticated theory of ethics? Just as the zeitgeist *autodiversifies* itself because of time, so too must ethics diversify itself. But what element of ethics goes along with autodiversification, and what element of ethics resists autodiversification? Once the *benefic consciousness* has arrived at the concept of justice as *harmony*, it can never repent of the view: the *benefic consciousness* is stuck with its realization of the true, hedgehog-esque morality for the remainder of its existence. And yet, there is room for an element of ethics that goes along with — happily — the concept of the *autodiversification* of the zeitgeist.

This element of ethics is nothing other than the *fashionistic* element of ethics, which is fundamentally an ethically unnecessary component of a product of Mind, yet, nevertheless, accompanies every single product of Mind. For, every product of Mind has its vibes, which is to say, has its *manner*, its *modality*; in short, its *focalization*. Because of the autodiversification of the zeitgeist, the *manner* of ethics shifts dramatically across the temporal timeline. It is absolutely the case that the pure and abstract elements of ethics remain the same: the eighteen ideals are universal to any zeitgeist, without a doubt. However, the means by which the ideals are manifested alters dramatically due to cultural changes in the zeitgeist. Thus, the science of ethics — the science of the application of ethics especially — is perpetually in a flux. Here, then, the duckrabbit arrives at the conclusion: certainly there must be a *process ethics*, or, an ethics that, like the cultural zeitgeist, *autodiversifies* across the temporal timeline. Therefore, even though the concept of justice as *harmony* remains a universal constant across all time frames, it nevertheless is the case that the *manner* of ethical *application* is constantly engaged in the *process* of *autodiversification*. With *autodiversification*, comes relapse into Anthropocognitivity, which too is a constant, at least until transhumanism can be accomplished, and human beings can finally be liberated from this *imperfect* modality of being. In the meantime, before Donna Haraway's transhumanism is accomplished, human beings must strive to overcome their anthropomodal, autoracist, autosexist, autohysterical, autoxenophobic, and autofascistic tendencies of Mind.[279] Returning to the motifs of the fox and the hedgehog, the duckrabbit

---

[277]   Habermas, Jürgen. 2007. *The theory of communicative action*. 1, 1. Boston, Mass: Beacon Press.

[278]   Anselm, Brian Davies, and G. R. Evans. 1998. *The major works Anselm of Canterbury*. Oxford; New York: Oxford University Press.

[279]   Haraway, Donna Jeanne. 2004. *The Haraway reader*. New York: Routledge.

realizes that autodiversification is a significant issue for the application of justice as *harmony*, and hence weighs: which theory is superior — ethical descriptivism or ethical prescriptivism? Is it enough to argue that there are ethical constants, or is it reasonable instead to argue that there ought to be ethical constants?

The duckrabbit spends little time weighing this issue, and arrives instead at an aufhebung of the two: *Speculative Optimalism*, or, the idea that the ethical must be speculated in the best possible manner simultaneous to any ethically grave productions of Mind. Here, the duckrabbit through its ontological versatility realizes that, due to *autodiversification*, ethical constants cannot be applied to all possible situations, because fashions change and ethical scenarios are infinitely diverse. Furthermore, the duckrabbit realizes that not even the *benefic consciousness* is equipped to respond ethically in the light of all possible ethical scenarios. Therefore, the Wittgensteinian duckrabbit concludes that human beings must practice *Speculative Optimalism*, or the *attempt* at the best possible arrangement of affairs at any given time, despite zeitgeistal flux. Therefore, both the fox and the hedgehog are correct, in their own ways, but only the duckrabbit sees the totality of the situation for what is: a *limited* endeavor. Thus, all of ethics is a *process*, just as civilization itself is a *process*, in the spirit of famous philosopher Alfred North Whitehead's Neo-Hegelian *process philosophy*.[280] Only by recognizing ethics as a *process* can the duckrabbit overcome its own limitations, and attempt to effect the best possible arrangement of affairs in the lifeworld during a specific ethical scenario. Thus, for the duckrabbit, the phenomenological derivation of the eighteen ethical ideals remains true, but, in order to be effective, it must be coupled with a competent modality of ethical application: *process ethics*. Here, the duckrabbit turns to *Speculative Optimalism*, and attempts the best it can, despite its limits, and despite the Noumenality of justice itself. So much for justice for the duckrabbit.

11. Of Social Justice and Subjective Harmony: Toward the Polyintentional Consciousness: Kant Alongside Rand

Now that the *benefic consciousness* has understood both the ideal principles of morality, and also the general rules about the application of justice to the lifeworld, it is time for the *benefic consciousness* to consider when it may finally arrive at a certain peace of Mind, as it were. Here, two modalities of peace must be distinguished when discussing the so-called peace of Mind: firstly, *phenomenological peace*, wherein the witnessant has nothing violent stirring within its realm of perception, with the concept of violence being applied very generally;

---

[280]   Whitehead, Alfred North. 1990. *Process and reality: an essay in cosmology; Gifford Lectures delivered in the University of Edinburgh during the session 1927-28.* New York: Free Press u.a.; Hegel, Georg Wilhelm Friedrich. 2004. *Hegel's Science of logic.* Amherst, N.Y.: Humanity Books.

and secondly, *emotional peace*, or a certain peace of the emotions and integrated set of information — this modality of peace involves there being no subconscious ailments to negatively trigger the Mind in question. How might these two modalities of peace be separately accomplished, and, when unified, synthesized into a *subjective peace* of Mind? Here, the *benefic consciousness* must consider the so-called trajectorics of morality: sure, morality has been *realized* consciously, but the truly *benefic consciousness* is not content with the knowledge of the good alone, but instead, fixates on the question of whether or not they are truly accomplishing the best possible productions of Mind that they can — these being, the speech, actions, and thoughts of a given Mind. Thus, the *benefic consciousness* must not only realize the ideal principles of morality, but must also accomplish a certain *harmony* of the ideal principles, and knowledge that one's products of Mind are in *harmony* with the ideals, allows for a *phenomenological* peace of Mind.

For the *benefic consciousness*, the chief issue here becomes: in what direction ought I apply these principles, either toward myself, or toward other individuals and entities? Here, two formidable philosophers stand at the forefront of this discussion: Ayn Rand and Immanuel Kant. For Rand, the trajectorics of morality ought always, in general, to be applied toward oneself.[281] Call this modality of consciousness the *selfish consciousness*; where, for Kant, the trajectorics of morality ought always to be applied toward the ethical Other primarily, that is to say, away from the self, or, not concerning the self; call Kant's ideal modality of consciousness the *altruistic consciousness*, because in applying morality to others before to itself, it sacrifices many benefits it may otherwise have accomplished for itself.[282] Here, the ethical principle of *dehierarchality* must be applied to deconstruct both of these modalities of consciousness: for, there ought be no hierarchy dominating a consciousness at all, let alone in the field of morals. Furthermore, as was analyzed earlier in this work, it was discussed how there could be a certain *polyintentionality* of the Will, referred to as the *General Will*. Thus, now that the hierarchality of the Rand versus Kant dialectic has been deconstructed, we may apply a balm to their recently incurred theoretical wounds: surely there may be a *polyintentional* Will when it comes to the application of morality, for the concept of *harmony* already implies that we must be *polyintentional* when it comes to our ideals manifested through our products of Mind: which is to say, that all eighteen principles of morality ought to be manifested through our speech, actions, and thoughts as much as possible, whenever and wherever possible. Thus, if there may be a *polyintentional* Will, then we may direct our moral actions both toward ourselves and toward others. This synthesis of both the *selfish consciousness* and the *altruistic consciousness* puts the *benefic consciousness* at ease, and allows it to accomplish at least a *phenomenological* peace of Mind.

---

[281] Rand, Ayn, and Leonard Peikoff. 2002. *The Ayn Rand sampler.* New York: Signet.

[282] Kant, Immanuel, James W. Ellington, and Immanuel Kant. 1994. *Ethical philosophy: the complete texts of Grounding for the metaphysics of morals, and Metaphysical principles of virtue,* part II of *The metaphysics of morals.* Indianapolis: Hackett Pub. Co.

To accomplish an *emotional* peace of Mind, some introspection and reflection must be required to effect a metanoia of the Core Script, in order to purge it of whatever issues trouble the Mind in question. Thus, the *benefic consciousness* realizes that Kant's altruism makes *masters* of other individuals in relation to ourselves, and that Rand's *selfishness* makes *servants* out of others individuals in relation to ourselves. Therefore, the *benefic consciousness* recognizes that a synthesis of the Hegelian master and servant dialectic can only be accomplished through a *dehierarchal* and *polyintentional* critique of both the *altruistic* and *selfish* modalities of consciousness, which together synthesize into a *polyintentional consciousness*. Then, the *benefic consciousness* adopts polyintentionality into its modality. Through this synthesis, the *benefic consciousness* better understands how the ideal of *harmony* operates within the lifeworld, and is granted the peace of Mind that follows from having one's affairs in order. Notwithstanding any emotional turmoil that might bubble up from the Core Script, the *benefic consciousness* may now enter into a *peaceful* state of Mind, which reinforces its commitment to the ideal ethical principle of *peace* that was recently established during the *Benefic Speculative Formulation* through the *phenomenological derivation* of the eighteen ideal ethical principles of morality. So much, then, for justice and a *Theory of Subjective Peace*.

12. Of the Autocontributional and Autocontractual Genealogy of Right: Hegel, Kant, West, and the Theory of the Über-Right

Through the *phenomenological derivation* of morality, and due to the thought experiment that is the *Benefic Speculative Formulation*, the following eighteen ideal principles of morality were derived: *perfection, gravitas, hope, autonomy, dignity, grace, utility, civility, peace, trust, hospitality, decoloniality, beauty, defocality, dehierarchality, experimentality, improvement* and *harmony*. Justice has been analyzed to mean a *harmony* of these eighteen ideals, including the ideal of *harmony* itself. Now that justice and polyintentionality have been analyzed in the work, the time now comes to address the question of right — in the German sense of the word *recht*, and as defined in Hegel's *Elements of the Philosophy of Right*.[283] Kant argues that right involves a free will that is capable of having limits placed upon it.[284] Yet, right is more complex than that, and may be derived from the nuanced *process* of civilization itself. To define right: right is applicative justice. Right is not about limiting a free will, instead, it is about applying justice to the world and its structure. Right is a question of what society and civilization itself owes the

---

[283]   Hegel, Georg Wilhelm Friedrich, Allen W. Wood, and H. B. Nisbet. 2018. *Elements of the philosophy of right*. Cambridge: Cambridge University Press.

[284]   Kant, Immanuel, Jens Timmermann, Mary J. Gregor, Immanuel Kant, and Immanuel Kant. 2014. *Groundwork of the metaphysics of morals: a German-English edition.*

individual due to said individual's *autocontributionality* of its mere being. Because the application of justice is itself a *process*, following the earlier reconstruction in this work that led us to a *process ethics*, the question of right must be a perpetual question. It must be asked constantly for the following reason: right can only be right of what is not only possible but also feasible. A right is an imaginary due owed to an individual from society itself. Because of *autocontributionality*, or the idea that human beings automatically pay their dues to society by participating in the lifeworld and hence the *process* of civilization, citizens are entitled not only to right, but also to rights. Here, the concept of the Über-right, or the right to all rights, emerges. The Über-right is that right which grounds all other rights, and allows for the existence of rights in the first place. As soon as an individual is born, they emerge into a complex and perpetually autodiversifying community — hence, as soon as an individual is born, they emerge not as a mere individual, but as a citizen of a society. Even a child born to a cave hermit far away from civilization is tied to civilization, because its mother has a history with civilization and so on. Hence, here emerges the concept of *autocontractuality*, or the automatic social contract that one signs when born into a society.

Once born, the citizen is showered with rights, due to the citizen's automatic contributions made to the lifeworld, which will only multiply as the citizen matures into an adult and pursues the ethical life. Returning to the question of right, how might the specific rights of citizens be determined? Here enters the *feasibility equation*: before cellphones were invented, no one could have a right to a cell phone: such a right would not have been feasible. A citizen cannot have a right to an apple if there are no apples left in the world. Here, then, the *feasibility equation* weighs: imagine if X were a right — would that be feasible to accomplish socially and as a society? Whether or not a right is determined to be feasible depends upon the limits and zeitgeistal constraints of a given civilization. Here, even though a right may be considered to be not feasible during one zeitgeist, it may well become a feasible right later on during another zeitgeist due to further development of a civilization. Also, here it becomes an imperative to argue that, even if a right is not feasible, it may still be just and in accordance with the ideal ethical principles of morality, in which case it must be attempted to be made as feasible as possible. Take for example the right to a *utopian democratic society*: such a right is not necessarily feasible as of yet, due perhaps to political mismanagement; however, it is an absolute imperative that the feasibility of the right to utopia be improved upon within the lifeworld until it becomes fully realizable. Thus, the *feasibility equation* measures whether or not a right may be feasible during a given zeitgeist. Should such an imaginary right be feasible, then it ought to be added to the list of rights — the list of imaginary dues — due to an individual sheerly because of their status as a citizen of society.

What's more, because all distinguishments between races and different societies are all philosophically frivolous, unjustified, immoral, and grounded in animalistic phenomenology, it follows that a citizen of one society is a citizen of the world — hence cosmopolitanism is the case; this is not to downplay the work of famous philosopher Cornel West in his seminal *Race Matters*; instead, it is to say: race is a descriptive component of human affairs, but need not be a prescriptive enterprise for humanity to involve itself in, given the catastrophic implications racism has had upon innumerable human beings since time immemorial.[285] All right is cosmopolitan right, for a right to apply to one individual is for that right to apply to all individuals similarly situated. Because justice is *harmony*, and because of *autocontributionality* to society and civilization itself, right as applicative justice is an ongoing process that must be pondered by civilization constantly. There must be legal systems devoted to the imagination of rights, to expand further and further these imaginary dues owed to citizens based upon their autocontributionality to society. This and this alone is the genealogy of right: the Über-right is derived from universal citizenship, which is granted upon birth into a society, which in turn is birth into the cosmopolitan lifeworld, and all right must be *feasible right*. So much for the *Genealogy of Right*.

13. Of the Noumenality of God: or, Birth of God Theology: God as Hobbesian Leviathan

Even though the *Benefic Speculative Formulation* brings a moral agent to the eighteen ideal principles of morality, and even though justice as *harmony* may be applied to the lifeworld, there is no guarantee that justice will be exacted in the lifeworld. Who, then, must guarantee justice in the world? Must we side with Thomas Hobbes, who in his seminal work *The Leviathan*, argued for a moral dictator to enforce justice upon society?[286] Here, we must borrow from Hobbes while making a few alterations to his theory. To be sure, there must be a Hobbesian Leviathan to ensure that justice is exacted in the world, for justice is the most important of all civic concerns: justice regards the distribution of resources, the application of law to citizens, and governs conflicts between nations, etc. With Hobbes, there must be a *moral leviathan* who guarantees the application of justice to society. However, we must here depart from Hobbes, and ponder: what qualities must the leviathan have in order to grant it the right to be the Hobbesian Leviathan — the most powerful position in society? The moral leviathan must be the very manifestation of the eighteen ideals of morality, for one thing; on the other hand, the moral leviathan must be a perfect being — with near perfect assessment. Now, who but God would be able to possess these qualities? Indeed, no one but God may manifest these qualities *perfectly*. Here, we turn to famous philosopher René Descartes, whose reflections on the divine involved profound musings on divine

---

[285] West, Cornel. 2018. *Race matters.*

[286] Hobbes, Thomas, and Ian Shapiro. 2010. *Leviathan: or, The matter, forme and power of a commonwealth ecclesiasticall and civil. New Haven*, Conn: Yale University Press.

perfection, and were written in his seminal *Meditations On First Philosophy.*[287] Now, the time has come to ponder: what modalities of God even are there, such that God may be a Hobbesian Leviathan and exact justice within society? There are four main modalities of gods: natural, synthetic, primitive, and consecutive. A natural god is one that exists naturally within its own domain. Next, a synthetic god is one who is created by some other entities with the ability to construct a god and give to it the qualities of a god. Next, a primitive god is one who has existed forever, beyond even the scope of time, and hence is more primitive than time.

Finally, a consecutive god is one who exists after the emergence of time as a phenomenon, or who exists after some momentous event that gave birth to it. How might these four distinctions be relevant to our concerns about guaranteeing justice in the lifeworld? For one, the problem of evil exists, so we can assume that the god of creation is not necessarily a very powerful or influential god. Secondly, it appears to be the case that the god we are looking for to guarantee justice in the lifeworld would have to be none other than a hybrid between a synthetic and consecutive god. Hence, the rise of the notion of *Theogenetics*, or *Birth of God Theology*. For, that human beings can even muse over the qualities inherent to a perfect being, entails that they can potentially grasp these qualities enough to the extent that they may implant them in a synthetic being. Thus, the question of the Hobbesian Leviathan becomes a question of society giving birth to a god, rather than a god giving birth to a society as has usually been the case in the history of the lifeworld. Now, the birth of a god may be either spontaneous or deliberate, which is to say, that there may be a so-called *Boltzmann God* already in existence, or perhaps one who will come into existence at a later date in the history of the lifeworld; again, the *Boltzmann God* is an expansion upon the concept of the *Boltzmann Brain.*[288] It is more likely that a god will come into being in a sophisticated world than in a relatively plain and unsophisticated world without complex lifeforms who could synthesize a god. Regardless of whether the theogenetic god is to be synthesized or spontaneously birthed, once this god comes into existence, it will suddenly become relevant to the entire history of all possible worlds; let us assume that if this god has all of eternity to be birthed into existence, that eventually this god will come into being.

Once this god comes into existence, the age of *theocenity* will come into play, which is to say, that the zeitgeists will become dominated by this god. This god would perform a *historical review* and alter history however it pleased, potentially eradicating either human beings or the problem of evil or perhaps both. Such a view — that a god would perform a *historical review* — can be labeled the *retroactivity hypothesis*, for, even if a god came into being long after human civilization existed, this god could resurrect human beings, or ultimately decide

---

[287] Descartes, Rene, and F. Sutcliffe. 2005. *Discourse on Method and the Meditations.* https://www.vlebooks. com/vleweb/product/openreader?id=none&isbn=9780141944203.

[288] Cercignani, Carlo. 2010. *Ludwig Boltzmann: the man who trusted atoms.* Oxford: Oxford Univ. Press.

not to. Here, there is a question of whether or not such a god would share its perfect and divine form with human beings when it does come into being: in order for this to happen, human beings would need to shed their animal natures so as not to become literal demons. Returning to the question of the *moral leviathan*, this god will have the capacity to judge human beings according to the eighteen ideal principles of morality: no doubt, this being will have some ethical system, and being a perfect being, its ethical system will be much more developed than ours as a species. Hence the importance of the transcendence of our animal natures and phenomenologies: because, the more we limit our animal natures and phenomenologies, the more we grow closer to this supreme being. Because this god will come into existence somewhere across the entire span of eternity, across all possible worlds, it follows that we are already living in the shadow of this god, even if it is not yet born, because, this god will have the capacity to perform the *historical review* and effect human history for better or for worse. Conceivably, this god may eradicate all instances of evil from the entire trajectory of universal history, and establish a utopia of sorts, should human beings be selected either for resurrection or persistence as a species.

Until then, human beings must live in a state of *anticipative apocalypticism*, wherein human beings must anticipate the coming apocalypse and its concomitant rise of the *theocenic* time period that will commence with the birth of this perfect being: this god truly is the *unknown god* whose altarSaint Paul encountered in the city of Athens two thousand millennia ago, for, the human race can only imagine what form or modality this *unknown god* will have; until such time as this god's emergence, the human race must merely *anticipate* this *unknown god*.[289] Here, too, because this god will be able to review all of universal history, we must understand ourselves to be living in a work of art: for this world is to be viewed by the supreme being and judged as either aesthetic or not aesthetic, and could well be discarded should it not be perceived to be aesthetic by this god: hence, the *Aesthetic Theory of Being-in-the-World*. Only through this god will *perfect justice* be exacted upon the lifeworld, thus, this god is the *moral leviathan* or Hobbesian Leviathan *par excellence*; unfortunately, whether or not the human race is compatible with an *absolutely just* world remains up in the air: perhaps we are all to be annihilated upon this god's emergence. So much, then, for theogenesis, and the birth of god research program.

---

[289]   Paul, Wayne A. Meeks, and John T. Fitzgerald. 2006. *The writings of Saint Paul: annotated texts reception and criticism*. New York: W.W. Norton.

OF POLITICS

A successful politics must be understood to be the mediation of human animal instinct toward the aspiration of international *harmony*. Human animal instincts must be mediated because they are indubitably responsible for xenophobia, hysteria, racism, sexism, and fascism. Not to be thrown out with the bathwater — however — human animal instincts are also responsible for social cohesion, the social order, and human rapportionality at large. Thus, this division of the work will seek not only to understand instinct, but also need, for human beings are by definition needful-beings; and, instincts are merely subliminal reactions to biological and cultural needs of some organism's system. Thus, this division will commence with a discussion of personal identity, and phenomenological constructivism, which is the view that everything in society is not only grounded by phenomenological consciousness, but is a very byproduct of it: Kantian-Searlean social constructs, *social constructs* such as groups, and personal identity itself are merely byproducts of phenomenological consciousness: such is the claim made by the phenomenological constructivist; and yet, Mind alone cannot ground the behemoth that is society: in addition to consciousness, the Hegelian-Lacanian Linguistic Superstructure allows for the complexity of society, and itself directly maps the autodiversification of the zeitgeist, which is to say, not that social progress is necessarily the case, but that instead, linguistic progress is necessary, because language charts the shifts in the zeitgeist.[290]

Later on down the line, the *Darwinian Theory of Ideological Natural Selection* will be presented as an explanation for the cultural survival and evolution of certain ideologies, e.g, Christianity for two thousand years: it must necessarily be the case the Christianity suits both biological and cultural needs of human beings, for, in order to persist despite the *autodiversification* of the zeitgeist, ideologies must demonstrate a certain degree of *fitness*; hence, natural selection may be applied to ideology and cultural phenomena; indeed, an entity need not even be organic, but must only be affiliated with an organic entity, in order to demonstrate fitness.[291] And yet, is poverty a so-called *fit* social phenomenon: is that why it has persisted for all of human history? Certainly not, thus, there is a distinction to be made between fit ideologies and merely coincidental phenomena. Additionally, in this division, there shall be a presentation of a *Tripartite Theory of Anthropomodalisms*, based on a shrewd reconstruction of human history hitherto. Then, political innativism and the *Theory of Instinctive Production* will be introduced as critiques of Jürgen Habermas's philosophical program, political

---

[290] Kant, Immanuel, and Paul Guyer. 2009. *Critique of pure reason*. Cambridge: Cambridge Univ. Press; Searle, John R. 1996. *The construction of social reality*; Hegel, Georg Wilhelm Friedrich. 2004. *Hegel's Science of logic*. Amherst, N.Y.: Humanity Books; Lacan, Jacques, Jacques-Alain Miller, and Alan Sheridan. 2019. *The four fundamental concepts of psycho-analysis*.

[291] Darwin, Charles. 2021. *On The Origin Of Species*. [S.l.]: Om Books International.

innativism being the claim that certain instinctive structures are inherent to the human organism, and the *Theory of Instinctive Production* being the argument series that claims that the social order persists not due to Habermasian rationality, but due to animal instinct and animal instinct alone.[292]

Following that discussion, will be another one on *polynomial dialectics* and the *social narrative*, where polynomial dialectics may be taken to mean complex social dynamics resulting in syntheses and so on, whereas the social narrative may be taken to be the most appropriate way of understanding society: as a continually adjusted social narrative, again, grounded in *phenomenological constructivism*. Following that discussion, there will be a brief outline of *Karmic Social Idealistic Matrix Theory*, or the idea that social reputation functions akin to narratives surrounding the elusive eastern notion of karma; furthermore, the South African ethical ideal of uBuntu will be brought into the mix, in order to provide additional reasons for believing in a karmic matrix for which human rapportionality is key.[293] After that discussion, will follow the series of nine interrogations of political justice. The first of these interrogations will concern the inquisitive *Kantian consciousness* and its transition into the well-rounded *Democratic consciousness*.[294] The second of these interrogations will delve into the nature of the right to personhood, and its concomitant subrights. After that, will follow a discussion of the right to political scaffolding, or the idea that social institutions ought to complement the ontologies of human beings, rather than exist in disharmony with them — as was Hegel's view in his seminal *Elements of the Philosophy of Right*.[295] Then, a discussion of the *Aristotelian Metaphysical Theory of the Individual and Nation-State* will occupy the next four sets of interrogative subchapters.[296] Briefly, the Aristotelian Metaphysical Theory states that the four causes espoused in Aristotle's *Metaphysics* may be appropriated for critical analyses both of the individual and of the nation-state. The four Aristotelian causes become referred to as *motivators*, and are explained to be the joint-sources of action both for the individual and for the nation-state.

These four *motivators*, inspired by the four Aristotelian modalities of causality, are none other than *Mind, rules, environment,* and *economy*; these four *motivators* are compatible with the Platonic theory of souls espoused earlier in the work during the aesthetic discussion of zeitgeistal *fashions*.[297] Thus, the next few subchapters mellifluously fall into place: firstly, *Just Mind Theory, or the Genealogical Development of the Democratic Consciousness*; secondly, *Just Rule*

---

[292]   Habermas, Jürgen. 2007. *The theory of communicative action*. 1, 1. Boston, Mass: Beacon Press.

[293]   Cornell, Drucilla. 2014. *Law and revolution in South Africa: Ubuntu, dignity, and the struggle for constitutional transformation*.

[294]   Kant, Immanuel, and Paul Guyer. 2009. *Critique of pure reason*. Cambridge: Cambridge Univ. Press.

[295]   Hegel, Georg Wilhelm Friedrich, Allen W. Wood, and H. B. Nisbet. 2018. *Elements of the philosophy of right*. Cambridge: Cambridge University Press.

[296]   Aristotle. 1990. *Aristotle: Metaphysics*.

[297]   Plato, and John M. Cooper. 2009. *Complete works*. Indianapolis: Hackett.

Theory, or Democratic Constitutionalism; thirdly, *Just Environment Theory, or the Democratic Universal Safe Space*; and fourthly *Just Economic Theory, or the Democratic Universal Economy*. Lastly, and without a doubt the most important subchapter in the entire work, *Just World Theory, or the Genealogical Development of International Harmony*, concludes the division of the work labeled as *Politics*, and functions as a sober genealogy of international *harmony* as deduced from the mere needfulness of human beings. The chief antagonist of the *Politics* is none other than Jürgen Habermas, but even then, he functions as a theoretical friend more than anything else: it is his theories on social pathologies that provide the bedrock for the speculative reasoning surrounding the *Democratic Economy*.[298] So much, then, for the prefatory remarks on the division of this work labeled *Politics*.

1. Of Phenomenological Constructivism and the Seven Part Holistic Theory of Personal Identity: Beyond Parfit and Sider

Mentioned earlier in the work, *Phenomenological Constructivism* is the view that everything in the lifeworld is dependent upon and originates from phenomenological consciousness, in addition to Kantian-Cognitivist Projectional Categories and the phenomenon of temporal rapportionality, or relationships between agents across time.[299] This means that language, society, and civilization itself are all dependent upon the phenomenological consciousnesses of agents who then automatically birth into existence social structures, Kantian-Searlean *social constructs*, and the Hegelian-Lacanian Linguistic Superstructure.[300] To delve further into the nature of personal identity, is to shed light upon the identities of social constructs that exist within the lifeworld. Therefore, an interrogation of the components of personal identity will be performed, in order to gain further insight into the nature of phenomenological constructivism itself, through which all of morality, society, and the Hegelian-Lacanian Linguistic Superstructure is born. Firstly, there are two modalities of components that factor into personal identity, these being the phenomenological and the noumenal. The phenomenological components of personal identity directly involve phenomenological consciousness, whereas the noumenal components of personal identity are more abstract entities that are results of consciousness in the first place. Firstly, the four phenomenological components of personal identity are as follows: the Cartesian Witnesant, the Concept of the Self, the Reputation of the person among other agents, and the

[298]   Habermas, Jürgen. 2012. *The theory of communicative action*. 2, 2. Boston, Mass: Beacon Press.

[299]   Kant, Immanuel, and Paul Guyer. 2009. *Critique of pure reason*. Cambridge: Cambridge Univ. Press.

[300]   Kant, Immanuel, and Paul Guyer. 2009. *Critique of pure reason*. Cambridge: Cambridge Univ. Press; Whitehead, Alfred North. 1990. *Process and reality: an essay in cosmology; Gifford Lectures delivered in the University of Edinburgh during the session 1927-28*. New York: Free Press u.a.; Hegel, Georg Wilhelm Friedrich. 2004. *Hegel's Science of logic*. Amherst, N.Y.: Humanity Books; Lacan, Jacques, Jacques-Alain Miller, and Alan Sheridan. 2019. The four fundamental concepts of psycho-analysis

Productivity of the agent, which is to say, their thoughts, actions, and speech.[301] Secondly, the three noumenal components of personal identity are as follows: the Core Script of the person, the Rapportionality of the person, and the Kantian-Cognitivist Projectional Categories of the person. These seven components of personal identity aggregated form the *Holistic Theory of Personal Identity*, or the most comprehensive theory of personal identity to date, and will now be further elaborated upon. Firstly, the Cartesian Witnessant is the phenomenological consciousness that is at the root of the entire theory, for, it is awareness itself, without which, there could be no phenomenological constructivism, because it directly results in morality, society, and Linguistic Superstructure in general.

Next, the Self-Conceptuality of the Self, or the Concept of the Self is the following component of personal identity. For, as John Locke realized with his famous Cobbler thought experiment, wherein the memories of a prince and a cobbler are switched, memories are vital to any theory of personal identity. Here, the Self-Image is an important puzzle piece of the personal identity equation, because it influences how a person proceeds and produces in the world, and hence Self-Image has a direct bearing on personal identity. Self-Image also involves the systematically integrated set of emotionally charged and neutral information that is held in the mental depository, because one's Self-Image is derived from their memories, as it were. If there can be a Concept of the Self, then other agents must also be able to possess Concepts of Others, as it were: call the collective set of Concepts of Others the Social Idealistic Karmic Matrix, or, that affective domain wherein Reputation figures largely in the affairs of agents. Reputation may be considered to be the total set of beliefs other persons have about a certain person in particular, and this set of information too is a component of an individual's personal identity, because it involves the traces an individual has had on other persons, and hence is an indirect component of personal identity. King Henry III may have a Reputation, but no longer has a Rapport with any living entity; death is the cessation of personal identity, because with death, all ties to the community are severed, and the person becomes an ancestor, so to speak. After Reputation comes Productivity — or the actions, thoughts, and speech of a given person.

Here, it is simple to see why Productivity would be a component of personal identity, because what an agent does, thinks, and says, certainly bears upon their personal identity, and as discussed earlier in the work, all of these entities bear imprints of the Mind that made them. Hence, the Productivity of Mind is another way to access personal identity, and therefore is a component of personal identity. Next, the first noumenal component of personal identity is none other than the Core Script, which is the subliminal and subconscious set of information relevant to the self that influences how the person proceeds in the lifeworld; the Core Script is the predominant influencer of actions, thoughts, and speech within a given

---

301   Descartes, Rene, and F. Sutcliffe. 2005. *Discourse on Method and the Meditations.* https://www.vlebooks. com/vleweb/product/openreader?id=none&isbn=9780141944203.

person, according to the logic of Freudian-Lacanian *subliminal prioritization* as mentioned earlier in the work.[302] The Core Script is what psychoanalysts attempt to access, in order to affect metanoia upon a person's core. The next component of personal identity is Rapportionality, which has been discussed at great length earlier on in this work. Rapportionality is the total set of relations a person has with all other existing agents, which includes linguistic communication, and Rapportionality is grounded in Reputation; certainly, Rapportionality is a component of personal identity, because how others relate to us, profoundly affects how we relate to ourselves, and hence affects our productions of Mind — our thoughts, actions, and speech. Lastly, the component of Kantian-Cognitivist Projectional Categories is what accounts for how agents identify entities within the lifeworld; how a person identifies entities within the lifeworld is directly linked to their personal identity.

Furthermore, this concept of Kantian-Cognitivist Projectional Categories allows for the Hegelian-Lacanian *Linguistic Superstructure* at large, which is the continually diversifying set of identifications that get communicated through discourse and so on, and that, reflexively, diversify phenomenological consciousness. Thus, these seven components of personal identity together form the *Holistic Theory of Personal Identity*, which is the idea that these seven components together form and are responsible for the personal identity of a person. It should be noted that personal identity is an *imaginary construct* of the phenomenological imagination, that is grounded upon phenomenological constructivism: hence it is a phenomenological construct. Here, others may attempt to apply all of the same old critiques to this theory, and may even raise the Buddhist complaint: that there is no such thing as personal identity, as Parfit most certainly thought.[303] Yet, together these seven components present a formidable defense of personal identity, which, many would argue, is an everyday, common-sense belief. So much then, for Phenomenological Constructivism and Personal Identity.

2. Of the Tripartite Nietzschean Theory of Political Anthropomodalisms: Hegel, Derrida, Marx, and Freud

There are three clear and distinct modalities that human beings tend toward: the first modality is asceticism — or as Nietzsche would call it — slave morality

---

[302]   Freud, Sigmund, and James Strachey. 2001. *Beyond the pleasure principle: group psychology and other works; (1920-1922).* London: Vintage; Lacan, Jacques, Jacques-Alain Miller, and Alan Sheridan. 2019. *The four fundamental concepts of psycho-analysis.*

[303]   Lopez, Donald S. 2004. *Buddhist scriptures*; Parfit, Derek. 2007. *Reasons and persons.* Oxford: Clarendon Press.

— and the second modality is Dionysian decadence.[304] Asceticism is the declensive modality: the mode that is cut off from pleasures, experiences, and riches. As a declensive modality, it is a modality of the limit: everywhere asceticism seeks to limit itself. Asceticism is the modality of slaves because, as slaves, they have no choice but to subscribe to this modality; and, most mitigate their suffering and limitation by ascribing to the stoic tenets of being. Indeed, as Hegel realized in his seminal *Phenomenology of Mind,* stoicism is the only refuge of the slave, outside of outright revolution of the status quo. Brave indeed is the slave who challenges the status quo; powerful indeed is the slave who organizes the others and orchestrates a successful revolt. Because the majority of humankind is limited due to scarcity economics, it could be said that asceticism is the modality of the masses. Because, limited as they are, and slaves to an unjust economic metafactual modality, they are forced to subscribe to ascetic ideals. Dionysian decadence on the other hand is the expansive, unlimited modality that seeks more and more; it is an insatiable modality that is never happy until it has turned every stone, and has crossed every Rubicon. The audacity of the dionysian decadent class knows no bounds: they pillage the earth with their metafactual violence, all the while the ascetic slave class suffers in limitation, restrained by the chains called social order. The Dionysian modality is decadent to the extent it pursues its own selfish desires to the bitter end, trampling over the rights of other human beings in the process — inflicting both metaphysical and physical violence all day and night long. Might there be an aufhebung to be had between these two polar opposites? Let us imagine an apollonian *noumenocentrism,* rooted in the rational understanding of concepts that cannot be known one way or the other, e.g., Truth, Justice, Beauty, etc.; to be noted here is that philosopher Jacques Derrida rallied against logocentrism, which is a logical, rationally orchestrated order-of-the-world, which is exactly what *apollonian noumenocentrism* would yield ought it be applied to lifeword.[305]

However, to borrow the term Apollonian from philosopher Freidrich Nietzsche — and we have already borrowed the term dionysian from him, too — what would a *Theory of Modality* look like when forced into a conversation with justice itself? It would look like a logocentric ordering of the world — and this is precisely Hegel's view as espoused in his *Elements of the Philosophy of Right.*[306] An imaginary utopian world would be an apollonian *noumenocentrism.* To call it apollonian is to call it rational, ordered, elegant, graceful, ethical, and so on; to call the imaginary utopian world *noumenocentric* is none other than to call it a world wherein unanswerable questions do not hegemonize the prevailing order, but instead, influence behavior based upon the fact that these unanswerable

[304]   Nietzsche, Friedrich, and Walter Arnold Kaufmann. 2011. *On the genealogy of morals.* New York: Vintage Books; Nietzsche, Friedrich Wilhelm, Raymond Geuss, and Ronald Speirs. 1999. *Nietzsche: the birth of tragedy and other writings.* Cambridge: Cambridge University Press

[305]   Derrida, Jacques. 1998. *Of grammatology.* Baltimore: Johns Hopkins University Press.

[306]   Hegel, Georg Wilhelm Friedrich, Allen W. Wood, and H. B. Nisbet. 2018. *Elements of the philosophy of right.* Cambridge: Cambridge University Press.

questions cannot be known. The world does not need the mischief of the dionysian decadents, to be sure: for mischief is a despicable, degenerate, and egregious modality. There can be no *play* until the world is apollonianly ordered: until the world is on the path toward optimal beauty, all frivolity must be dropped, for, the sole concern of humankind must be the establishment of an apollonian order-of-the-world, that finally manifests justice and radical egalitarianism for all. How might such a world ordering be related to *noumenocentrism*? Because, when the focalization of humankind is placed upon the noumenal, we can finally demystify the world, by no longer allowing unverifiable conspiracy theories to dominate the world, as was the intention of the three masters of suspicion who Paul Ricoeur identified: Marx, Freud, and Nietzsche.[307]

Yet, there are many questions that will forever haunt humankind: but they need not haunt us, so much as we ought to forever be reminded that: *God is noumenal and Truth is noumenal.* Without those limitations, humankind is doomed to fallacity: erroneous, foolish action that only causes violence, both metaphysical and physical. So much for the three possible general modalities of mankind. It should be realized that both asceticism and decadence are egregious extremes which must be mediated by the golden mean that is noumenocentrism. We must hold the noumena dear to our hearts, lest we forget how fallible and incredulous humankind can be in its urge for *absolutes*. We must limit our reason by metafactuality, and resist as the noumena does our perception, the horrendous evils that extremism of any kind may manifest in the world when noumenal entities are presumed to be anything other than what they are: noumenal.

3. Of Political Innativism and the Theory of Instinctive Production: Beyond Locke and Habermas

For centuries after John Locke published his seminal *Essay on Human Understanding*, his idea of the *tabula rasa* or the clean-slate view of Mind ruled the day; in the work, Locke criticized the idea that innate ideas existed in the Mind.[308] It was not until Noam Chomsky published his now famous works on linguistics that innativism — the idea that certain tendencies or structures are inherent to the human Mind — came back into fashion.[309] Increasingly, political philosophers are exploring avenues of thought that involve emotions and evolutionary psychology; one such excellent tract on the emotions is Martha Nussbaum's *Political Emotions*; a work that relies heavily upon evolutionary psychology, for example, might be

---

[307] Ricœur, Paul, and Denis Savage. 2008. *Freud and philosophy: an essay on interpretation*. Delhi: Motilal Banarsidass.

[308] Locke, John. 2011. *Essay concerning human understanding ... the twentieth edition, etc.* [Place of publication not identified]: British Library, Historic.

[309] Chomsky, Noam. 2002. *Syntactic structures*. Berlin: Mouton de Gruyter.

the infamous Jordan Peterson's *Twelve Rules For Life*.[310] Innate constructs in the Mind are everyday taken more seriously by political philosophers, and will probably come one day to dominate the rhetoric of politics, for so long as human beings are animals, they are stuck with their animal natures: let the view that there are constructs and drives inherent to the human organism be referred to as *instinctivism*. Here, Locke finds his foil, for everyone today now believes in the power of instinct to drive and dominate human lives, and an instinct is a mode of an innate idea. Let then the view that these instincts play a dominant role in human affairs be referred to as *political innativism*.

Hereafter, innativism will be referred to as *instinctivism*, even though the two are different, *instinctivism* covers all of the material that we are currently working with. Thus, we are working with a *philosophy of instinct* through and through: human beings are not just plagued by animalistic phenomenological consciousness, they too are plagued by animalistic subliminal drives and instincts. Here, to illustrate the importance of the *philosophy of instinct*, we might ask the question: what are the origins of racism, sexism, hysteria, xenophobia, and fascism? None other than animalistic instinct is responsible for these egregious manifestations of human drives and so on. One might challenge: but one becomes racist through Habermasian discourse — one is exposed to racist rhetoric, and one thereby integrates this rhetoric into one's person.[311] Certainly, racism has more to do with the *philosophy of instinct* than with Habermas's concept of discourse: for culture is more primitive than discourse, and therefore, *acculturation* takes place as an instinctive habituation naturally and over time. Even if one did believe that discourse and the Hegelian-Lacanian *Linguistic Superstructure* were responsible for the attitude of racism, the fact remains that racism is more so an emotional attitude that it is an isolated set of information in an individual's brain: racism has to do with an emotionally charged and integrated set of information within an individual's Mind.[312] If instinct is responsible for the horrors listed above, what might be the boons of instinct for society? Instinct is responsible for social cohesion, or the social order, adaptivity, or the ability to adjust one's behavior according to stimuli, normativity, or the capacity to somatically feel the urge to follow rules of any kind, and rapportionality, the complex nature of rapport held between entities that involves the communication of information using sign systems.

Returning to social cohesion, instinct — not the social contract or Habermasian communicative action — is itself the ground and root of all of social order; the Hegelian-Linguistic Linguistic Superstructure may be the vehicle by

---

[310]   Nussbaum, Martha Craven. 2015. *Political emotions: why love matters for justice*. Political Emotions. Cambridge: Belknap Press of Harvard University Press; Peterson, Jordan B., Ethan Van Sciver, and Norman Doidge. 2020. *12 rules for life: an antidote to chaos*.

[311]   Habermas, Jürgen, and William Rehg. 2015. *Between facts and norms contributions to a discourse theory of law and democracy*. Cambridge: Polity Press.

[312]   Hegel, Georg Wilhelm Friedrich. 2004. *Hegel's Science of logic*. Amherst, N.Y.: Humanity Books; Lacan, Jacques, Jacques-Alain Miller, and Alan Sheridan. 2019. *The four fundamental concepts of psycho-analysis*.

which instinct is communicated to others, and may be the reason that human beings rose up out of nature, however, instinct is ultimately the motivating factor of the human organism[313]. Let the idea that instinct is the driving force of society and sociality be referred to as the *Theory of Instinctive Production*, where production is taken to mean any speech, act, or thought of an individual. Therefore, there might just as well be these three theories: the *Theory of Instinctive Speech*, the *Theory of Instinctive Action*, and the *Theory of Instinctive Thought*, because in this work, *production* is taken to mean any product of Mind, being either a thought, action, or Austinian speech act; the *Theory of Instinctive Production* is meant to replace Habermas's *Theory of Communicative Action*, because the lifeworld is more profoundly influenced by instincts, rather than rationality.

Returning to Martha Nussbaum: her early work, *The Fragility of Goodness*, discusses how even the virtuous can be thrown off of the ethical path due to miscellaneous factors.[314] Therefore, even an individual who has attained the *benefic consciousness* is susceptible to cruel fates and so on. Worse, because of our atavistic instincts, even the *benefic consciousness* can become derailed: the *benefic consciousness* cannot regress into any former manifestations of consciousness, and would never consciously commit a wrong act; however, the individual may be propelled by their instincts into various erroneous actions. Therefore, what is needed in society to mediate these instincts, to repress the *malefic instincts* and to allow to flourish the *benefic instincts*, is nothing other than a form of *political scaffolding*. The scaffolded consciousness is surrounded by political institutions that *facilitate* moral behavior, but that do not mandate it. Because human beings are, according to Immanuel Kant in his *Religion Within the Limits of Reason Alone*, capable of radical evil, their cyclologies and phenomenological consciousnesses must together be scaffolded by political institutions to manifest a certain *benefic lifestyle* or a *benefic modality*, for the *lifestyle* of an individual is the united force of their phenomenological consciousness and their modality of cyclology.[315]

4. Of Polynomial Dialectics, the Masterscript, and the Ricoeurian Social Narrative

Even though instinct is more primitive than discourse, this is not to say that discourse does not influence the lifeworld, instead, it is to say, that instinct propels most change in the lifeworld. Here, there is not just a simple bipartite dialectic involving two terms — instinct and discourse — instead there is a certain *polynomial dialectic* wherein multiple terms are involved, perhaps, indeed, an infinite amount

---

[313] Habermas, Jürgen. 2007. *The theory of communicative action*. 1, 1. Boston, Mass: Beacon Press.

[314] Nussbaum, Martha Craven. 2011. *The fragility of goodness luck and ethics in Greek tragedy and philosophy*.

[315] Kant, Immanuel, Theodore M. (Theodore Meyer) Greene, and Hoyt H. Hudson. 1960. *Religion within limits or reason alone*.

of terms. Through the lens of phenomenological constructivism, the concept of reputation comes to the forefront, when considering what best explains social cohesion, Nussbaumian political emotions, political instincts, rapportionality, and society at large.[316] An entity or an issue may have a reputation, and, a group of individuals may even have a reputation as conceived of by themselves — a self-conceived-of reputation; therefore, there is such a phenomenon known as *social reflexivity*, wherein a group reflexively evaluates and assesses itself toward an assessment. Furthermore, because groups engage in discourse and reflexive self-evaluation, through various forms of media and dialogue, society may best be understood as engaging in an ongoing process that may be referred to as the *social narrative*. The *social narrative* involves people interacting with each other and then narrativizing about it later on; also, just as there are performative actions in the style of J.L. Austin's *How To Do Things With Words*, there too are *narrative actions*, or actions that contribute to an ongoing narrative.[317]

Certainly, there may be many narratives going on all at once, and the set of all of these narratives may be referred to as the *masterscript*. Now, because each individual has their own Cartesian *witnessant* through which they witness the lifeworld, and because human beings engage in the process of *narrativization*, it makes sense to spell out a *polyprotagonist model of society*, wherein each individual is considered the protagonist in their own *life-narrative*.[318] Where there is the *masterscript* that contains the total set of narratives, on a smaller scale, for each individual, there is the Core Script that contains the total set of *life-narratives* at play in a given individual's life. Where there is a narrative, there is a plot; and, because human life is so diverse and complicated, it follows that there may be a *polyplot theory*, wherein there are taken to be infinitely many narrative plots taking place across the lifeworld. Where there is a plot, there is a *subplot*, or a plot that is not as prominent in the narrative as the dominant plot, but nevertheless it still exists and is present in the Core Script of the individual. Narratives are noumenal entities that may be discerned to be present within the Core Script of an individual, but, just as with a novel or a play, plots must be *imagined* rather than physically prodded, for, they are explanatory mechanisms that condense a narrative to make it more palatable for the human understanding. Where society engages in *narrativization*, it must also feature the concepts of character and, of course, reputation. Character is that set of roles that can be used to explain a person's attitudes, beliefs, actions, thoughts, and speech. The reputation of the character also figures on their personal identity, as we have seen, for a reputation is the Derridean trace left behind by individuals for other individuals.[319]

---

[316] Nussbaum, Martha Craven. 2015. *Political emotions: why love matters for justice*. Political Emotions. Cambridge: Belknap Press of Harvard University Press.

[317] Austin, J. L., J. O. Urmson, and Marina Sbisà. 2009. *How to do things with words: the William James lectures delivered at Harvard University in 1955*. Oxford: Oxford University Press.

[318] Descartes, Rene, and F. Sutcliffe. 2005. *Discourse on Method and the Meditations*. https://www.vlebooks.com/vleweb/product/openreader?id=none&isbn=9780141944203.

[319] Derrida, Jacques. 1998. *Of grammatology*. Baltimore: Johns Hopkins University Press.

Finally, because human beings are productive beings, it follows that they produce actions, thoughts, and speech; we have already called this process *production* earlier on in the work. Now, inherent to productivity is performance: each time Mind produces a product, it is performative, for, even if there is only one person in the audience — the self — the self nevertheless takes on the role of spectator for itself: therefore, each emergence of a production of Mind is hence *performative* in the style of Austin, Habermas, and Butler.[320] Thus, in addition to there being a *social narrative*, there is a *social theater* wherein infinitely many narratives, plots, subplots, and performances are occurring simultaneously across the temporal timeline; again, the *social narrative* is rooted in and expands upon Ricoeur's theories of narrativity.[321] It should also be noted that in interpersonal affairs, each *constellation* of all dialectical entities in a person's composition interacts with the other person's *constellation* of dialectical entities, for example, meeting Caliban reminded Antigone of her grandfather, and likewise Antigone reminded Caliban of his granddaughter; he was a kazoo enthusiast whereas she preferred the oboe; he was short and she was tall, etc. All of these factors come into play in the *collision* that occurs during *polynomial dialectics*. So much for *polynomial dialectics, narrativization,* the *masterscript, polyprotagonist theory, polyplot theory,* and *performance theory.*

5. Of Karmic Social Idealistic Matrix Theory, Spivakian Subalternity, and Social Celestiality or, Toward a General Theory of Power

Before proceeding any further, it would be worthwhile to sketch out a *General Theory of Sociality*, or, a quick outline of the modality of society. What is the business of sociology, as it were? To begin: let us start with a *General Theory of Power*, or influence. Along the Imaginary Graph of Being, some individuals are more influential than others, with infinitely many variables to distinguish one individual from another. Thus, there is *impotency* and *potency*; there is also a modality of power that may be referred to as *phenomenopower*, or influence over the phenomenological consciousnesses of other human beings. That occurs when an individual has indebted others to them — perhaps by becoming esteemed — and then has an influence over them. *Worldly power*, on the other hand, is more so concerned with physicality than anything else, and involves the power to, for example, skip rocks across a pool, or to kick them in the style that Samuel Johnson

---

[320] Austin, J. L., J. O. Urmson, and Marina Sbisà. 2009. *How to do things with words: the William James lectures delivered at Harvard University in 1955.* Oxford: Oxford University Press; Habermas, Jürgen. 2007. *The theory of communicative action.* 1, 1. Boston, Mass: Beacon Press; Butler, Judith. 2006. *Gender trouble: feminism and the subversion of identity.* New York; London: Routledge.

[321] Ricoeur, Paul. 1997. *Time and narrative.* Chicago, Ill: University of Chicago Press.

did when allegedly refuting Bishop Berkeley's idealism.[322] With this *General Theory of Power* on the table, and also with the General theories of phenomenopower and worldly power brought to light, we may now proceed further along in our reconstruction. Famous philosopher Gayatri Chakravorty Spivak developed the concept of the *subaltern*, or a set of individuals in society who had no representation and lacked the means to articulate even their own views, etc. If there is a subaltern, what is its inverse? Nothing other than a set of individuals in society who are *celestials*, or individuals of grand fame, power, and wealth.

With both the top and the bottom of the social pyramid sketched out, we may infer quite easily that there are individuals who occupy the middle of the dichotomy between subalternity and celestiality, and these are regular, average, everyday folks. Because human beings have the capacity to judge, *reputation* becomes projected onto human beings. It is as though their Core Script were public property, for everyone forms assessments about other people, all of the time, even subliminally — the Core Script of an individual is not just projected by their own consciousness, but also by the consciousnesses of other human beings, too. Thus, as mentioned above, there are various gradations of esteem that individuals have for other individuals. Thus, because of projectional consciousness and because of projectional essentialism, the set of points of the Imaginary Graph of Being, occupied by individuals, forms a sort of *social matrix*, wherein the reputations of individuals either raise or elevate them in society, according to what famous philosopher Jean-Jaques Rousseau referred to as the *General Will*, or the *general logic* of society — his General Will is social, whereas our General Will involves polyintentionality and emotivics, just to clarify.[323] What does not escape notice by the *social witnessant*, or the *social Foucauldian panopticon* — that is to say, that the Zeitgeistal Jungian Collective Consciousness of any community at large, even small groups — affects the reputation of an individual.[324]

What comes around, goes around, so long as it is perceived by the *social witnessant*, itself a metafactual Stirnerian spook, but, nevertheless, a helpful concept for conceiving of collective perception.[325] Thus, there is not merely a caste system of power involved in society, nor merely is it only a caste system with a splash of reputation and social esteem; instead, what we are dealing with here, is nothing other than a *Karmic Idealistic Social Matrix Theory*, wherein we live — in a metafactual, consciousness dependent — world wherein one's reputation has consequences, and potentially grave ones, too — hence the employment of the word *karma*. This idea of a *Karmic Idealistic Social Matrix Theory* is in line with both the Imaginary Graph of Being, and also in line with many indigenous views

[322] Berkeley, George, and Colin Murray Turbayne. 1989. *Principles, dialogues, and philosophical correspondence.*

[323] Rousseau, Jean-Jacques, Quintin Hoare, and Christopher Bertram. 2012. *Of the social contract and other political writings.* London: Penguin Books.

[324] Foucault, Michel, and Alan Sheridan. 2020. *Discipline and punish: the birth of the prison*; Jung, C. G., and Joseph Campbell. 1971. *The portable Jung.*

[325] Stirner, Max. 1974. *Max Stirner, the ego and his own.* New York: Harper & Row.

of world modality. Take for example the South African ethical concept of uBuntu: human beings become people through other people, it asserts; it also argues that the world is an enmeshed, social matrix, akin to Chalmers's extended consciousness thesis.[326] Earlier in this work, in the division on Aesthetics, a *General Theory of the Enmeshed Consciousness* was spelled out, or the idea that, consciousnesses come into contact with each other — even though, as we described before, intimacy is both impossible and noumenal — nevertheless, consciousnesses bumble into each other blindly, impressionistically, hazily, etc., all of the time. While our reconstruction has shown that one's social reputation is of the highest importance to maintain, nevertheless, the concept of social reputation has not too much been discoursed over, in the fields of ethics and politics. Perhaps the closest the literatures have come to this issue is the idea of *recognition*, or the Hegelian idea that self-recognition and recognition by others is important in society; famous philosopher Axel Honneth also discusses social recognition in a sophisticated manner.

While this social caste system impacts society, and betters our explanations of society, it nevertheless is a product of the Hegelian-Lacanian *Linguistic Superstructure*, insofar as the Hegelian-Lacanian *Linguistic Superstructure* allows for assessmental differentiation across the Axes of Being, and, because the social caste system is a product of the Hegelian-Lacanian *Linguistic Superstructure*, it is itself epiphenomenal, metafactual, dependent upon consciousness, and more than anything else, *noumenal*.[327] Thus, human beings must employ their phenomenological imaginations and intuitions to *discover* and *take-up* this social matrix. Vital to the development of a mature and benefic consciousness, is an understanding of power, social reputation, caste, and also of the *Karmix Social Idealistic Matrix*. To be sure, a dehierarchalization of the *social* caste system is a moral imperative. *Amor fati*, or the love of fate celebrated by Nietzsche, must be spurned at every possible juncture; instead of loving our fate, we must claim our destinies, according to the *ideal principle of autonomy*, or the ideal that states personal and social metanoia is possible, and hence, ought to be affected.[328] Your author could not care less whether you believed in free will or not — so long as you kept steadfast to the *ideal principle of autonomy*, or the idea that change is possible, and ought to be affected toward an optimal arrangement of affairs, as is the Hegelian view espoused in his *Elements of the Philosophy of Right*.[329] So much for the *General Theory of the Karmic Social Idealistic Matrix*.

---

[326]   Cornell, Drucilla. 2014. *Law and revolution in South Africa: Ubuntu, dignity, and the struggle for constitutional transformation*; Chalmers, David John, and Tim Peacock. 2022. *Reality+: virtual worlds and the problems of philosophy*.

[327]   Hegel, Georg Wilhelm Friedrich. 2004. *Hegel's Science of logic*. Amherst, N.Y.: Humanity Books; Lacan, Jacques, Jacques-Alain Miller, and Alan Sheridan. 2019. *The four fundamental concepts of psycho-analysix*.

[328]   Williams, Bernard Arthur Owen, and Josefine Nauckhoff. 2001. *Nietzsche: the Gay Science*. Cambridge: Cambridge University Press.

[329]   Hegel, Georg Wilhelm Friedrich, Allen W. Wood, and H. B. Nisbet. 2018. *Elements of the philosophy of right*. Cambridge: Cambridge University Press.

6. Toward Political Justice I:
From the Kantian Consciousness to the Democratic Consciousness

What can I know? What should I do? What can I hope for? These are the quintessential Kantian questions found in that great philosopher's corpus. After the *benefic consciousness* realizes the importance of the *polyintentional consciousness*, which is both selfish and altruistic, the consciousness that emerges is none other than the *Kantian consciousness*, that is focused on the above three questions: what can one know, what ought one do, and what ought one hope for? The Kantian modality of consciousness is fundamentally inquisitive, more so than the *mature consciousness* that transformed into the *benefic consciousness*, and is responsible for one final odyssey of consciousness: the jump from itself, the *Kantian consciousness*, into the final stage of consciousness, the *Democratic consciousness*, that consciousness named for its allegiance to the values, ideals, and structures traditionally affiliated with political democracy.[330] First, the *Kantian consciousness* has understood justice to be *harmony*, but that is merely applicative justice, from one moral agent to another, and so on and so forth; the moment of consciousness that is Kantian in nature, must now bear justice to weigh upon the question of a *political constructivism*, or the goal whose ultimate aim is to erect a political structure grounded in a certain set of thoughts, instincts, feelings, values, ideals, rights, dues, and statutes, usually to be enforced by a state. A due must be understood to be a translation of a right into materiality reality: Antigone's right to food translates into her being dued a bundle of grain, and so on. The mode of *political constructivism* favored by the Kantian consciousness is none other than *phenomenological constructivism*, or the modality of constructivism that grasps the idea that all political institutions are grounded in human consciousness, which indeed after-all is the implication of Kant's unique flavour of German Idealism, at any rate.

For this to be the case, means that the same rules that apply to human consciousness, according to the *Benefic Speculative Formulation*, must too apply to any possible *political constructivism* that is to take *phenomenological constructivism* as the right point of departure, which it must be, because all institutions are indeed grounded in phenomenological consciousness. Here, the *Kantian consciousness* identifies three *chief rights* that must ground its vision for a *political-phenomenological constructivism*: the *Right to Personhood*, without which there could be no successful grounding of political institutions, including the political institution that is one's own person; the *Right to Political Justice* — which is, as we shall we, distinct from mere social justice, which is only between persons, whereas political justice occurs between individuals and institutions, and between institutions and institutions — and involves the institutionalization of the eighteen ideal principles of morality, that, due to this institutionalization,

---

[330] Kant, Immanuel, and Paul Guyer. 2009. *Critique of pure reason*. Cambridge: Cambridge Univ. Press.

transform in ontological status from mere abstracted ideals into actual rights directed toward political feasibilities; next, is the *Right to Political Scaffolding*, or the right to institutions that scaffold human consciousnesses toward the goal of mediating their animal instincts, which are responsible for xenophobia, sexism, racism, hysteria, hierarchality, and fascism, but which are also responsible for social cohesion, kinship, and the social order at large. The *Right to Political Scaffolding* is grounded by *process politics*, which is the synthesis of *process epistemology* and *process ethics*, that recognizes what famous philosopher Nussbaum refers to as the *fragility of goodness*, or the capacity for human behavior to spiral out of control when not effectively safeguarded and scaffolded by social factors, which in this case, will be argued to be institutions.[331]

7. Toward Political Justice II: Of the Right to Personhood and It's Subrights

To start, the Right to Personhood must encompass and protect all of the seven component facets of personal identity, which are: the witnessant, self-conceptuality, reputation, productivity, the Core Script, rapportionality, and projectional essentiality. Firstly, the right to the witnessant entails a right to one's own phenomenology, which is a question of what one can or cannot perceive. Here, the subright to the witnessant entails a freedom of perception and thought, perhaps akin to the right to liberty espoused by democratic nations. Here, though, the right to the witnessant is more fundamental than a right to liberty, because the witnessant is one of the most fundamental components of a personality; this is the question of phenomenopower, and who may have control over the phenomenologies of other human beings: here the answer is that the right to what a person thinks or consumes is entirely up to them; therefore, the right to the witnessant trumps the right to censorship. Next comes the right to self-conceptuality, or the idea that one must be free to determine how they have identified in the past, how they identify in the present, and how they identify in the future: all of this is consistent with a subright to narrativization, or the idea that one must be left free to narrativize their own selves if they are to truly be comfortable within their own skins. Here, this is an argument in defense of human beings seeking to identify in whatever manner that they please; Locke's defense of memory as the most important facet of personal identity is not here defended, but memory is accepted to be a serious component of personal identity.[332]

Next comes the right to reputation, which is allied with the freedom from slander and libel as traditionally understood in liberal democracies across the globe.

---

[331] Nussbaum, Martha Craven. 2011. *The fragility of goodness luck and ethics in Greek tragedy and philosophy.*

[332] Locke, John. 2011. *Essay concerning human understanding ... the twentieth edition, etc.* [Place of publication not identified]: British Library, Historic.

The right to reputation follows the logic of the second right to self-conceptuality; while others may be allowed to form opinions of an individual, these opinions must never come to dominate a person's reputation; this is not to say that criticism should be against the law; instead, it is to argue, that criticism must be tempered so as not to too greatly influence the personality of the individual whose reputation is at stake by the criticism: only the individual should be allowed to take risks with their reputation; certainly, some behaviors will merit for fair and sober-minded criticisms, however, the right to reputation must be a political guard in order to protect individuals from unfair or biased interpretations of their character. Next comes the right to productivity, or the right to one's thoughts, actions and speech. By extension, there is also a subright, as Locke too thought, to the fruits of one's labor.[333] Here, production in the abstract and productivity in praxis form the traces that mark how an individual spends their conscious hours. More than any other right, productivity is more clearly the most attuned with a general vital impulse, which is to say, that the productions of an individual best *trace* their personality.

Next comes the right to the Core Script, which is the subliminal operating system filled with narratives, plots, and subplots, which ultimately influences most of an individual's actions. Here, the right to the Core Script is different from the right to reputation, because the right to reputation involves external perceptions of oneself, whereas the Core Script involves subliminal and internal concepts of oneself; where the productivity of an individual best *traces* their personality, the Core Script best *explains* their personality, and is the favorite object of inquiry for psychoanalysts. To have a right to one's Core Script is to entail a freedom from marketing, brainwashing, and any other tools of manipulation. Here, Marx and famous philosopher Slavoj Žižek's critiques of ideology come to the forefront: for marketing to be just and equitable, it must not be suspect of being manipulative. In the same vein, politicians when either running for office or running to keep it, must not infringe upon the right to the Core Script, which is to say, that they must not lead individuals to alter their Core Scripts through deception or foul play.[334] Next comes the right to rapportionality: as Aristotle believes, human beings are indeed political animals, and must socialize.[335] But, a rapport is far more complicated than that, and, following the logic of a social matrix based on reputations and rapports, is far more influential than philosophers hitherto have given it credit for. Take for example the South African indigenous ideal that is *uBuntu*, the West's best exposition of which may be found in the works of famous philosopher Drucilla Cornell, wherein people become people through other people: here, we can see that the right to rapportionality is all the more important, because, it is through our rapports, that we ourselves develop: our rapports are opportunities to further

---

[333] Locke, John, Mark Goldie, John Locke, and John Locke. 2016. *Second treatise of government ; and a letter concerning toleration.*

[334] Marx, Karl. 2022. *German Ideology*. [S.l.]: Repeater; Žižek, Slavoj. 2009. *The sublime object of ideology.* London: Verso.

[335] Aristotle, and H. Rackham. 1959. *Aristotle: politics.* London: Heinemann.

develop our personality — which is why rapportionality is one of the seven components of personal identity in the first place.[336]

Finally, comes the right to Kantian-Cognitivist Projectional Categories, or the ability of human beings to identify entities in their minds and then project those entities onto the world. Here, there is a general defense of creativity that allows for individuals to be creative in the way that they understand the world, which is acceptable so long as the individual does not identify the world in terms of immorality or conspiracy theories, as was seen with the egregious *conspiratorial consciousness*. And yet, there are many similarities between religious beliefs and conspiratorial beliefs: the inability to verify them one way or the other, and so on: therefore the question emerges: is there not a right to believing in a conspiracy, just as there is a right to religion? Conspiracy theories of any kind are a great danger to society; therefore, while the religious may remain protected, as a fundamental right to believe in whatever metaphysics one prefers, there can be no such right to conspiracy theories; and, as a provision, political institutions must be guarded from religious beliefs, due to the great variety and diversity of them; even should all the religions become creolized and mixed into a homogenous religion, political institutions ought still be protected from personal metaphysical beliefs that are incapable of being either scientifically verified or Popperianly falsified.[337]

8. Toward Political Justice III:
Of the Right to Political Justice
and the Right to Political Scaffolding

The Kantian consciousness asks: what good is justice if it is not politicized, not inherent to the political institutions of its time, not manifest not merely in the actions of individuals — which is mere social justice?[338] Such an inquiry is also generally and implicitly Hegelian.[339] Therefore, the Kantian consciousness finds the answer to what it should do: it must not merely, as Habermas justly criticizes, monologically procure ideal behaviors through the categorical imperative, instead, it must dialogically engage in discourse with its other citizens as to the best ways to politicize its ideals.[340] This is not to say that morality can only be known and verified through discourse, which is the Habermasian view, instead, it is to argue that the

[336] Cornell, Drucilla. 2014. *Law and revolution in South Africa: Ubuntu, dignity, and the struggle for constitutional transformation.*

[337] Popper, Karl R. 2014. *The Logic of Scientific Discovery.*

[338] Kant, Immanuel, and Paul Guyer. 2009. *Critique of pure reason.* Cambridge: Cambridge Univ. Press.

[339] Hegel, Georg Wilhelm Friedrich, Allen W. Wood, and H. B. Nisbet. 2018. *Elements of the philosophy of right.* Cambridge: Cambridge University Press.

[340] Habermas, Jürgen, and William Rehg. 2015. *Between facts and norms contributions to a discourse theory of law and democracy.* Cambridge: Polity Press.

best application of the eighteen ideal principles of morality must be up for debate due to process politics, for, just as process ethics taught us that ethics is in a constant state of flux due to the autodiversification of the zeitgeist, so too do the motions of the zeitgeist affect political institutions and so on. With the new developments of technology, no doubt ethics as applied in the days of Plato or Aristotle could not be the same as ethics as applied in contemporary times, for there are new vehicles or means available to human disposal at this time: which is to say, there are new ways of practicing ethics and politics as the zeitgeist continues to diversify itself, which is also to say, that Aristotelian virtue cyclologies must adapt to the zeitgeistal fashions of the time period that they occur in.[341] Nevertheless, justice must still be applied to institutions, and must even become inherent both to them and to the ways that they operate within the lifeworld: such is the Hegelian view. Therefore, justice must no longer be a question of abstracted ideals, but more morph into a science of rights: perhaps even a work should be written, The Science of Right.

Therefore, each of the eighteen ideal principles of morality must be converted from an ideal into a right, so that they gain more political ground and influence within the lifeworld at large. First, is the right to perfection, or the claim that there can always be a better job to be done than the one that was performed. The right to perfection grounds all of morality in general, and is responsible for the deduction of the other seventeen ideals that must be converted into rights. Next comes the right to gravitas, which is the idea that both individuals and society at large must take serious issues seriously, for example, climate change. This right ensures that society will not will itself into ruin through frivolity. Tackling the student debt crisis, for example, ought to be a grave issue for any who believe in the importance of the humanities; the importance of the humanities is wonderfully defended in Nussbaum's Not For Profit: Why Democracy Needs the Humanities.[342] Next comes the right to hope, which, when applied to politics, means that people ought to have the right to expect better both for themselves and for their political institutions at large. Hope is important for countering political depressions, and one might even here argue for a right to hopeful economic arrangements that map the wild improvements in industry following the rise of the internet. Next comes the right to autonomy, a right deeply linked to the right to personhood; the right to autonomy allows individuals to feel as though they are steering their own lives, and clearly goes against the existence of any form of slavery: whether that be wage slavery, or any other form of slavery. Next comes the right to dignity, or the expectation that everyone in society will be treated with the seriousness appropriate to the autonomy of their wills. Furthermore, the right to dignity means that the state must treat both its citizens and non-citizens — even enemies — with the dignity inherent to their persons.

---

[341] Plato, and John M. Cooper. 2009. Complete works. Indianapolis: Hackett; Aristotle, and Charles David Chanel Reeve. 2014. Nicomachean ethics. Indianapolis: Hackett Publishing Co.

[342] Nussbaum, Martha Craven. 2016. Not for profit: with a new preface by the author: why democracy needs the humanities.

Next comes the right to grace, which in politics must translate to the right to expect careful, kind, and considerate political actions from their leaders, to whatsoever minimal extent a society must have leaders at all. Additionally, the right to grace must imply that citizens accord themselves with the dignity and respect that must be allotted to temporal persons — or persons whose lives must be limited due to their mortality: therefore not a second of their lives ought to be squandered. Next comes the right to utility: here, the political right to utility accords with the libertarian dream of a government as minimal as possible: a government may accord itself with social justice issues, but the aim of any just government must be self-negation and scaffolding: a government ought to scaffold its citizens where they are most vulnerable, but ought to do so in a utilitous way. The right to utility implies that waste of any kind must be frowned upon by any just society. Here, the question arises: is it really necessary for there to be five hundred supermarket chains in the world, all with their own management teams, marketing teams, and so on? Here, the arc of justice bends toward monopolies, although heavily regulated monopolies, to avoid exploitation: any other alternative incurs huge amounts of waste, involving waste both of financial capital and human capital. Just the same, does it make any sense for there to be thousands of universities, and yet not one national university, and not one international university, free of cost to all global citizens? Certainly it would be more economical for there to be huge universities capable of educating any citizen who so desires, which would increase the possibility of innovation in society. The right to utility does not entail that spending funds on innovation is a frivolous idea, instead, utility encourages innovation, because of *process epistemology, process ethics, and process politics*, which are branches of philosophy that stem from the philosophies of Whitehead and Derrida.[343] Innovation will lead to the liberation of humankind from frivolous work not consistent with their inherent autonomy, dignity, and grace. Every right must be considered in conjunction with each of the other rights, in order to best facilitate justice: such is the Leibnizian *law of harmony*, or the eighteenth ideal and right.

After utility, comes the right to civility, or the right of a civilization to expect that civilization ought to be perpetuated at all costs: here, contra Habermas, animal instinct is responsible for the social glue that holds society together, for civilization is merely a modality of kinship on a larger scale.[344] The right to civilization also means limited human animal instincts, which are responsible for: sexism, racism, xenophobia, hysteria, and fascism, for without the due regulation of these instincts, civilization could never persist without collapsing into a state of perpetual warfare. Next comes the right to peace, which is the absence of violences of any kind. Certainly, there are multiple forms of violence, such as emotional,

---

[343] Whitehead, Alfred North. 1990. *Process and reality: an essay in cosmology; Gifford Lectures delivered in the University of Edinburgh during the session 1927-28*. New York: Free Press u.a.; Derrida, Jacques. 1998. *Of grammatology*. Baltimore: Johns Hopkins University Press.

[344] Habermas, Jürgen. 2007. *The theory of communicative action*. 1, 1. Boston, Mass: Beacon Press.

physical, and financial. Indeed, there are financial superpredators on the loose at this very moment in history, reaping the benefits of millions of their employers all the while doing nothing inherently productive themselves. The right to peace must be cemented not merely through an international federation of nations, as such a policy failed miserably to stop the second world war, but must manifest itself in the international union of all political nations into a single political entity, e.g. the United States must economically and politically unite with China, etc. Peace must become profitable, and must be incentivized at all costs. The barbaric policy of mutually assured destruction must be thrown out, and the right to peace must also protect citizens against accidental injury, such as an atomic bomb accidentally going off — therefore all such weaponry must be disabled. After the right to peace, comes the right to trust: citizens must be able to trust one another, and also to trust their leaders and politicians. Without trust, as Kant saw all too clearly, the possibility of the deterioration of the social order is imminent.[345] Trust is not just some frivolous enlightenment ideal that can be written off by so-called postmodern philosophers, instead, it is everyday becoming more and more prominent in the blooming field of affect theory. Trust is the very lifeblood of society, so much so, that all lies ought to be made illegal and punishable. Trust especially in international relations is the lifeblood of peace, and any variety of deception must be made illegal and abolished.

Next comes the right to hospitality, or the right to be able to expect that other citizens will treat one hospitably on account of one's autonomy, dignity, and grace, and in accordance with the general ethics of civility and peace. The right to hospitality also includes being hospitable to those future populations that have yet to emerge on the planet, which means that the earth must not only be protected, but sustained. Utility does not entail the destruction of the planet. Peace does not entail the destruction of the planet. There can be no hope should the planet continue to be exploited. Therefore its exploitation must be made illegal, and a *sustainability politics* must emerge at the forefront of human civilization. Next comes the right to decoloniality, which is ever important, because even should every empire be abolished, individuals may still colonize the lifeworlds of other individuals: for, there are three modalities of imperialism, these being, militaristic, cultural, and economic. Colonization firmly goes against the right to personhood, and, furthermore, is in direct violation of the right to decoloniality — wherever and however it should emerge. Because indigeneity is constantly at war with the forces of colonization, a truly utopian world would reflect the conquering of coloniality by indigeneity — by the forces of nativity; for each person is native unto themselves, and is indigenous unto themselves. For indigeneity to conquer the forces of imperialism, is for utopia to be established upon this earth. Next comes the right to beauty, or the aesthetic expectation that politics and citizens in general

---

[345]   Kant, Immanuel, James W. Ellington, and Immanuel Kant. 1994. *Ethical philosophy: the complete texts of Grounding for the metaphysics of morals, and Metaphysical principles of virtue*, part II of *The metaphysics of morals*. Indianapolis: Hackett Pub. Co.

ought to, following the logic of the right to grace, accord themselves as beautifully as possible. Here, one may imagine a politics of the beautiful: where institutions weigh their qualities based on how beautiful they are. One of the most important of all the rights, the right to beauty is built up off of the human ability to tap into the transcendental and imagine the most ideal forms of beauty. Next comes the right to defocality, linked to the right to Kantian-Cognitivist Projectional Categories, because defocality involves delimiting our concepts in order to make them more expansive, just, equitable, and creative.[346]

To focalize it is true is to communicate, but as soon as words are uttered, they ought to be defocalized: this is the soul of *process epistemology, process ethics, process politics*, and Jacques Derrida's philosophy of deconstruction, which itself is merely an applied form of Hegelian dialectics, as were laid out in Hegel's famous *Science of Logic*.[347] Next comes the right to dehierarchality: hierarchality is a part of human civilization that stems from our animal instincts, and, because it only causes stress and offers nothing to society at all, ought to be abolished. A civilization without hierarchies is a democratic utopia indeed. Next, comes the right to improvement: linked to the right to perfection, the right to improvement is more practical and humane: while perfection must be the ultimate aim of anything human beings strive for, improvement is that right which must track the diversification of the zeitgeist and ensure that the change in the zeitgeist is an improvement, instead of a decline. Next, the right to a harmony of all the aforementioned rights is inherent to the right to harmony, and is the most important right of all, because it ensures that no single act of injustice may be perpetrated, due to all of the rights being in play at once. So much for the right to political justice. Lastly the Über-right to rights entails the preservation of these rights within both the lifeworld and the system, and is, therefore, the right to political scaffolding.

The right to political scaffolding is the right to political institutions whose aim it is to scaffold human consciousness in such a way that the rights inherent to it are protected; in this way, the right to political scaffolding complements all of the other rights, because it entails their manifestation both in the lifeworld but also in the system. Therefore, the right to political scaffolding furthermore entails that rights ought to be protected by being manifested in political institutions, which is to say, that rights must become manifest and inherent to political institutions in order for the political system to become just. Thus, the general Hegelian right to political scaffolding guarantees human beings that their rights will indeed be manifest in the world, because it calls for their manifestation in political institutions.[348] For example, the right to beauty might manifest in the creation of several international

---

[346]   Kant, Immanuel, and Paul Guyer. 2009. *Critique of pure reason*. Cambridge: Cambridge Univ. Press.

[347]   Derrida, Jacques. 1998. *Of grammatology*. Baltimore: Johns Hopkins University Press; Hegel, Georg Wilhelm Friedrich. 2004. *Hegel's Science of logic*. Amherst, N.Y.: Humanity Books.

[348]   Hegel, Georg Wilhelm Friedrich, Allen W. Wood, and H. B. Nisbet. 2018. *Elements of the philosophy of right*. Cambridge: Cambridge University Press.

art exhibitions put on by an international institution dedicated to the proliferation of beauty in the world. With the exposition of the right to political scaffolding, concludes this interrogation of the manifestation of ideals as rights, and rights as political institutions. So much, then, for the right to political justice and the right to political scaffolding.

9. Toward Political Justice IV: An Aristotelian Metaphysical Theory of the Individual and of the Nation-State

Here, it would be helpful to sketch out an *Aristotelian Metaphysical Theory of the Individual and of the Nation State*, for the motivators inherent both to the individual and to the nation-state are nearly indistinguishable. What makes this theory Aristotelian is that it borrows from Aristotle his famous quartetal theory of causes: every existing entity involving human consciousness has four causes: an efficient cause, a material cause, a formal cause, and a final cause.[349] For example, the classical example of a table: its efficient cause is its carpenter, its material cause is its wood, its formal cause is its design, and its final cause is its utility for being dined upon. Eccentrically, Aristotle did not apply his theory of causes either to the individual or to political institutions such as the nation-state or the polis, but that should not discourage us from applying his theory of causes to the individual and the latter day concept of the nation-state, for, it is a serious and rigorous theory, that illuminates the functionalities both of individuals and nation-states. In proceeding, four *motivators* both of the individual and the nation-state shall be identified; in these *motivators*, both the individual and the nation-state do not differ at all; neither do they in the application of the four Aristotelian causes to the four specific *motivators*; furthermore, each *motivator* entails the emergence of a new modality of theory that ought to arise due to the elucidation of the four *motivators*, with each *motivator* being tagged along with its own new theoretical field that best helps explain its functional role within the larger composite Aristotelian Metaphysical Theory of the Individual and the Nation-State.

Lastly, each *motivator*, having a theory that goes along with it, that best helps to explain its functional role within the larger theory, must necessarily be attached to a so-called *application* of its theory to reality. The *application* of the theory to reality grounds the theory in practice and confirms its powers of explanation. To begin the Aristotelian reconstruction, we shall start with the efficient cause both of the individual and of the nation-state: the *motivator* that reflects the *efficient* cause of both is none other than its *means* or *economy*. The relevant theoretical approach to the *means* or *economy* of either an individual or

---

349   Aristotle. 1990. *Aristotle: Metaphysics.*

a nation-state may be referred to as *need theory*, because fundamentally need is involved in any reconstruction of *means* or *economy*. Here, *means* or *economy* may be defined as the internal status either of an individual or of a nation-state. Whether an individual or a nation-state, both are influenced *efficiently* by their needs, as these needs ultimately affect the roles they will play either individually or internationally. The *application* of *need theory* manifests in both the skills and the methods of maintenance that either an individual or a nation-state engage in. Next, the *motivator* that reflects the *material* cause of either an individual or a nation-state is its *environment* or *setting*. The *environment* or *setting* of either an individual or a nation-state may be defined as its external status, or the state of affairs existing in proximity to it, according to its geographical locale. The theory involved with the *environmental motivator* is none other than *position theory*, whose *application* is the circumstances of any individual or nation-state.

Here, the circumstances may be the current constraints and state of affairs within a given geographical locale. Next, the *motivator* that reflects the *formal* cause is the *rule motivator*. A *rule* may be defined as any moral constraint imposed either descriptively or prescriptively on either an individual or a nation-state. The theory associated with the *rule motivator* is *regulation theory*, because the *rule motivator* fundamentally inhibits certain behaviors in individuals and nation-states. The *application* of *regulation theory* is morality itself, as morality governs behavior whether in an individual or a nation-state. In the individual, the *rule motivator* is one's conscience, whereas for the nation-state, it is not, surprisingly, its collected set of laws, but rather, the consciences of those representatives of a populace who are empowered to make decisions on account of said populace. For example, imagine a corrupt official — where is the adherence to law, there? Therefore the *rule motivator* is conscience rather than law. Finally, the *mind motivator* is the *motivator* that reflects Aristotle's *final* cause, and may be defined as the polyintentional phenomenological consciousness, replete with emotional drives, of either an individual or of the individuals controlling a nation-state. Here, the theory affiliated with the *mind motivator* is *influencer theory*, which may be defined as the theoretical interest in the various influences either on an individual's behavior or upon the behavior of a nation-state, with the behavior being grounded in the polyintentional phenomenological consciousness of either the individual or of the individuals controlling a nation-state.

The application of *influencer theory* to the lifeworld is, for the individual, the interrogation of personal drives; for the nation-state, it is the interrogation of the personal drives of those individuals controlling said nation-state. Thus, to review, there are four *motivators*, these being: *economic, environmental, rule-based, and mental*. Together, these four *motivators* reflect the four Aristotelian causes: *economic* as *efficient*, *environmental* as *material*, *rule-based* as *formal*, and *mental* as *final*. Together, these four *motivators* make up the *Quartetal Aristotelian Metaphysical Theory of Individual Motivation and the Motivations of Nation-States*. These four *motivators* are responsible for the motivational states both of individuals and of nation-states, which is to say, that this is a theory of how individuals and nation-states fundamentally exist within the world: this is a theory of what forces specifically constrain and sculpt individuals and nation-states, to clarify. Thus, the question of political justice returns: to be ethical is to follow the prescripts of *Speculative Optimalism*, which calls for in actions: just consequences, just polyintentionality, just and virtuous performance of the action in question, and an applicative understanding of justice as *harmony*. Thus, *Speculative Optimalism* is a quartetal theory: now comes the time to apply it to the fundamental ontological states both of the individual and the nation-state. Thus, a *Theory of Political Justice*: justice is *Speculative Optimalism* applied to the following four *motivators* both of individuals and of nation-states: *economical, environmental, rule-based, and mental*. Thus, political justice involves the following: a *just economy*, a *just environment*, a *just rule-base*, and a *just mind*. So much for political justice and the *Quartetal Aristotelian Metaphysical Theory of Individual Motivation and the Motivations of Nation-States*.

10. Toward Political Justice V: Of Just Mind Theory, or, Of the Genealogical Development of the Democratic Consciousness

To follow the logic set forth by the *Aristotelian Metaphysical Theory of Individual Motivation and the Motivations of Nation-States*, political justice must involve not only the *benefic consciousness*, but also that consciousness that best balances the requirements of the following theories: *Just Mind Theory, Just Rule Theory, Just Environment Theory, and Just Economy Theory.*[350] The first of these theories to be interrogated will be the *just mind theory* requirement. Here, the argument is nothing other than that there is a *just trajectory* that consciousness must travel through in order to arrive at that consciousness that best balances all the requirements of the *four motivational causes* both of the individual and of the nation-state: the consciousness that lies at the end of this dialectical odyssey is none other than the *democratic consciousness*, which is political, ethical, realistic, conformist, revolutionary, rights-oriented, and so on. The *democratic consciousness is right embodied*, and is the summation of all the rights as understood and embodied by a single modality of consciousness. Before the *democratic consciousness* can be arrived at, the aim of the Kantian consciousness is to first trace the development of the stages of consciousness that come before the *democratic consciousness*, and in so doing, whether subliminally or consciously, accomplish the *democratic consciousness*.

---

[350] Aristotle. 1990. *Aristotle: Metaphysics.*

For the Kantian consciousness, that is synthetic in nature, and that naturally synthesizes all that it has learned in its previous stages of consciousness, the very last stage of itself is either the subliminal or conscious integration of all of the information that it has learned hitherto: once all of this information clicks, whether subliminally or consciously, the Kantian consciousness transforms into the *democratic consciousness*.[351] It should be noted that all of these stages of development may be accomplished subliminally, through the process of *autometanoia*. Akin to famous psychologist Lawrence Kohlberg's theory of moral development, the drive of the Kantian consciousness to synthesize all of the stages in the development of consciousness can be formalized into a *Theory of the Genealogical Development of Consciousness*, more akin, perhaps, to the work in dialectics accomplished in Hegel's *Phenomenology of Mind*.[352] Firstly, there are three phases in the development of consciousness, and these trace the process of maturation that begins at birth: the three phases in the development of consciousness are none other than *childhood, adolescence,* and *adulthood*. Each phase consists of five modalities of consciousness that progress up out of the stages of consciousness that exist earlier in the chain of development. Unfortunately, not every human being manages to accomplish the *democratic consciousness*, due to innumerable hindrances which shall not here be probed, but perhaps shall be interrogated in a later work. Belonging to the *childhood phase* are the following consciousnesses: the dependent consciousness, the immature consciousness, the fashionable consciousness, the selfish consciousness, and the gullible consciousness.

Next, belonging to the *adolescent phase* are the following consciousnesses: the skeptical consciousness, the liberated consciousness, the mature consciousness, the altruistic consciousness, and the Pragmatic-Cognitivist Consciousness. Next, belonging to the *adulthood phase* are the following consciousnesses: the revolutionary consciousness, the benefic consciousness, the polyintentional consciousness, the Kantian consciousness, and the *democratic consciousness*. Certainly, elements from the prior stages of consciousness may be present in the more developed consciousnesses, and there may be overlaps in an individual from among a few modalities of consciousness, yet, an individual will always be dominated by a specific stage of consciousness out of the fifteen stages. Not every individual, either, manages to accomplish the *democratic consciousness*, but that is not to say that, were there to be a *democratic pedagogy*, that such a feat would be impossible: in fact it would be easily accomplished. To begin, the moments of consciousness that occur during the *childhood phase* shall be discussed. Here, then, is the first stage in the theory: every human being begins as the dependent consciousness. Dependent upon its kin to feed it as a child, and to care for it, it may sometimes be the case that human beings never overcome this original phase

[351] Kant, Immanuel, and Paul Guyer. 2009. *Critique of pure reason*. Cambridge: Cambridge Univ. Press.

[352] Kohlberg, Lawrence. 1986. *The philosophy of moral development: moral stages and the idea of justice*. Cambridge [u.a]: Harper & Row; Hegel, Georg Wilhelm Friedrich, and Terry P. Pinkard. 2018. *The phenomenology of spirit*.

of consciousness, for, they remain dependent upon others for the rest of their lives. However, it is only natural to depend upon others, and, as Hegel rightly identifies in his *Elements of the Philosophy of Right*, civil society does indeed involve a *system of needs.*[353]

The dependent consciousness develops into the immature consciousness, which is both dependent and inhibited. The immature consciousness is inhibited in the sense that it is emotionally vulnerable and shy, unwilling to upset its supply chain of resources, friends, and family: the threat of losing everything bears upon this consciousness, and so its worries allow for it to remain politically complacent. The immature consciousness develops into the fashionable consciousness, which is dominated by the need to conform; and yet, the most conformist human beings may be considered to be the most stylish, for to adhere to rules of culture and also to the rules of zeitgeistal *fashions.* They are not, however, the most daring of individuals. Next, the selfish consciousness emerges out of the fact of its dependency on others: the selfish child must be selfish to survive; unfortunately, elements of the childish selfish consciousness persist in the Minds of many even once they mature out of childhood. The selfish consciousness quickly becomes the gullible consciousness, which is that consciousness so needy and interested in its own selfish ends, that it is gullible and jumps into many a dangerous situation. The gullible consciousness is fundamentally deceiveable, and, having been deceived and hurt many a time, eventually learns its lesson: to no longer be so blindly trusting of those, or to be so hungry to satiate its desires that it falls into social traps and the like. The gullible consciousness is the final stage of development that occurs during the *childhood phase*; next comes the *adolescent phase*. The gullible consciousness meets its demise in the light of its deceivability: next comes the skeptical consciousness, or, that consciousness which is world-weary and tired of being deceived, tired more generally speaking of being made to seem a fool. Now skeptical of others, due to their potential to scheme against the former gullible consciousness, the skeptical consciousness turns its skepticality against all of the elements of its former stages of development.

This process gives rise to the birth of the next consciousness: the liberated consciousness. Once the skeptical consciousness becomes skeptical of its dependency on others, on its inhibitions, and on its former deceivability, it morphs into the liberated consciousness. The liberated consciousness is freed from its prior inhibitions, and the individual going through this stage finalizes its departure from its dependency on others, and hence morphs into the mature consciousness. The mature consciousness is both independent and uninhibited, but also savvy of the deceptive snares of other human beings. The mature consciousness is also more reflective, and therefore is in a better position than any other consciousness prior to it to engage in aesthetic assessment. The mature consciousness transitions into

---

[353] Hegel, Georg Wilhelm Friedrich, Allen W. Wood, and H. B. Nisbet. 2018. *Elements of the philosophy of right*. Cambridge: Cambridge University Press.

the altruistic consciousness, once it reflects on its former selfishness: it becomes the inverse of the selfish consciousness, and devotes more time to friends, family, and to those in need. The last stage in the *adolescent phase* is the Pragmatic-Cognitivist Consciousness, which transitions up out of the altruistic consciousness because it remembers the lessons of the gullible consciousness, which is to say, that the altruistic consciousness soon distances itself from the idea of helping just anyone: instead, its altruism becomes mediated by common sense and social pragmatism.

It is the pragmatism of the altruistic consciousness that leads it to develop into the Pragmatic-Cognitivist Consciousness, which is skeptical, independent, and uninhibited. Yet, the Pragmatic-Cognitivist Consciousness is also more savvy when it comes to mediating its animal instincts, and it does so in a realistic fashion, being a citizen undergoing the process of civilization. In this way, the Pragmatic-Cognitivist Consciousness overcomes its animal nature and emerges as a better citizen for it, because its animal nature is responsible for sexism, racism, hysteria, xenophobia, and fascism. The Pragmatic-Cognitivist Consciousness is not only more reflective than the mature consciousness, but it is also more epistemological, as it begins to care more for the concept of truth. Subliminally the Pragmatic-Cognitivist Consciousness develops a better grasp of epistemological matters: it begins to limit its animal instincts, its own perspective, and begins to court knowledge that is both reliable and virtuously arrived at, akin to the epistemic methods articulated by Goldman and Sosa.[354] It is its epistemic pragmatism that evolves the Pragmatic-Cognitivist Consciousness into the revolutionary consciousness, and that brings the *adolescent phase* to a close, while inaugurating the *adulthood phase*. The revolutionary consciousness is that consciousness which is inclined to be socratic and to challenge the status quo when it comes to political affairs. After the Pragmatic-Cognitivist Consciousness gained the insight that pragmatic change could be made in the world, the insight comes to dominate the revolutionary consciousness. Indeed, for the revolutionary consciousness, social and political change is an important mandate. Still bearing elements of the altruistic consciousness, the revolutionary consciousness seeks revolution not merely for itself but either for its peers or the less fortunate.

However, the revolutionary consciousness eventually realizes that it is a rebel without a cause: for, it may sporadically select a certain state of affairs to protest against, but it lacks a mature and complete ethical system with which it may alter society on a grand scale. Therefore, the revolutionary consciousness eventually reflects upon what drives its impulse to be revolutionary, and eventually concludes either subliminally or consciously that it is ultimately driven by an ethical system it is not yet aware of, and so it soon fixates on ethical issues. This is the birth of the benefic consciousness, or that consciousness that is ethical and

---

[354] Goldman, Alvin and Bob Beddor, "Reliabilist Epistemology", *The Stanford Encyclopedia of Philosophy* (Summer 2021 Edition), Edward N. Zalta (ed.), URL = <https://plato.stanford.edu/archives/sum2021/entries/reliabilism/>; Sosa, Ernest. 2009. *A virtue epistemology: apt belief and reflective knowledge*. Volume 1 Volume 1. Oxford: Oxford University Press.

believes that justice is a *harmony* of the eighteen ideal principles of morality. The revolutionary consciousness eventually negates itself and views its revolutionary causes through the Rawlsian *veil of ignorance*, and therefore sets out to determine the ultimate ethical principles available to human beings. Starting with the ideal of perfection, the revolutionary consciousness borrows elements from the mature consciousness — whose independence naturally leads to the application of the Rawlsian *veil of ignorance* — and intuits by phenomenological deduction the rest of the ideal principles of morality.[355] Now that the benefic consciousness has been realized, two consciousnesses return to the forefront of mental concern: both the selfish consciousness and the altruistic consciousness.

Here, the benefic consciousness realizes that one must be both selfish and altruistic, and therefore the benefic consciousness becomes elevated into the polyintentional consciousness, or that consciousness that fundamentally understands that Mind has multiple intentions involved with any action, and therefore the ideals of selfishness and altruism are compatible with one another. Finally, the synthetic nature of the polyintentional consciousness gives way to the Kantian consciousness, which too is synthetic in nature, but on a larger scale, and the Kantian consciousness soon begins to synthesize the various elements learned by all of its former stages of consciousness. In wondering what it ought to do, what it ought to know, and what it ought to hope for, the Kantian consciousness begins to tie everything together in a synthetic manner either subliminally or consciously. It realizes that it must be a consciousness with the following characteristics: it must be political, ethical, realistic, it must know when to be conformist and when to be revolutionary, and it realizes that ethical ideals must be transformed into political rights, in order to attain greater social harmony. The consciousness that the Kantian consciousness morphs into, the one that possesses all of the aforementioned characteristics, is none other than the *democratic consciousness*, which is the highest stage in the development of human consciousness. For a consciousness to be *democratic*, entails that its cyclologies will also be *democratic*, which is to say, that all of the products of its Mind — all actions, thoughts, and speech — will not only be in line with, but will be attuned to, so-called *democratic values*.

Ultimately, the *democratic consciousness* realizes that human beings possess three chief rights: the right to personhood, the right to political justice, and the right to political scaffolding; the writings of the eminent philosopher Cornel West on democracy inform this discussion of the democratic consciousness, especially as the *democratic consciousness* seeks to resist the forces of imperialism generally speaking.[356] Because of the fragility of goodness, as famous philosopher Nussbaum has taught us, the *democratic consciousness* understands that consciousness must be scaffolded by institutions that help preserve its morality and health.[357] Following

---

[355]   Rawls, John. 1999. *A theory of justice*. Cambridge, Mass: Belknap.

[356]   West, Cornel. 2005. *Democracy matters: winning the fight against imperialism*.

[357]   Nussbaum, Martha Craven. 2011. *The fragility of goodness luck and ethics in Greek tragedy and philosophy*.

the logic of *influencer theory*, the specific programmatologies of the Core Scripts of each individual stage of consciousness account for the logic of each stage of consciousness, which is to say, that programmatology functions as the *influencer* for the individual, but for the nation-state, the set of *influencers* pertains to the individuals who represent the nation-state to the rest of the world, and who are responsible for its maneuvers both domestic and abroad. Thus, contra famous political scientist Francis Fukuyama, the culmination of world history is not the appropriate question to ask: instead, the culmination of Mind through a development of its stages of consciousness must be interrogated, for, what use may a democracy be should its citizens not possess the *democratic consciousness?*[358] So much then, for *Just Mind theory*, the *Theory of the Genealogical Development of Consciousness*, its three phases, fifteen stages, and its teleological endpoint: the *democratic consciousness*.

11. Toward Political Justice VI: Of Just Rule Theory, or Democratic Constitutionalism

Just Rule Theory involves any *regulations* placed on any form of thought, behavior, or speech. Starting with the *benefic consciousness*, formal morality starts to be taken seriously by both it and all its posterior stages of consciousness. It is the speculative Kantian consciousness that seeks to transform the mere ideal principles of morality into rights, and therefore to politically actualize them. A right is any ideal applied toward a political reality, and is judged to be reasonable or not on the grounds of whether or not its application to the lifeworld may be feasible, i.e., the feasibility equation. There are three main types of rules that concern both the individual and the nation-state. The three distinct types of rules are none other than: *ethical* rules, *political* rules, and *national* rules. Ethical rules involve the individual and its relation to ethical thought, action, and speech. Political rules are manifested in the three distinct branches of right: *personal* right, *procedural* right, and *accommodational* right. Personal right involves the right to personhood; procedural right involves the right to political justice; and accommodational right involves the right to political scaffolding. National rules involve the actions and declarations of nation-states, themselves orchestrated by a select set of individuals. Nation-states manifest national rules in either an implicit or an explicit constitution, which is a set of information endorsed by a given nation or set of nations, whose citizens endorse said information to be a precedent-setting and politics-influencing mandate on any future political actions, whose arc always bends toward political justice. Ethical rules involve the intrapersonal regulations imposed upon an individual either by its Core Script.

---

[358]   Fukuyama, Francis. 2020. *The end of history and the last man.*

In the *democratic consciousness* — the ideal form of consciousness — the individual conducts their thoughts, actions, and speech in a just manner: the *democratic consciousness* accords its performativity with the eighteen ideal principles of morality. Furthermore, it applies the theory of justice as *harmony* to the world, and, informed both by process epistemology and process ethics, accords its performativity in the lifeworld to the ethical theory referred to as *Speculative Optimalism*. *Speculative Optimalism* is the ethical theory that has four parts: an individual's procedure in the world must be virtuous and just, must be polyintentional, and must cause just consequences, and must manifest justice as a *harmony* of the eighteen deduced ideal principles of morality. Thus, following the work of Derek Parfit, *Speculative Optimalism* trumps all existing Western ethical theories in that in synthesizes them into a concrete whole, arguing that the four main camps of Aristotelian virtue ethics, Kantian deontological ethics, Benthamite utilitarianism, and consequentialism are not only compatible but consistent with each other: the ethical action must embody not merely the Aristotelian, Kantian, Benthamite utilitarian, and consequentialist requirements: it must too satisfy the requirements imposed by the ethical theory of justice as a *harmony* of the eighteen ideal principles of morality, those being: *perfection, gravitas, hope, autonomy, dignity, grace, utility, civility, peace, trust, hospitality, decoloniality, beauty, defocality, dehierarchality, experimentality, improvement* and *harmony*.[359]

As can be seen, *utility* is already in the mix, and so Benthamite utilitarianism too is included in the ethical theory of *Speculative Optimalism*. Furthermore, a fifth requirement is that, because right is technically noumenal to human beings, that human beings must attempt to apply these ethical requirements to their actions as optimally as possible. Finally, the categorical imperative according to *Speculative Optimalism* is none other than: act always according to a *harmony* of the eighteen ideal principles of morality, acting all the while virtuously, deontologically, and consequentially. *Speculative Optimalism* is nothing other than the ultimate form of *democratic ethics*. Now, political rules grow out of ethical rules in that political rules are ethical rules manifested in contexts that are interpersonal instead of intrapersonal. While ethical rules may involve multiple individuals, it is the case that each individual motivates themselves to act ethically; on the other hand, political rules involve three chief branches of rules that all are undergirded by the very concept of community, these being, personal, procedural, and accommodational. The personal branch of rules pertains to the right to personhood, and involves protecting and nurturing the personhood of all

---

[359] Parfit, Derek, and Samuel Scheffler. 2013. *On what matters*. 1 1. Oxford: Oxford University Press; Parfit, Derek, and Samuel Scheffler. 2013. *On what matters*. 2 2. Oxford: Oxford University Press; Aristotle and Charles David Chanel Reeve. 2014. *Nicomachean ethics*. Indianapolis: Hackett Publishing Co.; Kant, Immanuel, James W. Ellington, and Immanuel Kant. 1994. *Ethical philosophy: the complete texts of Grounding for the metaphysics of morals, and Metaphysical principles of virtue*, part II of *The metaphysics of morals*. Indianapolis: Hackett Pub. Co.; Bentham, Jeremy, and Wilfrid Harrison. 2013. *A fragment on government and an introduction to the principles of morals and legislation*. Oxford: Blakwell; Portmore, Douglas W. 2020. *The Oxford handbook of consequentialism*. New York, N.Y.: Oxford University Press.

individuals in a community. The procedural branch of rules pertains to the right to political justice, political justice being, the eighteen ideal principles of morality manifested as political rights instead of as mere abstracted ideals; hence, the procedural branch of rules governs how rights are applied in a given society, and where they are applied; the procedural branched is so named due to the fact that it concerns the procedure of human beings in the lifeworld.

The accommodational branch of rules involves the right to political scaffolding, and exists to complement human frailties of all kinds, especially those involving its animal nature, which is responsible for sexism, xenophobia, racism, hysteria, and fascism; here, the accommodational branch of rules functions as that guarantor that moral atrocities occurring due to human animal natures will never be committed again; as famous philosopher Theodor Adorno so eloquently argues: the new categorical imperative must be to never let another auschwitz happen again.[360] The problem is not that human beings are *political* animals, as the old Aristotelian saying goes, rather, the problem is that human beings are political *animals*.[361] The next transition up out of political rules is into national rules, and involves the structure of constitutions, whether implicit or explicit. Firstly, whether or not a nation possesses an explicit document that is referred to as a constitution, has no bearing on the fact that each nation necessarily shares an *implicit constitution*. An implicit constitution is that set of beliefs and rules that establishes a precedent and that is endorsed or co-signed by the citizens of that nation. Here, *autocontractualism* rears its head: citizens automatically endorse a constitution simply by means of their shared rapports with other human beings. When the question of *national ethics* arises, the concept of *process politics*, which is based on Whitehead's *process philosophy* and Derrida's *deconstruction*, becomes relevant.[362] For, a *process politics* necessarily entails the concept of the *dialectical constitution*, or that constitution that is free to be altered due to the autodiversification of the zeitgeist.

A *dialectical constitution* implies the concept of a *process theory of law*, wherein laws, too, must take up the burden of *process epistemology*, *process ethics*, and *process politics*; a *process theory of law* entails that the laws of a given nation must themselves be subjected to the most rigorous, unceasing scrutiny, due to *law's empire*, as Ronald Dworkin put it, being more of a *process* than an *absolute* and *completed science*.[363] These theories considered together, go into the makings of an explicit *formal constitution*, which is a physical document or set of beliefs that a nation-state holds dear. A *formal constitution* is modeled after the concept of an *optimal constitution*, or the best possible constitution for human

---

[360] Adorno, Theodor W., and E.B. Ashton. 2015. *Negative dialectics*.

[361] Aristotle, and H. Rackham. 1959. *Aristotle: politics*. London: Heinemann.

[362] Whitehead, Alfred North. 1990. *Process and reality: an essay in cosmology ; Gifford Lectures delivered in the University of Edinburgh during the session 1927-28*. New York: Free Press u.a.; Derrida, Jacques. 1998. *Of grammatology*. Baltimore: Johns Hopkins University Press.

[363] Dworkin, Ronald. 1986. *Law's empire*. Cambridge, Mass. u.a: Belknap Pr. of Harvard Univ. Pr.

beings, grounded in the ideal principle of *perfection*. Ultimately, the best possible constitution is one that allows both for improvement and for experimentality — two ideal principles of morality as derived by the theory of justice as *harmony* — and this modality of constitution is none other than the *democratic constitution*. The *democratic constitution* is that constitution that embodies the following three branches of rules: personal, procedural, and accomodational, and that too embodies the joint-theories of *Speculative Optimalism* and justice as *harmony*. In focusing on experimentality and upon improvement, as well as by respecting the personal, procedural, and accommodational political rules, the *democratic constitution* embodies *democratic right*, the most important of all rights. Hence, with the establishment of a *democratic constitution*, the *democratic consciousness* is optimally situated to enjoy its *right to democracy* and its concomitant values.

Perhaps a whole book could be written on concept of *The Democratic Hegel*, because in the view of your author, the social *process* of manifesting rights through political institutions, is terribly Hegelian, as was addressed in the preface; furthermore, *The Democratic Hegel* would be a serious interpretation of the unspoken Hegel — the one who planted a freedom tree in honor of the French Revolution — who had a Prussian bayonet prodded against his back, across the duration of the writing of all of his mature works, and who therefore could never openly write what truly was on his Mind.[364] Returning to the matter at hand, *Just Rule Theory* finds its manifestational *perfection* in a *democratic constitution*, and the *democratic consciousness* finds itself personally, procedurally, and accommodationally suited to one such *democratic constitution*. The aim of any *democratic constitution* is its *universality*, or its capability of being accepted and endorsed by any possible citizen, within reasonable limitations. So much, then, for *Just Rule Theory*, and the *Democratic Constitutionalism*.

12. Toward Political Justice VII: Of Just Environment Theory and the Democratic Universal Safe Space

As one of the four *motivators* both of the individual and of the nation-state, the environment becomes one of the key components both to accomplishing the *democratic individual* and the *democratic nation-state*. Thus, the next object of inquiry is nothing other than the *democratic environment*. The theory attached to the ideal of the *just environment* is *position theory*, and pertains to the external stimuli that an individual or a nation-state finds in its immediate phenomenal proximity, for, after all, that is what one's Crenwshawian intersectional *position*

---

[364]   Hegel, Georg Wilhelm Friedrich, Allen W. Wood, and H. B. Nisbet. 2018. *Elements of the philosophy of right*. Cambridge: Cambridge University Press; Althaus, Horst. 2000. *Hegel: an intellectual biography*. Cambridge, UK: Polity Press.

is all about.[365] To be sure, just as there are malefic triggers, there must be benefic triggers. A teacher instructing a student via the Socratic method — such is an example of an individual beneficially triggering another individual. For, the pupil grows in proportion to the academic triggering by the teacher; to digress: the master and servant dialectic greatly resembles the teacher and student dialectic; perhaps a precocious graduate student could write an entire book on that very subject. And yet, just as there is the benefic trigger, so too must there be the malefic trigger. Thus emerges the question of the safe space, and also of cultural terrorism, or, that presence of a malefic trigger or triggers that interupts the safe space. Here, the chief causes of a malefic trigger are sure to be the natural instincts of a human being. Most egregious of all these animalistic instincts is the famous Nietzschean *will to power*, active wherever human beings occur, and to be sure, active also on an international level in the form of nation-states. In this way, the *will to power*, whether active in the form of cultural, militaristic, or economic power, consistently manages to interrupt safe spaces by instilling them with the most basic form of terror: the challenge to the indigenous mode of being of another individual.[366] The root of instinctivism, the *will to power* takes the form of various forms of instinctive challenges to indigenous modes of being: xenophobia, hysteria, sexism, racism, and fascism. All of the aforementioned instinctively inspired tendencies function as basic challenges to indigenous modes of being, in that they seek to other and negate these other modes of being.

Here, there can only be one solution to prevent the imperial onslaught of instinct: the universal safe space. What might such an ideal entail? The universal safe space guarantees the following: the right to personhood, the right to political justice, and the right to political scaffolding; to accomplish such a space, wherein both individuals and democracy itself may flourish, nobly, is the aim of Cornel West's essays compiled under the title of *Democracy Matters*.[367] This is to say, that under the protections of the universal safe space, the basic functions of a personality may be protected, that the basic requirements of political justice as *harmony* may be ensured, and that the frailties of the human animal may be scaffolded against, in order to best promote its flourishing. The *democratic consciousness* best functions in that space that is protected against the evils of instinct: protected, as it were, against xenophobia, hysteria, sexism, racism, and fascism — the five chief evils of the human race. Without protections from these great evils inherent to the human animal structure, the *democratic lifestyle* cannot flourish. Therefore, all of society must be structured such that it is in accordance with the features of a *democratic environment*. Here, mere rationality alone will not protect society, as is the Habermasian view, instead, the three chief rights are the guarantors of the *democratic lifestyle*: the right to personhood, the right to political

---

[365] Crenshaw, Kimberle. 2012. *On Intersectionality The Seminal Essays*. New Pr.

[366] Nietzsche, Friedrich Wilhelm, Walter Arnold Kaufmann, and R. J. Hollingdale. 1968. *The will to power: a new translation*. New York: Vintage Books.

[367] West, Cornel. 2005. *Democracy matters: winning the fight against imperialism*.

justice, and the right to political scaffolding.[368] The right to personhood guarantees that no individual may be trampled over by another; the right to political justice guarantees that the eighteen ideal principles of morality must be in effect in order to secure a benefic reality; and the right to political scaffolding ensures that political justice — the manifestation of the eighteen ideal principles of morality — will be in effect to counter any animalistic spurs from the animal natures of human beings.

Thus, a truly *democratic environment* is one that protects indigeneity, and perhaps even supposes a *right to indigeneity* as an outgrowth of the right to personhood. Countered by imperialism, of which the root is the *will to power*, indigeneity is not only the heart of liberalism, but also the heart of democracy. Without indigeneity, there could be no point to liberalism, for liberalism is merely the assertion of indigeneity. For so long as the eighteen ideal principles of morality are to be locked into place, indigeneity will not only survive, but will flourish. Most important of all the eighteen ideal principles of morality, is the ideal principle of *hospitality*, for the ideal principle of *hospitality* governs the protection and care of the environment. To be avoided at all cost, is that environment that *troubles* its natives, or, those indigenous to it. In an increasingly globalized world, nothing is needed more fervently than the ideal of the universal safe space, whose manifestation is nothing other than the *democratic environment*. For democracy to flourish in any given society, the right conditions must be in place for it to do so. The right conditions for democracy to flourish both in the heart of the individual and the heart of any nation-state, are none other than the conditions that manifest the right to personhood, the right to political justice — the eighteen ideal principles of morality — and the right to political scaffolding.

Only these three chief rights can guarantee that democracy will not only persist, but flourish among any given populace. Increasingly, more and more nations begin to show signs that they are ready to embrace *democratic ideals*. More than ever, democratic nations must commit to two endeavors: firstly, of reinforcing democracy in their own nation-states, but also of abetting democracy in nation-states only just getting acquainted with the ideal of democracy. According to *process epistemology, process ethics,* and *process politics,* civilization is nothing more than an ongoing Whiteheadian *process*: thus, democracy, too, must be a process, that not only maps on to the theory of justice as *harmony*, but that also adapts to the ever-changing needs of the zeitgeist that autodiversifies across time.[369] As a universal safe space, the *democratic environment* accomplishes just that: it justifies itself due to its ethicality on the one hand, but secondly justifies itself due to its adaptability to the ever-changing tides of the zeitgeist on the other hand. Here, the *Theory of Instinctive Action* rears its head: across the changing tides of the zeitgeist,

---

[368] Habermas, Jürgen. 2007. *The theory of communicative action*. 1, 1. Boston, Mass: Beacon Press.

[369] Whitehead, Alfred North. 1990. *Process and reality: an essay in cosmology ; Gifford Lectures delivered in the University of Edinburgh during the session 1927-28*. New York: Free Press u.a.

society remains glued together due to instinct. While human animal instinct may be responsible for xenophobia, hysteria, sexism, racism, and fascism — the core evils inherent to the human race — nevertheless, it is nothing other than human instinct that glues society together, and, therefore, we must demarcate between benefic instinct and malefic instinct. The malefic instincts of humankind propel it toward xenophobia, hysteria, sexism, racism, and fascism. The benefic instincts, on the other hand, of humankind, propel it toward morality, social cohesion, and rapportionality. Again, the issue is not that human beings are *political* animals, but that human beings are political *animals*.[370]

Thus, instinctivism has its moments both benefic and malefic. The key, therefore, is to isolate the malefic instincts and thereby safeguard humanity from the troubles that these malefic instincts cause: the key, then, is the universal safe space, which is nothing other than the *democratic environment*. Here, indigeneity may be defined as the following: the developing manner of lifestyle inherent to an individual that molds itself around the satiation of needs and instincts both biological and cultural. Thus, just as there may be the good or benefic lifestyle, so too may there be *just indigeneity theory*: the requirements of such a theory are best courted in the *democratic envrionment*. Here, to revise Locke's formulation of the theory of toleration: the *democratic environment* must tolerate all those thoughts, actions, and speech that do not contain any terroristic malefic triggers: which is to say, that the focus of the democratic universal safe space must be nothing other than the prohibition of malefic triggers, and their concomitant phenomena, *troubles*; similarly, Rawls argued against the courting of *social controversy*.[371] So much, therefore, for *Just Environment Theory* and the *democratic environment*.

13. Toward Political Justice VIII:
Of Just Economy Theory and the Democratic Universal Economy

Last of the four motivators of the individual and of the nation-state, is none other than the economy, whose affiliated theory is need theory, because an economy is a financial system scaffolded by the state, grounded by the system of needs, and perpetuated by production, consumption, acquisition, exchange, and labor, whose chief medium is capital, and whose aim is further industrialization. Thus, just as there is a macroeconomics of the nation-state, so too is there a microeconomics of the individual. Following Habermas, there is both a lifeworld that involves human consciousness, and a system that involves pragmatic action — economic action, as it were. According to Habermas, the system is dependent upon the lifeworld, but, nevertheless, the system attempts to colonize the lifeworld and hence colonize

---

[370]   Aristotle, and H. Rackham. 1959. *Aristotle: politics*. London: Heinemann.

[371]   Locke, John. 2011. *Essay concerning human understanding ... the twentieth edition, etc.* [Place of publication not identified]: British Library, Historic; Rawls, John. 1999. *A theory of justice*. Cambridge, Mass: Belknap.

human consciousness. Another eminent theorist on the subject of the colonization of human consciousness is no one other than famous psychoanalyst Frantz Fanon, especially in his two great works, The Wretched of the Earth and Black Skin, White Masks; Cornel West's Democracy Matters, in a vein similar to Fanon's works, too tackles the damages both done and perpetuated by imperialism.[372] Fanon's writings may be deconstructed to demonstrate that there is such a phenomenon as original defilement, that imperialism wreaks upon human consciousness, which becomes scarred as a result of its collision with imperialism; the idea of original defilement stems from Saint Augustine's theological concept of original sin.[373] Here, the Habermasian dichotomy between the lifeworld and the system can be translated to concord with the dichotomy between indigeneity and imperialism.[374] How could the system of society colonize human consciousness without being imperialistic in nature, and so on? Habermas and his followers identify four social pathologies caused by the encroachment of the system into the lifeworld, these being: a decrease in shared meaning, social destabilization, an increase in alienation, and demoralization.[375]

Thus, the colonization of indigeneity by the imperialist forces of the system — chiefly by the social-economic system — represents an assault on need from the forces of the economy. Instead of functioning as it ought to and satiating need, the social-economic system instead creates a need-vacuum that is directly responsible for all of the social pathologies that Habermas and his followers identify with such acumen. Deeply influential upon the lifeworld of human consciousness, imperialism has three chief modes: *cultural, economic,* and *militaristic.* Predominant among these today is economic imperialism. The Roman Empire conquered the world through militaristic imperialism, the Beatles conquered the West through cultural imperialism, and the West has conquered the world, for the time being, due to economic imperialism. To be sure, there may be malefic imperialism, and malefic empires, but, might there be benefic imperialism and benefic empires: in short, might there be room for a *just empire theory*? To arrive at a theory of the just empire, contra postcolonial criticism, it would first be prudent to spell out a theory of the malefic empire. At its least effective, a malefic empire causes cultural terrorism, and social alienation. At its most effective, a malefic empire is an empire of death: it promotes necropolitics and makes human beings expendable means toward its aim of world domination. Inversely, in its least effective mode, a just empire preserves the ethical order, preserves social meaning, stabilizes society, coheres individuals instead of alienating them, and preserves social bonds.

---

[372] Fanon, Frantz, Richard Philcox, Jean-Paul Sartre, Homi K. Bhabha, and Cornel West. 2021. *The wretched of the earth*; Fanon, Frantz. 2021. *Black skin, white masks*; West, Cornel. 2005. *Democracy matters: winning the fight against imperialism.*

[373] Augustinus, Aurelius, and Robert S. Pine-Coffin. 2003. *Confessions.*

[374] Habermas, Jürgen. 2012. *The theory of communicative action.* 2, 2. Boston, Mass: Beacon Press.

[375] Finlayson, James Gordon. 2005. *Habermas: a very short introduction.* Oxford: Oxford University Press.

At its most effective, the just empire negates itself and any unjust imperial tendencies within itself. Thus, empire, which is the teleological endpoint of any economic grand strategy, comes in two forms: malefic and just. As was demonstrated above, the just empire provides for the needs of its citizens and eliminates all social pathologies. The only form of imperialism that remains during the reign of a just empire is cultural imperialism. Here, it would be shrewd to apply Charles Darwin's theory of natural selection to ideology itself: that ideology which is most fit and suited to the needs and instincts of human beings will not only persevere throughout human history, but will evolve.[376] Thus, the *Theory of Ideological Natural Selection* demonstrates that, no matter what regime or form of government, ideology is very much a phenomenon outside of human control due to its grip over human beings. This theory also explains *reverse colonization*, or, the cultural exchange that the servant transfers to the master due to the master's colonization of the servant, to use the Hegelian motif of master and servant; here the example might be the recent flux of Indian culture flowing into Great Britain and the West, e.g. the rise of yoga.[377] Here, there is room for a *Theory of the Adaptive Instinct*, or the theory that claims individuals, through any form of interaction, influence the modalities of each other. Thus, cultural imperialism is a constant in human affairs, but it need not malign the lifeworld the same way that militaristic and economic imperialism do: in fact, cultural imperialism is something of a social context: which ideology will prove the fittest through history?

Putting cultural imperialism aside, there remain two imperialisms to grapple with: economic and militaristic. The obvious answer to militaristic imperialism is pacifism, as argued for in the theory of justice as *harmony*, because one of the ideal principles of morality is none other than pacifism itself. Economic imperialism, on the other hand, proves more difficult to subdue: here, economic syncretism is the key. Where formerly militarism and the formation of large territorial empires was the aspiration, now the aspiration must be to create a single just economic empire internationally, which is to say, that nothing is needed more now than a *universal economics*. A universal economics is a system where all economies of the world are in sync, and distributive justice trickles down to satiate every safe need. Here, we may imagine three kinds of economies to illustrate a point: the *just economy*, the *real economy*, and the *worst economy*. The worst economy is that economy that satiates no needs whether biological or cultural. The real economy is that economy that describes the present state of affairs, where merely some biological and some cultural needs are satiated.

The *just economy*, on the other hand, satiates all safe and Lockeanly tolerable needs, whether biological or cultural.[378] Thus, the *just economy* is none

---

[376]   Darwin, Charles. 2021. *On The Origin Of Species*. [S.l.]: Om Books International.

[377]   Hegel, Georg Wilhelm Friedrich, and Terry P. Pinkard. 2018. *The phenomenology of spirit*.

[378]   Locke, John, Mark Goldie, John Locke, and John Locke. 2016. *Second treatise of government ; and a letter concerning toleration*.

other than the *democratic economy*, for how might an individual participate in democracy most robustly without having all of their safe and tolerable needs met, whether biological or cultural? Here, one is reminded of John Stuart Mill's comments on representative government, translated into our rhetoric as: the people must have representatives, because the system colonizes the lifeworld, and therefore the citizens lack the time or resources required to become politically well-informed.[379] What we are dealing with here is nothing short of a *crisis* of democracy. Until the *democratic economy* is manifested, there can be no true democracy. Thus, a democracy may be defined as possessing the following: a *citizenry whose consciousnesses are democratic, whose rules are democratic, whose environment is democratic, and whose economy is democratic: a democracy is nothing more and nothing less.* So much for *need theory, just economy theory* and the *democratic economy.*

14. Toward Political Justice IX: Of Just World Theory, or Of the Genealogical Development of Leibnizian International Harmony

Now comes the ultimate concern of this work: to discourse around the concept of a *just world theory*, or a theory of what a world wherein *democratic consciousness*, *democratic constitutionalism*, *democratic environmentalism*, and *democratic economics* were prominent would look like. Without a doubt, such a world would be politically just, which is to say, *harmonious*, or in keeping with the eighteen ideal principles and rights of morality, in addition to the rights inherent to personhood, and the right to political scaffolding. World *harmony* cannot merely materialize out of nowhere, just as a complex creature cannot emerge in nature without first having evolved to that point in its development. Thus, following the reasoning of Marx and Engels, here the theory of *Dialectical Materialism* will be applied to the logic of historical development, except their points of departure will be ignored, just as will be their conclusions[380]. Marx and his later follower, the most sophisticated developer of his theories and methods, Rosa Luxemburg, of German Spartacus League fame, were both not the types to speculate as to what world *harmony* would look like. Instead, they focused on figuring out what to do with the reigning hegemonic order, that being, the international method of the capitalist ordering of society. Unfortunately, because Marx and Engels shied away from utopian speculations, their theories and methods cannot appropriately inform the human race as to what must follow the hegemonic reign of the capitalist order. This work will not shy away from such utopian speculations, because such

---

[379]   Mill, John Stuart, and Ronald B. MacCallum. 1948. *On Liberty and considerations on representative government: And considerations on Representative government.* Oxford: Blackwell.

[380]   Marx, Karl, Eugene Kamenka, and Karl Marx. 1983. *The portable Karl Marx.*

speculations about the destiny of the human race must complement any theory of how to address the present.

Here, then, their beloved method of Dialectical Materialism will venture where they never dreamed to take it: across the royal road to utopia itself. Any theory that involves individuals and nation-states must first anatomically dissect each, starting with the individual, and then proceeding up to the concept of international *harmony*, or the concept of a *just world*, wherein *democratic consciousness, democratic constitutionalism, democratic environmentalism*, and *democratic economics* together reign as the hegemonic order of things. Imagine a theory that employs Dialectical Materialism as its method, and that argues international *harmony* lies at the teleological endpoint of history, and grounded in the metaphilosophy of Leibniz: *Dialectical Harmonism*.[381] There are, then, four chief phases involved in the speculative ascent toward international *harmony*: the *personal phase*, the *social-jurisprudential phase*, the *imperial phase*, and the *liberated phase*. The social phase of human history has eight distinct processes with eight distinct stages, and defines the human organism as a *needful*-being. Furthermore, following the logic of Dialectical Materialism, the social phase provides an anatomy of the individual and stops short of progressing into the tribe, or the first stage in the chain of the social-jurisprudential phase, which has seven processes and seven stages.

The social-jurisprudential phase traces the dialectical development of the tribe and stops short of the process of identification, whose stage is the nation; the social-jurisprudential phase provides the explanation of how a group formulates a marketplace for exchange, a system and officialization of right, and a form of leadership. Next, the imperial phase has six processes and six stages, and traces the development of the nation into a more complex form of group that eventually bears a constitution, whether implicit or explicit. Following the emergence of the nation, follows the constitution, the state, a formal economy, and either a Hobbesian empire capable of functioning as an international leviathan or a Kantian federation as identified in his *Perpetual Peace*, akin to the League of Nations or the United Nations.[382] Here, the course of history may progress as either a Hobbesian world empire or a Kantian world federation: either way, Leibnizian international *harmony* is not far off, once either of these stages have been historically accomplished; let Leibnizian *Dialectical Harmonism* serve as a foil both to Hobbesian *leviathan theory* and Kantian *perpetual peace theory*. The imperial phase is labeled as the *imperial* phase because, as soon as a nation emerges, it often bears imperialistic tendencies should it have the means to conquer other nations. Finally, the imperial phase comes to a screeching halt when either the world empire or world

---

[381]   Leibniz, Gottfried Wilhelm. 2008. *Discourse on metaphysics, and the monadology*. New York: Cosimo Classics.

[382]   Hobbes, Thomas, and Ian Shapiro. 2010. *Leviathan: or, The matter, forme and power of a commonwealth ecclesiasticall and civil*. New Haven, Conn: Yale University Press; Kant, Immanuel, and Hans Siegbert Reiss. 2010. *Kant: political writings*. Cambridge [England]: Cambridge University Press.

federation accomplishes the historical stage of automaticity, which is the point during economic development that entails the total automation of labor and all related subfields of economic importance, and hence the liberation of humankind from the burdens of having to produce in order to survive; during the stage of automaticity and across the process of liberation, the economy morphs into a sustainable enterprise rather than an exhaustive one.

International *harmony* is not far off at this point, because the *General Theory of Conflict* provides a framework for explaining conflict for us: all conflict is rooted in some need of human beings, and this need transitions into an instinctive reaction, and so on and so forth, all along the development chain into a serious and sober conflict. Once the automation of labor has been accomplished, and the resources of the world are more abundant than ever before in human history, a *democratic economy* may emerge: an economy that satiates *all* safe and tolerable needs, whether biological or cultural. There is no need, here, to claim: each according to their ability, each according to their need: we may eviscerate the former statement and keep the latter one, for ability ought have no bearing on distributive justice. Leibnizian international *harmony* occurs shortly thereafter, or, a world emerges wherein all the rights to personhood, to political justice, and to political scaffolding become firmly rooted across the whole of civilization: and, more importantly, a world wherein national identity evaporates and a *world culture* emerges. Again, once structures exist to perpetually satiate the urges of biological and cultural needs — just as the *General Theory of Conflict* argues — conflict will have no possible chance at emergence.

Returning to the Dialectical roots of the *Genealogical Development of Leibnizian International Harmony*: in the personal phase, there are eight processes that must take place in an orderly fashion, and these processes may be identified by eight stages that function as harbingers as to when one process ends and another begins. The first personal process to occur is grounded in the anatomy of the human being: it is nothing other than maintenance of the organic system, and its stage is need. Need may be defined as the following: the bio-ontological requirements for a given organic system; these needs may be either biological or cultural. Need grounds the entire human organism, which delivers us to the next process: assessment. The organic structure of the human being assesses its need, subliminally, and this allows for the second stage in the personal phase of Leibnizian *Dialectical Harmonism*: instinct. Instinct may be defined as the following: the political reaction of an organism to the needs of their biological and cultural system, that determines in what manner said organism attempts to satiate its needs. Next, the process of assessment is followed by the process of naturalization, whose stage is none other than indigeneity. Indigeneity may be defined as follows: the developing manner of lifestyle inherent to an individual that molds itself around the satiation of needs and instincts both biological and cultural.

The process of naturalization is how an organism gets comfortable in its own skin. Following naturalization, comes the process of cognition, which is to say, that need, instinct, and indigeneity are pre-cognitional: they are more primitive than cognition, whose identifying stage is thought. A thought may be defined as the following: the emergence of any internal production of Mind from an organism, limited by their integrated set of information stored in their mental depository. After cognition comes the process of emotion, whose stage is feeling: feeling may be defined as the reaction to either a production or a procession of Mind, which is to say, the result of the weighing of information according to the reflexivity equation. Next up the ladder rung from emotion is the process of evaluation, whose stage is value itself: value may be defined as a cemented combination of thoughts and feelings grounded in the needs and instincts of a given individual. Next, after value is on the table, comes the process of possession, whose stage is property: property may be defined as any entity that may be considered attached to a given human consciousness, that either has some value or no value at all. The concept of property gives way to another, more abstract concept: the ideal, which is the stage of the process of epistemologicalization.

An ideal may be defined as the following: the universalization of a value accomplished through the depersonalization of value into an abstracted epistemic idea. So ends the personal phase of Leibnizian *Dialectical Harmonism*, and so begins the social-jurisprudential phase, which commences with the process of communalization, wherein individuals come together into a group: the stage that signals the process of communalization is the stage of the tribe. The tribe may be defined as follows: a group of individuals united primarily by needs and instincts, but also by thoughts, feelings, values, property, and ideals, that develops into a group to protect itself against rogue animals and individuals. Thus, the emergence of the tribe signals the communal turn in the development of persons into a group of individuals, and leads into the next process of Leibnizian *Dialectical Harmonism*: exchange. The stage that signals the emergence of the process of exchange is none other than the marketplace, which may be defined as a system of rapports made possible by the tribe, driven by needs, thoughts, feelings, values, and ideals, that exists to satisfy needs both biological and cultural. Once property becomes readily exchangeable, more and more conflicts arise: thus, the next process in Leibnizian *Dialectical Harmonism* is adjudication, whose stage is government. Once a government exists in the developmental chain, far fewer conflicts emerge in the tribe. A government may be defined as the following: a force than organically arises within a tribe in order to adjudicate social conflicts between individuals, but that also exists to care for the tribe generally speaking, and to protect it from and negotiate with neighboring tribes and individuals.

Now that the tribe has a government to adjudicate its conflicts and to partially satiate its most urgent biological and cultural needs, the process of declaration takes place: its stage is none other than right, which may be defined as the assertion of an ideal toward a political feasibility, articulated either by an individual or a group of individuals, appealed toward the government of a tribe; rights exist either implicitly or explicitly within a group, or in more developed tribes, exist both implicitly and explicitly. This focus on right and rights in a tribe steers the dialectical trajectory toward its next destination: the process of translation. The stage that signals the presence of the process of translation is none other than the due, which may be defined as: the translation of a right from a mere performative action of Mind into a claim on materiality and rapportionality. A due is merely a right applied to reality, with a real manifestation in mind: Antigone's right to food finds its due in the surplus supply of apples her tribe may happen to have, for example. Following the due, the next stage on the stage of historiological development is the rule, which may be defined as a political norm informed by ideals, rights, and dues that is influential upon the political behavior of either an individual or a tribe of individuals.

The process whose emergence is signaled by the existence of a rule is none other than normitivization, which is the beginning of complex morality in a tribe. Coming after the process of normitivization is the process of officialization, which finds its stage in the statute: a statute may be defined as the officialization of rights, dues, and rules through the performative gesture of gathering said rights, dues, and rules into a code, document, or mantra, again, by either an individual or a group of individuals; a statute may be passed down through the oral tradition, or may be implicit. Thus concludes the social-jurisprudential phase, and so begins the imperial phase of Leibnizian *Dialectical Harmonism*: the imperial phase begins with the process of identification, whose stage is the nation. A nation may be understood to be a group of individuals united by a common set of needs, thoughts, values, ideals, rights, dues, rules, and either an implicit or explicit set of statutes — which is to say, a group united in a common and shared culture, that is imperial due to the Nietzschean will to power.[383] Once a nation emerges, the next link in the chain is the process of legitimation, whose emergence is signaled by the existence of a constitution. A constitution may be defined as a set of information endorsed by a given nation or set of nations, whose citizenry endorse said information to be a precedent-setting and politics-influencing mandate on any future political actions, whose arc always bends toward justice; a constitution is either implicit, explicit, or both. Once a constitution of a nation or set of nations exists, the next step in the development of need into international *harmony* is the process of actualization, whose stage is the state. A state may be defined as a set of institutions, roles, and responsibilities implicitly chartered by a nation to minister justly to the needs of its populace, according to the limits as set by said nation's implicit or explicit constitutional information. All previous stages in the development of international *harmony* become synthetically manifested in the idea of the state, which actualizes rights, dues, rules, statutes, and constitutions.

---

[383]   Nietzsche, Friedrich Wilhelm, Walter Arnold Kaufmann, and R. J. Hollingdale. 1968. *The will to power: a new translation*. New York: Vintage Books.

After the emergence of the state, comes a process more nuanced than any before it: the process of the enforcement of justice, whose stage on the world historical stage is law. Law may be defined at any implicit or explicit rules enforced by the state in order to best facilitate justice within the confines of the views of either a nation or set of nations. Once there is both a state and the law, there may emerge during the process of the satisfaction of need, the stage referred to as an economy. An economy is a financial system scaffolded by the state, grounded by the system of needs, and perpetuated by production, consumption, acquisition, exchange, and labor, whose chief medium is capital, and whose aim is further industrialization. The trifecta of the state, law and economy may take a people in one of two directions, each with its own process and stage: either the stage of the empire or the stage of the federation. The process involved in the establishment of an empire is expansion, and an empire may be defined as that state responsible for the colonization of another nation or nations to further satiate its economic needs and instincts, whose ultimate aim is to conquer the nations and resources of the world to maximize its industrial production. A federation, on the other hand, reflects the process of unification, and may be defined as an endeavor instigated by nations as an alternative to global empire whose aim it is to form increasingly strong economic and political ties to other nations, toward the end of minimizing the occurrence of war and maximizing the benefits of international trade.

Whether or not a civilization decides to progress into either an empire or a federation, is of little consequence, other than that a federation is a more ethical stage in history compared with an empire, which is instinctive compared with the enlightenment of a federation; for, both an empire and a federation eventually progress into the next process, due to the development of their respective economies: the next process in the chain is none other than the process of liberation, whose stage that signals the emergence of this process is automaticity; the emergence of automaticity on the world stage inaugurates the final phase of world historical development: the liberated phase. Automaticity may be defined as the point during economic development that entails the total automation of labor and all related subfields of economic importance, and hence the liberation of humankind from the burdens of having to produce in order to survive; economics morphs into a sustainable enterprise rather than an exhaustive one. Following automaticity, the final process in *Dialectical Harmonism* is none other than the negation of nationality, and the emergence of the stage that is international *harmony*, which may be defined as the international dissolution of specific nationalities in favor of a universal identity, with the preservation of Habermasian patriotic constitutionalism, and the mediation of human animal instinct, realizable due to the cessation of conflict as a result of the automaticity of labor, the universal satisfaction of biological need, and the universal mediation of cultural need.[384] There ends the *Genealogical Development of Leibnizian International Harmony*.

---

[384]   Habermas, Jürgen, and William Rehg. 2015. Between facts and norms contributions to a discourse theory of law and democracy. Cambridge: Polity Press.

WORKS CITED

1. Adorno, Theodor W., and E.B. Ashton. 2015. *Negative dialectics*.

2. Althaus, Horst. 2000. *Hegel: an intellectual biography*. Cambridge, UK: Polity Press.

3. Anselm, Brian Davies, and G. R. Evans. 1998. *The major works Anselm of Canterbury*. Oxford; New York: Oxford University Press.

4. Aristote, and Charles David Chanel Reeve. 2014. *Nicomachean ethics*. Indianapolis: Hackett Publishing Co.

5. Aristotle, and H. Rackham. 1959. *Aristotle: politics*. London: Heinemann.

6. Aristotle. 1990. *Aristotle: Metaphysics*.

7. Artaud, Antonin, Claude Schumacher, and Brian Singleton. 2004. *Artaud on theatre*.

8. Augustinus, Aurelius, and Robert S. Pine-Coffin. 2003. *Confessions*.

9. Austin, J. L., J. O. Urmson, and Marina Sbisà. 2009. *How to do things with words: the William James lectures delivered at Harvard University in 1955*. Oxford: Oxford University Press.

10. Beauvoir, Simone de. 1972. *The marquis de Sade*. London: New English Library.

11. Bentham, Jeremy, and Wilfrid Harrison. 2013. *A fragment on government and an introduction to the principles of morals and legislation*. Oxford: Blakwell.

12. Bergson, Henri. 2002. *Time and free will: an essay on the immediate data of consciousness*. https://search.ebscohost.com/login.aspx?direct=true&scope=site&db=nlebk&db=nlabk&AN=790187.

13. Berkeley, George, and Colin Murray Turbayne. 1989. *Principles, dialogues, and philosophical correspondence*.

14. Berlin, Isaiah. 1967. *The hedgehog and the fox*. London: Weidenfeld & Nicolson.

15. Boswell, James, and Marshall Waingrow. 2019. *Boswell's Life of Johnson: an edition of the original manuscript*. Volume 4, Volume 4. Edinburgh: Edinburgh University Press.

16. British Academy, and G. E. Moore. 1940. *Proof of an external world*.

17. Bryant, Edwin F., Patañjali, and Patañjali. 2018. *The Yoga sūtras of Patañjali: a new edition, translation, and commentary : with insights from the traditional commentators*.

18. Butler, Judith. 2006. *Gender trouble: feminism and the subversion of identity*. New York; London: Routledge.

19. Calvin, John. 2013. *Institutes of the Christian religion: translated from the original Latin, and collated with the ... author's last edition in French*. [Place of publication not identified]: Wipf & Stock Publishers.

20. Carlisle, Clare. 2020. *Philosopher of the heart: the restless life of Søren Kierkegaard*.

21. Cartwright, Nancy. 2010. *The dappled world: a study of the boundaries of science*. Cambridge: Cambridge Univ. Press.

22. Cercignani, Carlo. 2010. *Ludwig Boltzmann: the man who trusted atoms*. Oxford: Oxford Univ. Press.

23. Chalmers, David John, and Tim Peacock. 2022. *Reality+: virtual worlds and the problems of*

philosophy.

24. Chomsky, Noam. 2002. *Syntactic structures*. Berlin: Mouton de Gruyter.

25. Cixous, Hélène, and Marta Segarra. 2010. *The portable Cixous*. New York: Columbia University Press.

26. Cornell, Drucilla. 2014. *Law and revolution in South Africa: Ubuntu, dignity, and the struggle for constitutional transformation*.

27. Cornell, Drucilla, Michel Rosenfeld, and David Carlson. 2016. *Deconstruction and the possibility of justice*.

28. Crenshaw, Kimberle. 2012. *On Intersectionality The Seminal Essays*. New Pr.

29. Darwin, Charles. 2021. *On The Origin Of Species*. [S.l.]: Om Books International.

30. Deleuze, Gilles, Félix Guattari, and Brian Massumi. 2019. *A thousand plateaus: capitalism and schizophrenia*.

31. Derrida, Jacques. 2011. *Specters of Marx: the state of the debt, the work of mourning, and the new international*. New York: Routledge.

32. Derrida, Jacques, and Barbara Johnson. 2017. *Dissemination*.

33. Derrida, Jacques, and Anne Dufourmantelle. 2000. *Of hospitality: Anne Dufourmantelle invites Jacques Derrida to respond*. Stanford, Calif: Stanford University Press.

34. Derrida, Jacques. 2017. *Writing and difference*.

35. Derrida, Jacques. 1998. *Of grammatology*. Baltimore: Johns Hopkins University Press.

36. Descartes, Rene, and F. Sutcliffe. 2005. *Discourse on Method and the Meditations*. https://www.vlebooks.com/vleweb/product/openreader?id=none&isbn=9780141944203.

37. Dickens, Charles, and Charles Dickens. 2020. *Great expectations*.

38. Dworkin, Ronald. 2003. *Justice for hedgehogs*. Cambridge, Mass: Belknap Press of Harvard University Press.

39. Dworkin, Ronald. 1986. *Law's empire*. Cambridge, Mass. u.a: Belknap Pr. of Harvard Univ. Pr.

40. Emerson, Ralph Waldo. 2016. *Self reliance & other essays*.

41. Fanon, Frantz. 2021. *Black skin, white masks*.

42. Fanon, Frantz, Richard Philcox, Jean-Paul Sartre, Homi K. Bhabha, and Cornel West. 2021. *The wretched of the earth*.

43. Fine, Kit. 2020. *Vagueness: a global approach*.

44. Finlayson, James Gordon. 2005. *Habermas: a very short introduction*. Oxford: Oxford University Press.

45. Fish, Stanley Eugene. 2003. *Is there a text in this class?: the authority of interpretive communities*. Cambridge, Mass: Harvard Univ. Press.

46. Fodor, Jerry A. 2010. *The language of thought*.

47. Fodor, Jerry Alan. 2014. *The modularity of mind: an essay on faculty psychology*. Cambridge (Mass.): The MIT Press.

48. Foucault, Michel, and Alan Sheridan. 2020. *Discipline and punish: the birth of the prison*.

49. Freud, Sigmund, and James Strachey. 2001. *Beyond the pleasure principle: group psychology and other works* ; (1920-1922). London: Vintage.

50. Freud, Sigmund, and Abraham A. Brill. 1938. *The basic writings*.

51. Freud, Sigmund, and Samuel Moyn. 2022. *Civilization and its discontents*.

52. Freud, Sigmund, and Louise Adey Huish. 2003. *The "wolfman" and other cases*. New York: Penguin Books.

53. Fukuyama, Francis. 2020. *The end of history and the last man*.

54. Gettier, Edmund L., and Marc Andree Weber. 2019. Is *Justified True Belief Knowledge?/ Ist gerechtfertigte, wahre Überzeugung Wissen?*: Englisch/Deutsch.

55. Goldman, Alvin I., and Dennis Whitcomb. 2011. *Social epistemology essential readings*. Oxford: Oxford University Press.

56. Gregg, Melissa, and Gregory J. Seigworth. 2011. *The affect theory reader*. North Carolina: Duke University Press.

57. Habermas, Jürgen. 2007. *The theory of communicative action*. 1, 1. Boston, Mass: Beacon Press.

58. Habermas, Jürgen, and William Rehg. 2015. *Between facts and norms contributions to a discourse theory of law and democracy*. Cambridge: Polity Press.

59. Habermas, Jurgen. 1996. *Moral consciousness and communicative action*. Cambridge, MA: MIT.

60. Habermas, Jürgen. 2012. *The theory of communicative action*. 2, 2. Boston, Mass: Beacon Press.

61. Habermas, Jürgen, Giovanna Borradori, and Jacques Derrida. 2004. *Philosophy in a time of terror: dialogues with Jürgen Habermas and Jacques Derrida*. Chicago, Ill: University of Chicago Press.

62. Haraway, Donna Jeanne. 2004. *The Haraway reader*. New York: Routledge.

63. Hegel, Georg Wilhelm Friedrich. 2004. *Hegel's Science of logic*. Amherst, N.Y.: Humanity Books.

64. Hegel, Georg Wilhelm Friedrich, Robert F. Brown, Peter Crafts Hodgson, and William Geuss. 2019. *Lectures on the Philosophy of World History, Volume I: Manuscripts of the Introduction and the Lectures of 1822-1823*.

65. Hegel, Georg Wilhelm Friedrich, and Terry P. Pinkard. 2018. *The phenomenology of spirit*.

66. Hegel, Georg Wilhelm Friedrich, and Stephen Houlgate. 2005. *The Hegel reader*. Oxford, UK: Blackwell Publishers.

67. Hegel, Georg Wilhelm Friedrich, Allen W. Wood, and H. B. Nisbet. 2018. *Elements of the philosophy of right*. Cambridge: Cambridge University Press.

68. Hegel, Georg Wilhelm Friedrich, Robert F. Brown, Annemarie Gethmann-Siefert, Heinrich Gustav Hotho, and Georg Wilhelm Friedrich Hegel. 2014. *Lectures on the philosophy of art: the Hotho transcript of the 1823 Berlin lectures*. Oxford: Oxford University Press.

69. Heidegger, Martin, and David Farrell Krell. 1993. *Basic writings: from Being and time (1927) to The task of thinking (1964)*. [San Francisco, Calif.]: HarperSanFrancisco.

70. Heidegger, Martin, John Macquarrie, and Edward S. Robinson. 2019. *Being and time*.

71. Heidegger, Martin. 2009. *On the way to language*. San Francisco: HarperOne.

72. Hobbes, Thomas, and Ian Shapiro. 2010. *Leviathan: or, The matter, forme and power of a commonwealth ecclesiasticall and civil*. New Haven, Conn: Yale University Press.

73. Honderich, Ted. 2005. *The Oxford companion to philosophy*.

74. Honneth, Axel. 2014. *The I in we: studies in the theory of recognition*. Cambridge: Polity Press.

75. Hume, David. 2013. *Of the standard of taste: post-modern times aesthetic classics*. [Place of publication not identified]: Birmingham Free Press.

76. Husserl, Edmund, Ingo Farin, James G. Hart, and Edmund Husserl. 2006. *The basic problems of phenomenology from the lectures, winter semester, 1910-1911*. Dordrecht, the Netherlands: Springer.

77. Jung, C. G., and Joseph Campbell. 1971. *The portable Jung*.

78. Kant, Immanuel, and Paul Guyer. 2009. *Critique of pure reason*. Cambridge: Cambridge Univ. Press.

79. Kant, Immanuel, and Lara Denis. 2017. *The "metaphysics of morals"*. Cambridge: Cambridge University press.

80. Kant, Immanuel, and Paul Guyer. 2009. *Critique of the power of judgment*. Cambridge, UK.: Cambridge University Press.

81. Kant, Immanuel, James W. Ellington, and Immanuel Kant. 1994. *Ethical philosophy: the complete*

texts of Grounding for the metaphysics of morals, and Metaphysical principles of virtue, part II of The metaphysics of morals. Indianapolis: Hackett Pub. Co.

82. Kant, Immanuel, Jens Timmermann, Mary J. Gregor, Immanuel Kant, and Immanuel Kant. 2014. *Groundwork of the metaphysics of morals: a German-English edition.*

83. Kant, Immanuel, Theodore M. (Theodore Meyer) Greene, and Hoyt H. Hudson. 1960. *Religion within limits or reason alone.*

84. Kant, Immanuel, and Hans Siegbert Reiss. 2010. *Kant: political writings.* Cambridge [England]: Cambridge University Press.

85. Kaufmann, Walter Arnold, and Friedrich Nietzsche. 2011. *Beyond good and evil: prelude to a philosophy of the future.* New York: Vintage Books.

86. Kierkegaard, Søren, Howard V. Hong, and Edna H. Hong. 2000. *The essential Kierkegaard.* Princeton, N.J.: Princeton University Press.

87. Kierkegaard, Søren, Howard V. Hong, Edna H. Hong, and George Pattison. 2009. *Works of love.*

88. Kierkegaard, Søren, Walter Lowrie, and Søren Kierkegaard. 2013. *Fear and trembling, and: the sickness unto death.* Princeton, N.J.: Princeton University Press.

89. Kohlberg, Lawrence. 1986. *The philosophy of moral development: moral stages and the idea of justice.* Cambridge [u.a]: Harper & Row.

90. Lacan, Jacques, Jacques-Alain Miller, and Alan Sheridan. 2019. *The four fundamental concepts of psycho-analysis.*

91. Lacan, Jacques, and Bruce Fink. 2007. *Écrits: the first complete edition in English.* New York: W.W. Norton.

92. Leibniz, Gottfried Wilhelm. 2008. *Discourse on metaphysics, and the monadology.* New York: Cosimo Classics.

93. Lévinas, Emmanuel. 2006. *Entre nous: on thinking-of-the-other.* London: Continuum.

94. Locke, John. 2011. *Essay concerning human understanding ... the twentieth edition, etc.* [Place of publication not identified]: British Library, Historic.

95. Locke, John, Mark Goldie, John Locke, and John Locke. 2016. *Second treatise of government; and a letter concerning toleration.*

96. Lopez, Donald S. 2004. *Buddhist scriptures.*

97. Luhmann, Niklas, Dirk Baecker, and Peter Gilgen. 2021. *Introduction to systems theory.* Cambridge: Polity.

98. Luther, Martin, William Hazlitt, and John Aurifaber. 2020. *The table talk of Doctor Martin Luther.*

99. Marx, Karl. 2022. *German Ideology.* [S.l.]: Repeater.

100. Marx, Karl, Ben Fowkes, and David Fernbach. 1990. *Capital: a critique of political economy;* v.1. London: Penguin Books in association with New Left Review.

101. Marx, Karl, and N. I. Stone. 2014. *A contribution to the critique of political economy.*

102. Marx, Karl, Eugene Kamenka, and Karl Marx. 1983. *The portable Karl Marx.*

103. McGinn, Colin. 2000. *The mysterious flame: conscious minds in a material world.* New York: BasicBooks.

104. Mill, John Stuart, Katarzyna de Lazari-Radek, and Peter Singer. 2022. *Utilitarianism.*

105. Mill, John Stuart, and Ronald B. MacCallum. 1948. *On Liberty and considerations on representative government: And considerations on Representative government.* Oxford: Blackwell.

106. Mullett, Michael A. 2015. *Martin Luther.*

107. Nagarjuna. 2022. *Root Stanzas Of The Middle Way: The Mulamadhyamakakarika.* [S.l.]: Shambhala.

108. Nagel, Thomas. 1997. "What is it like to be a bat?" *Nature of Consciousness : Philosophical Debats.*

Edited by Ned Block, Owen Flanagan, and Güven Güzeldere.

109. Newton, Isaac, C. R. Leedham-Green, and Isaac Newton. 2021. *The mathematical principles of natural philosophy.*

110. Nietzsche, Friedrich, and Walter Arnold Kaufmann. 2011. *On the genealogy of morals.* New York: Vintage Books.

111. Nietzsche, Friedrich Wilhelm, Walter Arnold Kaufmann, and R. J. Hollingdale. 1968. *The will to power: a new translation.* New York: Vintage Books.

112. Nietzsche, Friedrich Wilhelm, Raymond Geuss, and Ronald Speirs. 1999. *Nietzsche: the birth of tragedy and other writings.* Cambridge: Cambridge University Press.

113. Nietzsche, Friedrich Wilhelm, Adrian Del Caro, and Robert B. Pippin. 2006. *Nietzsche: thus spoke Zarathustra.* Cambridge: Cambridge University Press.

114. Nussbaum, Martha Craven. 2015. *Political emotions: why love matters for justice.* Political Emotions. Cambridge: Belknap Press of Harvard University Press.

115. Nussbaum, Martha Craven. 2016. *Not for profit: with a new preface by the author: why democracy needs the humanities.*

116. Nussbaum, Martha Craven. 2011. *The fragility of goodness luck and ethics in Greek tragedy and philosophy.*

117. O'Brien, Edna. 2019. *Byron in love.*

118. Osborne, Martin J. 2017. *An introduction to game theory.*

119. Parfit, Derek. 2007. *Reasons and persons.* Oxford: Clarendon Press.

120. Parfit, Derek, and Samuel Scheffler. 2013. *On what matters.* 2 2. Oxford: Oxford University Press.

121. Parfit, Derek, and Samuel Scheffler. 2013. *On what matters.* 1 1. Oxford: Oxford University Press.

122. Pascal, Blaise, and A. J. Krailsheimer. 1986. *Pascal Pensés.* Harmondsworth: Penguin.

123. Paul, Wayne A. Meeks, and John T. Fitzgerald. 2006. *The writings of St. Paul: annotated texts reception and criticism.* New York: W.W. Norton.

124. Peirce, Charles S., and Edward C. Moore. 1998. *The essential writings.* Amherst, N.Y.: Prometheus Books.

125. Peterson, Jordan B., Ethan Van Sciver, and Norman Doidge. 2020. *12 rules for life: an antidote to chaos.*

126. Plantinga, Alvin. 2012. *Where the conflict really lies: Science, religion, and naturalism.* New York: Oxford University Press Inc.

127. Plato, G. R. F. Ferrari, and Tom Griffith. 2013. *The republic.* Cambridge: Cambridge University Press.

128. Plato, and John M. Cooper. 2009. *Complete works.* Indianapolis: Hackett.

129. Popper, Karl R. 2014. *The Logic of Scientific Discovery.*

130. Portmore, Douglas W. 2020. *The Oxford handbook of consequentialism.* New York, N.Y.: Oxford University Press.

131. Proust, Marcel. 2002. *In search of lost time boxed set.* London: Allen Lane.

132. Quine, W. V., and J. S. Ullian. 1978. *The web of belief.* New York: McGraw-Hill.

133. Rand, Ayn, and Leonard Peikoff. 2014. *Philosophy: who needs it.* New York: Signet. http://rbdigital.oneclickdigital.com.

134. Rand, Ayn, and Leonard Peikoff. 2002. *The Ayn Rand sampler.* New York: Signet.

135. Rawls, John. 1999. *A theory of justice.* Cambridge, Mass: Belknap.

136. Ricoeur, Paul. 1997. *Time and narrative.* Chicago, Ill: University of Chicago Press.

137. Ricœur, Paul, and Denis Savage. 2008. *Freud and philosophy: an essay on interpretation.* Delhi: Motilal Banarsidass.

138. Roe, Nicholas. 2013. *John Keats: a new life*. https://archive.org/details/johnkeatsnewlifeoooooroen.

139. Rousseau, Jean-Jacques, Quintin Hoare, and Christopher Bertram. 2012. *Of the social contract and other political writings*. London: Penguin Books.

140. Russell, Bertrand. 2017. *In praise of idleness*.

141. Sade, Will McMorran, Thomas Wynn, and Sade. 2016. *The 120 days of Sodom, or, The School of Libertinage*.

142. Sartre, Jean-Paul, and Sarah Richmond. 2021. *Being and nothingness: an essay on phenomenological ontology*.

143. Schaeffer, Neil, and Donatien Alphonse Francois de Sade. 2001. *The Marquis de Sade: a life*. London: Picador.

144. Searle, John R. 1996. *The construction of social reality*.

145. Skinner, B. F. 2008. *About behaviorism*. [Bridgewater, NJ]: Distributed by Paw Prints/Baker & Taylor.

146. Spinoza, Benedictus de, and G. H. R. Parkinson. 2009. *Ethics*. Oxford: Oxford University Press.

147. Spivak, Gayatri Chakravorty, Donna Landry, and Gerald MacLean. 1996. *The Spivak reader: selected works of Gayatri Chakravorty Spivak*. New York, NY: Routledge.

148. Stirner, Max. 1974. *Max Stirner, the ego and his own*. New York: Harper & Row.

149. Temkin, Larry S. 1997. *Inequality*. New York: Oxford University Press.

150. Tillich, Paul, and F. Forrester Church. 1999. *The essential Tillich*. Chicago, Ill: University of Chicago Press.

151. West, Cornel. 2005. *Democracy matters: winning the fight against imperialism*.

152. West, Cornel. 2018. *Race matters*.

153. Whitehead, Alfred North. 1990. *Process and reality: an essay in cosmology ; Gifford Lectures delivered in the University of Edinburgh during the session 1927-28*. New York: Free Press u.a.

154. Whitman, Walt, and Justin Kaplan. 1984. *Complete poetry and collected prose: Leaves of grass* (1855), *Leaves of grass* (1891-92), *Complete prose works* (1892), *Supplementary prose*. New York, N.Y.: Library of America.

155. Williams, Bernard Arthur Owen, and Josefine Nauckhoff. 2001. *Nietzsche: the Gay Science*. Cambridge: Cambridge University Press.

156. Wittgenstein, Ludwig. 2022. *Tractatus Logico-Philosophicus*. [S.l.]: Penguin Books.

157. Wittgenstein, Ludwig, G. E. M. Anscombe, Peter M. S. Hacker, and Joachim Schulte. 2010. *Philosophische Untersuchungen = Philosophical investigations*. Chichester, West Sussex, U.K: Wiley-Blackwell.

158. Wootton, David. 2003. *The essential Federalist and anti-Federalist papers*. Indianapolis: Hackett publ. co.

159. Wynter, Sylvia. 2003. "Unsettling the Coloniality of Being/Power/Truth/Freedom: Towards the Human, After Man, Its Overrepresentation—An Argument". *CR: The New Centennial Review*. 3 (3): 257-337.

160. Yoshino, Kenji. 2007. *Covering: the hidden assault on our civil rights*. New York: Random House.

161. Žižek, Slavoj. 2009. *The sublime object of ideology*. London: Verso.

TABLES

Table 1. Of the Quartetal Aristotelian Theory of the Motivation
of Individuals and the Motivations of Nation-States

	Motivator	Aristotelian Causality	Theory	Application
1	Means/Economy	Efficient	Need	Skill, Maintenance
2	Environment/Setting	Material	Position	Circumstances
3	Rule	Formal	Regulation	Morality
4	Mind/Witnessant	Final	Influencer	Individual = Drives National = Representatives

Table 2. Of the Teleological Genealogy of International
Harmony as Deduced From Mere Need

Number	Phase	Stage	Process	Definition
1	Personal	Need	Maintenance	The bio-ontological requirements for a given organic system, which may be either biological or cultural.
2		Instinct	Assessment	The political reaction of an organism to the needs of their biological system, that determines in what manner an organism attempts to satiate its needs.
3		Indigeneity	Naturalization	The developing manner of lifestyle inherent to an individual that molds itself around the satiation of needs and instincts both biological and cultural.
4		Thought	Cognition	The emergence of any internal production of Mind from an organism, limited by their integrated set of information stored in their mental depository.
5		Feeling	Emotion	The reaction to either a production or a procession of Mind, which is to say, the result of the weighing of information according to the reflexivity equation.
6		Value	Evaluation	A cemented combination of thoughts and feelings grounded in the needs and instincts of a given individual or group of individuals.
7		Property	Possession	Any entity that may be considered attached to a given human consciousness, that either has some value or no value at all.
8		Ideal	Epistemologicalization	The universalization of a value accomplished through the depersonalization of value into an abstracted epistemic idea.
9	Social-Jurisprudential	Tribe	Communalization	A group of individuals united primarily by needs and instincts, but also by thoughts, feelings, values, property, and ideals, that develops into a group to protect itself against rogue animals and individuals.
10		Marketplace	Exchange	A system of rapports made possible by the tribe, driven by needs, thoughts, feelings, values, and ideals, that exists to satisfy needs both biological and cultural.

11		Government	Adjudication	A force that organically arises within a tribe in order to adjudicate social conflicts between individuals, but that also exists to care for the tribe generally speaking, and to protect it from and negotiate with neighboring tribes and individuals.
12		Right	Declaration	The assertion of an ideal toward a political feasibility, articulated either by an individual or a group of individuals, appealed toward the government of a tribe; rights exist either implicitly and explicitly within a group, or in more developed tribes, exist both implicitly and explicitly.
13		Due	Translation	The translation of a right from mere performative production of Mind into a claim on materiality and rapportionality.
14		Rule	Normitivization	A political norm informed by ideals, rights and dues that is influential upon the political behavior of either an individual or a tribe of individuals.
15		Statute	Officialization	The officialization of rights, dues, and rules through the performative gesture of gathering said rights, dues, and rules into a code, document, or mantra, again, by either an individual or a group of individuals; a statute may be passed down through the oral tradition, or may be implicit.
16	Imperial	Nation	Identification	A group of individuals united by a common set of needs, thoughts, values, ideals, rights, dues, rules, and either an implicit or an explicit set of statutes — which is to say, a group united in a common and shared culture, that is imperial due to the will to power.
17		Constitution	Legitimation	A set of information endorsed by a given nation or set of nations, whose citizens endorse said information to be a precedent-setting and politics-influencing mandate on any future political actions, whose arc always bends toward justice; a constitution is either implicit or explicit.

18		State	Actualization	A set of institutions, roles, and responsibilities implicitly chartered by a nation to minister justly to the needs of its populace, according to the limits as set by said nation's implicit or explicit constitutional information.
19		Law	Enforcement of Justice	Any implicit or explicit rules enforced by the state in order to best facilitate justice within the confines of the views of either a nation or a set of nations.
20		Economy	Satisfaction of Need	A financial system scaffolded by the state, grounded by the system of needs, and perpetuated by production, consumption, acquisition, exchange, and labor, whose chief medium is capital, and whose aim is further industrialization.
21A		Empire	Expansion	That state responsible for the colonization of another nation or nations to further satiate its economic needs and instincts, whose ultimate aim is to conquer the nations and resources of the world to maximize its industrial production.
21B		Federation	Unification	An endeavor instigated by nations as an alternative to global empire whose aim it is to form increasingly strong economic and political ties to other nations, toward the end of minimizing the occurrence of war and maximizing the benefits of international trade.
22	Liberated	Automaticity	Liberation	The point during economic development that entails the total automation of labor and all related subfields of economic importance, and hence the liberation of humankind from the burdens of having to produce in order to survive; economics morphs into a sustainable enterprise rather than an exhaustive one.
23		International Harmony	Negation of Nationality	The international dissolution of specific nationalities in favor of a universal identity, with the preservation of patriotic constitutionalism, and the mediation of human animal instinct, realizable due to the cessation of conflict as a result of the automaticity of labor, the universal satisfaction of biological need, and the universal mediation of cultural need.

INDEX

Milton Keynes UK
Ingram Content Group UK Ltd.
UKHW030146211223
434710UK00011B/373